Narrative Writing
Learning a New Model for Teaching

George Hillocks, Jr.

HEINEMANN
Portsmouth, NH

Heinemann
A division of Reed Elsevier Inc.
361 Hanover Street
Portsmouth, NH 03801–3912
www.heinemann.com

Offices and agents throughout the world

© 2007 George Hillocks, Jr.

The author and publisher wish to thank those who have generously given permission to reprint borrowed material:

Excerpts from *Teaching Writing as Reflective Practice* by George Hillocks, Jr. Copyright © 1995. Published by the Teachers College Press. Reprinted by permission.

Excerpts from *Black Boy* by Richard Wright. Copyright © 1937, 1942, 1944, 1945 by Richard Wright; renewed © 1973 by Ellen Wright. Published by permission of HarperCollins Publishers.

"Abandoned Farmhouse" from *Sure Signs: New and Selected Poems* by Ted Kooser. Copyright © 1980. Reprinted by permission of the University of Pittsburgh Press.

Library of Congress Cataloging-in-Publication Data
Hillocks, George.
Narrative writing : learning a new model for teaching / George Hillocks, Jr.
　　p. cm.
　Includes bibliographical references and index.
　ISBN-13: 978-0-325-00842-4
　ISBN-10: 0-325-00842-6
　　1. English language—Composition and exercises—Study and teaching (Secondary).
2. Narration (Rhetoric)—Study and teaching (Secondary).　I. Title.
LB1631.H523 2007
808.042′0712—dc22　　　　　　　　　　　　　　　　　　　2006020004

Editor: Lisa Luedeke
Production: Elizabeth Valway
Cover design: Gina Poirier
Composition: House of Equations, Inc.
Manufacturing: Louise Richardson

Printed in the United States of America on acid-free paper
11　10　09　08　07　RRD　1　2　3　4　5

Dedicated to my students in the
University of Chicago
Master of Arts in Teaching English Program,
1971–2002

CONTENTS

FOREWORD

There is an old saying that "the proof is in the pudding." We are in an era of high stakes accountability for K–12 education. Schools are being pressured to use curricula based on scientifically-based research. For many years in Chicago African American and Latino youngsters were dropping out of high school at rates of seventy percent or better; and yet no one was particularly bothered by these staggering statistics.

I, for one, have no problems with high stakes accountability. However, there are cautions to consider in this environment. A number of subjects have received short shrift in the process. Writing, particularly writing narratives, is one of the casualties. Writing is no longer routinely tested. The second caution is that studies of scientifically-based research are not routinely carried out in low achieving urban school settings. In many cases, the research studies are experimental studies of fundamental theories with limited empirical research specifying what it means to translate these theories into practice.

George Hillocks steps into this fray with a monumentally important book, *Narrative Writing: Learning a New Model for Teaching*. This book is important for a number of reasons: It provides a compelling illustration of what is necessary to make complex processes of problem solving explicit to students; in this case, the complex process is the constructive act of composing written narratives. It demonstrates the *generativity* of learning in this domain. Hillocks shows how learning to write rich narratives offers access points for understanding the rhetorical moves employed by writers of great fiction, expands what students understand about rhetoric more broadly (i.e. critical semantic manipulation, functional uses of sentence structures, elements of narrative genres), and shows how this can transfer to writing in other genres. He also makes a persuasive argument for the functions of narrative composing for identity development. *Narrative Writing* also represents a pedagogical tour de force, illustrating with a multitude of exemplars from real classrooms in urban schools the fundamental logic of careful *pedagogical planning*. Finally, Hillocks offers a potent *model of teacher learning* from the MAT (Master of Arts in Teaching) program he originated at the University of Chicago to prepare novices to teach English.

Making Complex Processes of Problem Solving Explicit

A persistent challenge in K–12 education is what pedagogical practices best make complex processes of problem solving explicit. As research has demonstrated, the act of composing involves complex problem solving (Flower and Hayes 1981, Hillocks 1986, Scardamalia, Bereiter, and Steinbach 1984, Smagorinksy and Smith 1992). These constructive processes are no less complex than one finds in reading comprehension or in problem solving in mathematics and the sciences. As Hillocks' prior research has so clearly demonstrated, novices do not learn to reason about what features their compositions should have or how to produce such features simply by examining models or being given linear directions like steps in the five paragraph theme, or by receiving definitions of terms, or simply learning descriptive grammar.

However, it is rare that we see very clear, grounded illustrations of making these constructive processes explicit. Each chapter of this book contains multiple examples of strategic lessons that show the nuts and bolts of the composing process. Hillocks describes in detail how students learn to incorporate detail and figurative language, create dialogue, represent the internal states of characters, and make scenes come alive. There are plenty of publications with descriptions of lessons about composing, but few are rooted in conceptions of the domain that are deeply rooted in the literary arts. This disciplinary clarity is evident as Hillocks moves from analyses of how great writers from Mark Twain to Toni Morrison create imaginary worlds on the page to illustrations of how middle and high school students in historically under-achieving urban schools come to approach similar rhetorical questions and achieve deeply aesthetic representations and re-interpretations of personal experiences in writing. As readers, we are able to step inside the heads of master and novice teachers as they engage in the messy, but necessarily systematic work of making the complex explicit. I raise this as a truly important contribution of this book because the default norm in too many schools serving students from low-income backgrounds and students of color is to dumb down the curricula. Making learning explicit is translated as telling simplistic rules. While Hillocks makes a compelling argument in the domain of written composition, what he has done here has strong implications for teaching in other domains as well.

My own research in what I call *Cultural Modeling* is a direct outgrowth of George's theories in composition, applied to reasoning about literary texts (Lee 1993, 1995b, 2001, in press). In Cultural Modeling, we use the examination of cultural data sets to help students make public emergent forms of reasoning about making sense of satire, irony, symbolism, and unreliable narration. Cultural data sets are akin to what George calls *gateway activities*. In our work, such activities are grounded in the everyday experiences of youth, such as a form of talk called *signifying* in African American English or contemporary rap lyrics. I hope my efforts to make complex problem solving explicit in the domain of response to literature offer one example of how George's ideas have application in a wide array of domains (Ball 1992, Ballenger 1997, Conant 1996).

The Generativity of Narrative Composing

A second important contribution of this book is Hillocks' argument about why teaching narrative writing is important. Fundamentally, he argues narrative writing is generative. He shows us what students learn about language, about genres, about reading, and about themselves through the iterative problem-solving processes that such writing demand. The argument is important because, after the accomplishments of the last decade in increasing attention to writing in K–12 education, we are now facing a conservative reaction embodied in public legislation for high-stakes accountability. One unfortunate by-product has been to narrow the curriculum, particularly in schools in low-income communities and schools with large percentages of students of color. I believe Hillocks is exactly on the mark in the reasons he offers for teaching narrative writing. I will discuss his initial reason about the role of narrative in the presentation of self (Bruner 1990, Miller, Mintz, Hoogstra, Fung, and Potts 1992, Ochs, Taylor, Rudolph, and Smith 1992, Scollon and Scollon 1981). Hillocks draws on the work of my Northwestern University colleague Dan McAdams' research on narrative, identity, and generativity (McAdams 1993, McAdams 2006, McAdams, Josselson, and Lieblich 2006). Professor McAdams has shown what people's stories of personal experience reveal about how people see themselves and how they position and present aspects of themselves in particular settings.

We know that motivation in school is a labyrinthine matter. Old folks say, "you can bring a horse to water, but you can't make him drink." Adolescence is a particularly cumbersome life stage. Youth are learning to navigate new roles in preparation for adulthood. Peer relationships, including knowledge about sexual identity, are heightened during this period. High schools are typically more impersonal than elementary or middle schools; and the subjects of the high school curriculum are typically far removed from students' everyday experiences and life goals as they incompletely understand them. These are part of the normative developmental challenges of transitioning from adolescence into adulthood in western societies. However, youth living in communities of persistent inter-generational poverty and who are from ethnic and racial communities facing persistent inter-generational stigmatization must learn to wrestle with additional challenges (Spencer 1987, 2000). This wrestling can make them stronger or it can greatly lessen abilities to adapt to future opportunities. For these youngsters, I believe that learning to write narratives of personal experience in ways that invite critical reflection on how the self is presented through language can be empowering. As Hillocks has so elegantly demonstrated in this book, how to engage in such teaching in ways that empower students rhetorically and personally is a lesson that our schools sorely need.

Models of Teacher Learning

Teaching narrative writing as generative, making complex problem solving explicit, and personal empowerment cannot happen without teachers who understand the conceptual, technical, and pedagogical principles that are needed. Hillocks' research in the area of teacher learning may be the greatest contribution of this work. I know George Hillocks as a teacher—a master teacher. He was my Ph.D. dissertation advisor. I had the extraordinary opportunity to work with him directly in the MAT program he describes in this book. In 2004, George received the Distinguished Service Award, a lifetime achievement award from the National Council of Teachers of English. One of the most moving parts of the ceremony was when close to thirty of his prior MAT and Ph.D. students came up from the audience and stood behind him. George was almost in tears at the outpouring of love and appreciation from his former students. What is more telling is that each of these former students is now a practicing scholar-researcher in his or her field. I am talking primarily here about those students, MAT and Ph.D., who have gone on to pursue careers as secondary English teachers. Some of them are the teachers whose work he describes in this book. They research their teaching. They publish their findings in practitioner and research journals. They continue to dialogue with one another about practice on websites and list servs set up by members of the group. They collaborate in research enterprises with George. As a cohort, they represent precisely the quality of reflective teaching for which the National Board for Professional Teaching Standards calls. They are testimony not only to George's compassion and commitment as a teacher and mentor, but more importantly to the theoretical model for teacher learning that George describes in this book and illustrates through the careful examination of the MAT Composition Workshop that he developed for more than thirty years at the University of Chicago.

The MAT Composition Workshop reflects several foundational principles that have proven clearly effective and that I think are applicable to both preservice and inservice teacher learning. George understands that teaching itself involves complex problem solving. Whether teaching composition or other subjects, teachers need deep understanding of many domains and must learn to coordinate such knowledge dynamically on the performance floors of classrooms. The detailed descriptions of novice teachers learning through teaching gives the reader an insider view of the myriad trade-offs that teachers must weigh in their planning and enactment. Although the details in this book come from George's elaborate documentation of the enactment of the MAT Composition Workshop during the 1994–1995 academic term, it actually represents the compilation of thirty years of systematically working through this model in middle and high schools in the Chicago area. He is honest in sharing what he learned along the way, including what he learns in microlessons he himself teaches in the middle and high school classrooms. I was inspired by George when I decided to teach myself, in both my dissertation research and the research in cultural modeling that followed. George's history as a teacher and researcher not only stands alongside the ground-breaking work of people like Magdalene Lampert (2001) and Deborah Ball (Ball and Cohen 1996) in mathematics (esteemed college professors who also taught in elementary school math classrooms and documented their teaching in order to examine fundamental propositions about learning mathematics); George's stance in this regard pre-dates Lampert, Ball, and the rest of us.

Conclusion

This is a book about what students and teachers need to know about teaching adolescents to write great narratives. In that regard, it is groundbreaking in its intellectual rigor, its clear disciplinary focus, and its deeply detailed explications of pedagogy. But it is also uses teaching narrative to adolescents as a grounded exemplar of ideas that have currency in teaching complex problem solving in other domains, in making what we teach a resource to leverage youth's personal development in trying times, and in illustrating with highly informative examples how teachers—novice and experienced—learn to tackle the rigorous problems of teaching. When George Hillocks (1975) first wrote the monograph *Observing and Writing* in 1971, he began the incubation of some of the most powerful ideas about teaching composition. These ideas have emerged full blown in *Narrative Writing*. and I believe it will become another of George's many classic works.

Carol D. Lee, Ph.D.
Professor of Education and Social Policy
School of Education and Social Policy—Program in the Learning Sciences
Northwestern University
Evanston, Illinois

References

Ball, A. 1992. "Cultural Preferences and the Expository Writing of African-American Adolescents." *Written Communication* 9 (4): 501–532.

Ball, D., and D. Cohen. 1996. "Reform by the Book: What Is—Or Might Be—the Role of Curriculum Materials in Teacher Learning and Instructional Reform?" *Educational Researcher* 25 (9): 6–8.

Ballenger, C. 1997. "Social Identities, Moral Narratives, Scientific Argumentation: Science Talk in a Bilingual Classroom." *Language and Education* 11 (1): 1–14.

Bruner, J. 1990. *Acts of Meaning*. Cambride, MA: Harvard University Press.

Conant, F. 1996. "Drums in the Science Lab." *Hands On* 19 (1): 7–10.

Flower, L., and J. R. Hayes. 1981. "A Cognitive Process Theory of Writing." *College Composition and Communication* 32: 365–87.

Hillocks, G. 1975. *Observing and Writing*. Urbana, IL: National Council of Teachers of English.

———. 1986. *Research on Written Composition: New Directions for Teaching*. Urbana, IL: National Conference on Research in English/ERIC Clearinghouse on Reading and Communication Skills.

Lampert, M. 2001. *Teaching Problems and the Problems of Teaching*. New Haven: Yale University Press.

Lee, C. D. 1993. *"Signifying As a Scaffold for Literary Interpretation: The Pedagogical Implications of an African American Discourse Genre."* Urbana, IL: National Council of Teachers of English.

———. 1995b. "Signifying As a Scaffold for Literary Interpretation." *Journal of Black Psychology* 21 (4): 357–81.

———. 2001. "Is October Brown Chinese: A Cultural Modeling Activity System for Underachieving Students." *American Educational Research Journal* 38 (1): 97–142.

———. in press. *The Role of Culture in Teaching and Learning Academic Literacies: Conducting Our Blooming in the Midst of the Whirlwind*. NY: Teachers College Press.

McAdams, D. P. 1993. *The Stories We Live By: Personal Myths and the Making of the Self*. New York: The Guilford Press.

———. 2006. *The Redemptive Self: Stories Americans Live By*. New York: Oxford University Press.

McAdams, D. P., R. Josselson, and A. Lieblich, eds. 2006. *Identity and Story: Creating Self in Narrative (The Narrative Study of Lives)*. Washington, DC: American Psychological Association.

Miller, P. J., J. Mintz, L. Hoogstra, H. Fung, and R. Potts. 1992. "The Narrated Self: Young Children's Construction of Self in Relation to Others in Conversational Stories of Personal Experience." *Merrill-Palmer Quarterly* 38 (1).

Ochs, E., C. Taylor, D. Rudolph, and R. Smith. 1992. "Storytelling as a Theory-Building Activity." *Discourse Processes* 15 (1): 37–17.

Scardamalia, M., C. Bereiter, and R. Steinbach. 1984. "Teachability of Reflective Processes in Written Composition." *Cognitive Science* 8: 173–90.

Scollon, R., and S. B. K. Scollon. 1981. *Narrative, Literacy and Face in Interethnic Communication*. Norwood, NJ: Ablex.

Smagorinksy, P., and M. Smith. 1992. "The Nature of Knowledge in Composition and Literary Understanding: The Question of Specificity." *Review of Educational Research* 62 (3): 279–305.

Spencer, M. B. 1987. "Black Children's Ethnic Identity Formation: Risk and Resilience in Castelike Minorities." In *Children's Ethnic Socialization: Pluralism and Development* edited by J. Phinney and M. Rotheram, 103–16. Newbury Park, CA: Sage.

———. 2000. "Identity, Achievement Orientation and Race: 'Lessons Learned' About the Normative Developmental Experiences of African American Males." In *Race and Education* edited by W. Watkins, J. Lewis, and V. Chou. Allyn & Bacon Press.

ACKNOWLEDGMENTS

Many people have made it possible for me to write this book during all of these years. One is Dean Frank Thomas, whom I went to see soon after my arrival at the University of Chicago in 1971. Coming from a state university, I expected to be told what to teach. I imagined that there would be a set of courses for the Master of Arts in Teaching English program. Dean Thomas looked at me with a trace of amusement and said, "We hired you as the expert to develop and run the MAT program in English." He nodded in my direction and continued, "*You* have to decide what to do and what to teach to make the program the best it can be." I was astonished. I did not have to abide by some set program. I could do it the way I thought best! The department chairs of education continued to allow me that freedom until the Division of Social Sciences closed the Department of Education in 2001, at which time the MAT English program moved into the Humanities Division. The program continued for the next year, but Dean Janel Mueller, of the Humanities Division, closed it in 2002.

The freedom allowed me to make my own decisions about curricula and course work, at least for the English education part. I decided that there was no better way to help my students learn to teach than to coach them as they tried different strategies in a workshop on writing for at least a few weeks. It was very time-consuming, but after those thirty-one years, I would make the same decision again. So I thank my chairs in education for that freedom: Dean Thomas, Philip Jackson, Charles Bidwell, Larry Hedges, Robert Dreeben, and John Craig.

I could not run three workshops at one time, but I managed to gather an amazing crew of assistants, most of whom, but not all, were doctoral students, many of whom were graduates of the MAT program. Doctoral students who were not graduates of the MAT program had to assist me as an adviser to a group of MAT students before they would take one on their own. MAT graduates who assisted with workshop groups include Dorothea Anagnostopoulis, Jane Curry, Larry Johannessen, Elizabeth Kahn, Steve Littell, Bruce Novak, Peter Smagorinsky, Michael Smith, and Deborah Stern. Other doctoral students who took on groups of MAT students in the workshop include Carol D. Lee and Kendra Sisserson. There were also skilled teachers who helped me: Faye Kachur and James F. McCampbell. Without all of these wonderful assistants, the workshops would not have fared as well as they almost inevitably did.

I am also grateful to all of the schools and the teachers who let us come into their classes to teach. But most of all I am grateful to all the sixth, seventh, eighth, and ninth graders who have affected my life and the lives of my MAT students. They were generous, tolerant of us, trusting, and willing to take the chances we asked of them. We could not have asked for more.

I also am in great debt to those MAT students who scored so many compositions for the study in Appendix A: Carolyn Blair, Julianna Cucci, Shirley Ho, and Kevin Perks, who scored, and Jamie Kowalczyk, who coded, mixed, and then sorted and re-sorted the papers. Rater reliabilities tell how conscientious they all were.

I also thank my longtime friend Larry Ludlow, Chair of Statistics at the School of Education at Boston College, who advised me on several problems I had with running SPSS (Statistical Package for the Social Sciences), which is no picnic for an English major.

Without the MAT students themselves, this book obviously would not exist and my life would not be the same. They have given me knowledge, joy, and love. A teacher cannot ask for more. They will live in my heart as long as I breathe.

WHY AND HOW TO TEACH NARRATIVE

Many state writing assessments ask students to write narratives. But there are better reasons for teaching narrative than preparing students for state assessments. First and perhaps most important, work on narrative, if we make it personal, is a way to examine the stories of our lives. Beyond that, it allows students to contribute to the body of literature they will study, understand more fully how the works of professional writers are constructed, and learn techniques that will be useful in other kinds of writing. But it will do these things only if our students learn the strategies for producing narratives of high quality.

The experiences we have are the basis of our dispositions, our worldviews, our characters, our ways of thinking, and our ability to undertake and integrate new experiences. They are, in every meaningful sense, who we are. When the experience (even one that is seemingly trivial) is gone, our memories of it remain and become part of us. The way we integrate them into the stories of our lives determines our identities, how we see ourselves. Take this poem by Countee Cullen:

Incident

Once riding in old Baltimore,
Heart-filled, head-filled with glee,
I saw a Baltimorean
Keep looking straight at me.
Now I was eight and very small,
And he was no whit bigger,
And so I smiled, but he poked out
His tongue, and called me, "Nigger."
I saw the whole of Baltimore
From May until December;
Of all the things that happened there
That's all that I remember.

What obviously counts in this poem is the emotional impact of the experience on the poet, which is still fresh when he recalls it years later.

Smagorinsky and Smith (2002) tell us that according to McAdams (1989), people do not have a single, static self but instead play multiple roles. Building on the work of

Jung and more modern social-cognitive psychology, McAdams addresses the idea of the multiple roles that people play through his concept of the imago. Imagoes are the various characters, the "(mes) within me" (McAdams 1989, 207), who play leading roles in different parts of one's life story. According to McAdams, no single imago can define the complex amalgam of roles that any individual plays. Yet he argues that "'a major goal in life—perhaps *the* major goal—is to discover or compose the right story for one's own life' [28; emphasis in original]. That is, people seek to compose life stories that somehow integrate different and often opposing imagoes" (Smagorinsky and Smith 2002, 305).

I believe that writing about an experience allows us to reflect on that experience and helps bring it into perspective as a part of our developing lives and life stories whether the reflection appears in the work or not. Writing about an experience helps transform it from what may appear at the time to be a life-shattering event to a more objective memory that can be viewed in the context of other events and integrated with other experiences to be understood in a different way.

Writing provides ways of dealing with experiences that are not available without the writing. I wish I had known that when I was ten and spent every day quaking in fear of the bully Mars (really!), who had been in my elementary school far longer than most and as a result was much taller and stronger than the rest of us, or when I was thirteen and clutching the shale high on a cliff that threatened to crumble and drop me one hundred feet or more to the bottom of a waterfall, which I had climbed along the face of the cliff to see, or when I was seventeen and in love with a red-haired girl who refused, all summer long, to skate with me or even speak to me at the open-air roller rink. I think I did have an inkling of it by the time I was thirty-eight and my son and daughter and I kept a monarch caterpillar alive on milkweed so that we could watch it transform into a bright lime-green chrysalis with its thin gold-beaded ridge at the top, then into a black chrysalis that we thought might be dead, then into a transparent outer shell through which we could see the tiny patchwork of orange and black that was the wings, and finally, after staying up all night for fear of missing the transformation, into a monarch butterfly breaking the shell of the chrysalis, slowly unfolding its wings to their full span, resting on my son's shoulder and drying those wings, moving them slowly up and down, and flying off to a rose bush and from there to a treetop and out of sight.

I have since written about these and other experiences, as a student in school and later as a teacher in pieces I've shared with my own classes. I believe writing about them has put them into perspective for me and given me greater insight into my own joys and fears. I wrote about the experience with Mars for an English assignment in high school. My teacher, as part of a unit on narrative, had asked us to write a story about an experience that had been important for us in some way. She suggested that we write about one that had made us frightened, angry, or surprised. I chose the experience with Mars because it had certainly been important and because it had not only frightened me but also angered me and finally surprised me. She provided no instruction in how to write an effective narrative other than having us read a couple of stories by Edgar Allan Poe, one of which was "The Pit and the Pendulum." I no longer have that tenth-grade effort, which is probably just as well. (I do remember that in high school I used no dialogue, because I was never sure where the commas went, and I could not bother to look it up.) But the events it chronicled were similar to the following version, written to use as an example of a narrative in the classes I teach.

The Bolt Bandit

Bang! Pop! Crack! Crack! It was the season for throwing bolts at recess in the fifth grade. We had gone through playing marbles and tops, but now was the season for throwing bolts. It was easy and fun and relatively cheap. You needed only two bolts, one nut, and many kitchen matches. You screwed one bolt into the nut, took the head off a kitchen match and placed it in the opening of the nut, and then screwed the second bolt in the other side of the nut firmly but not so tight that it would crush the match head. We would throw the bolts down onto the concrete as hard as we could to make the match head explode. The bolts would bounce away and we would go collect them and do it all over again. It was great fun, not really a game because we hadn't developed a way to compete against each other yet. We all cheered when anyone accomplished a little explosion.

It was great fun except when Mars was there. He was rumored to be going on fifteen and was still in the sixth grade. Someone had said the teachers might pass him on to high school whether he passed the sixth grade or not. We all hoped so. He was bigger than any of the rest of us by several inches. He always wore long pants, instead of knickers like the rest of us, and wore his hair slicked back with a pompadour in the front. Ronnie said he was trying to look like a hood. There was no doubt about it; he was a crook all right. When we played marbles, if he didn't win, he would simply take all the marbles. Then he would put the marbles on the ground in a little clutch and stand over them daring us to push him away and take the marbles back. When no one did, he would say, "See, they're mine. You guys don't want them." We were all afraid of him and hated when he was around. My stomach would churn and my chest got so tight it hurt.

On one fall day, Mars was there standing off to one side. After five of us threw our bolts, he ran over to the bolts and snatched them up before we realized what was happening. We walked toward him tentatively. When we were about ten feet away, Mars ostentatiously took a bolt set from his pocket, sniffing it to detect the smell of an explosion. "This one didn't go off," he said. "You little creeps can't do nothin' right." (He didn't say *creeps*. He used a slang word for *stool*, one of his favorites.) He made a big show of putting the bolts back into his pocket.

Jimmy was standing off to my left and said, "Well, you better give them back to us."

"What you mean, you little creep? What you mean I'd better give 'em back? I ain't givin' nothin' back to none of youse. You throwed 'em at me. When little creeps throw things at me, I keep what I want."

I was keeping my mouth shut, but Ronnie said, "You better give 'em back, or I'll tell the principal you stole 'em."

"You ain't tellin' the principal nothin'. Here's yours, you little creep." With that Mars threw a bolt set at Ronnie. I ducked, but Ronnie cried out. When I looked over at him his forehead was bleeding and he was holding his hand to it. I could see blood seeping through his fingers, and he was wailing. When I looked back at Mars, he was walking deliberately toward us. I could feel myself quaking even as I stood frozen in place. Mars was walking right up to Ronnie with a snarl on his mouth. "Shut the hell up, you big sissy," he said as he pushed Ronnie into me. My stomach was churning in fear, but I felt I had to stand up to him. After all, I was a Cub Scout and every week we swore to help other people at all times. We even talked about how helping others demanded some level of courage. But I knew I was a coward. What I really wanted to do was run away. Then Mars pushed Ronnie into me again. By this time, Ronnie had blood all over his face and neck. Stomach churning and chest tight, I bit my lip and forced myself to step in front of Ronnie.

I held my arm out to keep Mars away. Dumb move, I thought, as soon as I realized where it was. "Leave him alone," I said. "If you hurt him again, you're gonna get it."

"Oh yeah?" said Mars. "Who's gonna to give it to me? You, you little sissy creep?" With that he grabbed my arm, twisted it behind my back and pushed me to the ground, face down. "So what are you gonna give me?" He had his knee in my back, and with his free hand he rubbed my face in the gravel next to the pavement for what seemed like a very long time. "Nothing but a damned weakling sissy," he crowed. "Little creep."

Suddenly the school bell rang. I had never been so glad to hear it ring to end recess. Then I heard Mrs. Welch yelling, "You boys! You boys! What is going on there?" What a stupid question, I thought. Mars gave my head one more push into the gravel as he got up and then ran off. I lay still for a minute thinking that I was not dead at least. When I turned my head to the side and opened my eyes, I saw Mrs. Welch's black oxford shoes about a foot from my face. "George, is that you George?" she said. "I am surprised at you. You should be ashamed of yourself, fighting in the school yard. What will your father say?" That was the question I did not want to think about.

"Don't know," I mumbled as I struggled to stand up. I heard her gasp as my head came up to hers.

"Well," she said, "I was going to take you to the principal, but you are going to see the nurse first." With that, she took me by an elbow and pushed me towards the building. "You are a mess," she announced as if I didn't know. What about Mars, I wondered. He was in this too.

When we arrived at the school dispensary, Ronnie was already bandaged. He looked at me sheepishly as Mrs. Welch ushered me through the door. Miss Conklin, the nurse, looked at me, her eyes wide in disapproval. She was a gray-haired woman who also wore oxford shoes and did not take kindly to cleaning up and bandaging little boys. "You have quite a set of scratches here," she said. She led me to a chair, lowered me into it and took my head into her hands to examine the scratches. After what seemed an eternity, she declared, "I think you'll live, no thanks to your propensity for fighting." I wanted to tell her that I was not fighting, just trying to keep Ronnie from getting hurt more. But I did not know what *propensity* meant. So I said nothing, which she took to be a confession of guilt. "I see nothing that will require stitches. I'm going to clean up these scratches, treat them with iodine, and deliver you to the principal."

I gulped, "Yes, ma'am," knowing very well how iodine would sting. I was afraid even of iodine. When Miss Conklin finished with me, she showed me my face in a mirror. It reminded me of a red and white dragon I had seen in a Chinese painting at the Museum of Art. Before I had time to think much about it, Miss Conklin was towing me down the hall by the elbow to the principal's office. She opened the door and pushed me through it to face a scowling secretary who said, "Is this another one of them?" Without waiting for an answer from Miss Conklin, she continued, "Sure looks like it to me. Looks like you been in a fight with a bag of cats." She laughed in appreciation of her own humor. "Mrs. Whitney will see him as soon as she's through with the other one." Miss Conklin pointed to a chair, said, "Wait there," and left the room. I sat avoiding the glances of the scowling secretary by looking steadfastly at the pattern of the carpet. I considered what the principal might say to me, but dismissed it because it was not nearly so important as what Dad would say. I did not want him to know I was afraid, a coward, that I had lost another fight. But I could not lie to my father. Lying just didn't work. Once I lied to him about practicing my piano lesson when I had not. I was working on Mozart's "Turkish March" (as it was called in my music book), which I actually liked, but when my mother wanted to hear me play it, it was just as slow and with as many mistakes in the left-hand chording as two weeks prior. My mother had said only, "Well, that needs some work yet." She was clearly not happy. She looked at my father and said, "I'll leave this to you."

When she was gone, Dad looked me in the eye and said, "I thought you told me that you had been practicing every day." He said something about my responsibility to practice and being honest, another Cub Scout virtue. He was not angry but, worse, disappointed and maybe disgusted. I decided that I would never lie to him again. So I would have to tell him the truth when he asked about my dragon face. I would have to confess that I had been beaten up once again by a bully of whom I was deathly afraid. That was going to be worse than dealing with Mars.

I hung my head in shame. I did not want to go home. When I got home, I would have to face Grandma, who would be upset by my appearance. Then I would practice until my parents arrived home from work. Just thinking about the prospect of facing them all made my stomach churn. I considered running away. The New York Central trains stopped in the railroad yards not far from the school. Maybe I could hop on one. Maybe I could find Uncle Bob's train and ride in the cab with him all the way to Buffalo or maybe New York City. I had been in the cab with him once when I was little, in the first grade. I tried to remember what his train looked like, but I couldn't. Maybe he didn't even drive the same train every day. I heard a door open and my head snapped up as the principal called my name. "George," she said, "come into my office, please."

When I was seated on a big chair at her large conference table, she said, "Now, George, I want you to tell me the truth. What happened during recess today?" I squirmed. It was against the code to squeal on someone, even the dreaded Mars.

"We were just playing," I said, "and then some guy took our stuff." It was clear from her eyes that that explanation would not be enough, and I dropped my head to look at my hand, my chest tightening by the second.

"What stuff are you talking about?" she asked, stretching the word *stuff* into at least two syllables in a tone that indicated she already knew the answer. "A word like *stuff* is not very helpful to me, and I need to know what happened."

"Well," I said, "uh, we were just playing with bolts, you know, bolts." I looked at her. Clearly that was not going to get me off the hook. She made a little huffing sound and looked at me expectantly. I squirmed in my big chair. After a couple of false starts, I explained the procedure of putting the match head between two bolts held together by a nut and throwing the bolts end down to make a little explosion.

"That does not sound like a game to me. That sounds like a dangerous activity."

"It isn't really a game, because nobody wins or loses. But it's not dangerous. Nobody gets hurt," I said. "We stand in a line and throw the bolts at the ground where nobody is. We hear the little explosions, and, and that's it."

She looked at me for a moment. Then she said, "Well someone was hurt today. I have already sent Ronnie home to see a doctor. He may need stitches on his forehead. So do not tell me that it is not a dangerous game. Now, I need you to tell me who threw the bolt at Ronnie."

"Well, we didn't throw it at Ronnie. He was playing with us. I mean, why would we throw it at him?"

"George, you are evading my question. I did not say that you threw the bolt. I am asking *who* threw it. Did you see who threw the bolt?"

I looked at my hands. I knew I was trapped. I was going to have to tell. My chest felt like one big knot. "Yes, ma'am," I said.

She waited expectantly for more. When I remained silent, she began to look angry. "George, I don't think you understand how serious this is. Mrs. Welch told me that she saw you fighting with Mars. Ronnie told me that you stepped in front of him and pushed Mars away and the next thing he knew you were on the ground in a fight with Mars. Now, depending on whether Ronnie's parents decide to press charges, this could go to court, and I suspect that we could have a case of criminal assault and battery. People go to jail for that. Now, I am asking again, who threw the set of bolts?" I sat amazed. "You admitted you saw the person who threw the bolt. Who was it?"

I looked at my hands. "Mars threw the bolt at Ronnie," I said. Now I was a squealer too, a coward, a weakling, and a squealer.

"Thank you, George. I am going to have to write a letter to your parents explaining the condition of your face and the steps that need to be taken. I am very pleased you told the truth, even though it took you a long time," she said. "Your parents will appreciate that." Yeah, and they'll know I was a coward, a weakling, and a squealer, I thought. "You go to your science class now. It's almost over. After school, stop by my office to pick up my letter to your parents. I'll ask that they call me to say it was delivered. Be sure to do it." She looked sternly at me over her gold-rimmed spectacles.

"Yes, ma'am." I turned and left the office, the secretary harrumphing at me over her typewriter. I went to class avoiding all the eyes I could. The problem was that everyone knew I had been sent to the office. That was a very big deal, and they would all want to know what had happened. I nodded my head and said, "Nothing happened." But they could tell, I was sure, that more than nothing had taken place.

At the end of the day I went to get the letter for my parents. The principal was not there, but the secretary handed me the letter with a look that suggested to me that she thought I was a despicable worm. "Be sure to take that home," she said. I left without saying a word. I wanted out of the school, but I was not eager to go home. I did not want to see any of the kids, so I walked very slowly. I went to the old frame house that was our neighborhood branch of the Cleveland Public Library. I found the section where the Doctor Doolittle books were shelved. I recognized several that I had read and found one that I had not. I took it to a table to read for a bit to see if I would like it. I knew I would. I figured it would help cheer me up. When I looked up at the clock, it was already 3:45. I was going to be late and Grandma would be having a fit already. I checked out the book and started home. The underpass for the New York Central tracks was clear of kids. So I began to trot. When I arrived home at four o'clock, sure enough, Grandma was waiting at the door. "Oh, God in Heaven," she said, "what's happened to you? Are you alrecht? Och, let me see these cuts on your face." After nearly forty years in the States, Grandma retained her thick Scots accent. I protested that I was fine, that they did not hurt, but she insisted on dabbing more iodine on my wounds as she called them. With every dab, I could tell, she was becoming more and more angry. Finally, she put up the iodine and stood before me, clenched fists on her hips. "Wha did this to ye, Geordie? Tell me, this instant!"

I had learned not to mess with Grandma. So I said, "It was a guy at school."

"You tell me his name." She went to one of the kitchen drawers and pulled out my great grandfather's hammer. "I'll gie that boy a bat i' the lug."

"No, no, Grandma. You can't do that. He's really big. He's way taller than even Daddy."
My Grandma was tiny, under four feet six, but what she lacked in size, she made up for in
determination. "Here, I have a letter for Mom and Dad. From the principal. I think the boy
is in trouble already. The principal said he might have to go to court."

She took the envelope and examined it. "Weel then, we'll hae to wait till they come home,
won't we? I'll put the letter here so your mither can see it when she comes in." She put the
letter on the kitchen table on top of the mail. "You go and practice your piano. You've got
ten minutes before they're here."

I went to the piano and began playing "Turkish March." I was getting better at it. The
speed was up a bit and the mistakes in the left hand were gone most of the time. I played
the first two parts over several times. When I heard the door open, I tried to increase the
tempo and concentrated, hoping to make as few egregious errors as possible. At the same
time, I was listening hard for what my parents might say. All I could hear were low voices,
a kind of murmuring. I continued playing for another several minutes, even switching to
exercises that I was supposed to practice every week but hated. I was so agitated I don't know
how I was able to concentrate on the music. At least, I could not think about what Mom
and Dad would say.

Then I heard my Dad say, "Geordie, come doon the stairs wi me. I want to hae a talk wi'
ye." He still had a Scots accent like Grandma's.

"Okay," I finally choked out. "I'm coming." I rose from the piano bench, went to the
kitchen, averting my face from my mother, and hurried down the stairs, stomach churning
as it had at recess. Dad was standing by his workbench, his favorite spot. He took one look
at my face and chuckled. "You look like you've been in the war, laddie."

"It looks worse than it is," I said.

"Maybe so. Maybe so. Let me see you over here." I moved closer to him under his light.
He inspected me closely. "So tell me what happened," he said. "I want the truth, no balo-
ney." His voice was very soft in his most serious way. I did not want to tell him, to disap-
point him in his only son. I felt the tears in my eyes and knew I was on the verge of crying.
"I got in a fight," I nearly sobbed.

"Well, I can see that. How else would your face get in such a mess? The last time your
face looked like this was when you went sledding in the woods and ran into a tree. And, as
I remember, the tree won in that confrontation. You didn't have a fight with a tree today,
did you?"

"No," I said, "it wasn't nearly as bad as hitting the tree." Dad chuckled at the memory
and for a moment I chuckled with him.

"I'm happy to hear that. So tell me about this lesser accident you had."

I told him about playing bolts. He knew about that because he had helped me pick out
bolts that were the right size from his tools and equipment. We had even experimented with
them to find the size to get the loudest bang. "Then, one time after we threw them, Mars
ran over and took them all and put them in his pockets. I was angry, but I was afraid and
didn't say anything at all." I felt tears coming down my cheeks. I could not look my father
in the face. "But a couple of guys said he had to give them back. Mars said no he wouldn't.
Then he took one and threw it really hard at Ronnie and hit Ronnie in the forehead. He
was bleeding. It looked bad to me, and Mars came up and he was going to hit Ronnie some
more. He is really a mean guy. I was so scared I could hardly move because I knew he was
going to beat me up next. I really don't know what happened, but I tried to push Mars away

from Ronnie. The next thing I knew he had my arm twisted behind my back, and he had me on the ground and was rubbing my face in the gravel. I'm sorry, Dad," I said, "I didn't want to be so scared and get beat up again." I was sobbing now.

"Well, Geordie, bein' scared's no sic a bad thing. If ye'r no scared at the recht things, ye'd be a damn fool. Aye, it's true. Ye know, in 1917 and 18, I was in the trenches in France for many months. We'd be shelled by the Huns every morning. I never knew a soldier during my time there who wasn't afraid most of the time, afraid during the shelling, waiting for it to start, afraid even after it stopped when we had to find the dead and wounded and take them back behind the lines. When ye see a danger tae yersel, it's natural to be afraid. It's what keeps ye alive, or gives ye a better chance in a war or a situation like you were in today." I sniffed and drew my sleeve across my runny nose. Dad handed me his handkerchief. "What makes the difference among men is not fear. Nearly all men are afraid of certain things. What makes the difference is their ability to do what they hae to do despite the fear. Do ye ken what I mean?" I was not sure I understood, but I nodded that I did. "Now, from what yer principal says in her letter, you acted to save Ronnie, and, apparently, so says Ronnie. From what you say, you acted to help Ronnie in spite of yer fear. Now that's a mark of a courageous man. And I'm proud of ye. Do ye ken what I'm tellin' ye?" If Dad was proud of me, it really did not matter if I understood.

But Dad was not finished. "Be that as it may," he said, "you've a serious problem with yer fightin'. Dinnae put yer arm oot so yer opponent can take it and twist it behind yer back. That's foolishness. Keep yer arms in so ye can defend yersel against blows. Put them oot to jab with as much force as you can and aim for somethin' vital. But bring it back quickly. Like this." He demonstrated a right jab, then a left. He bent down and pulled the box with our boxing gloves from under his bench. "Put on a pair," he said and began to put on a pair himself. We practiced jabbing and defending against jabs until Mom called us for dinner. As I sat down at the table, I noticed that my scratches no longer hurt and that the tight pain in my chest had completely disappeared.

I hope this story suggests the way in which my self-image changed as a result of the experience. I was lucky to have a father who was willing to try to understand my twisted sense of self, a task he undertook on many occasions. In this instance, I firmly associated courage with winning the fight. How could a loser be courageous? Only winners receive applause. At the time, his calling me courageous seemed inappropriate. I assumed he did it to make me feel better, and it did. I thought I had to learn to be courageous, and I like to think I did. Perhaps I had the germ of courage in me at ten, as my father had assured me, but I did not believe him until I wrote the story.

The Place of Narrative in the Writing Curriculum

Some critics charge that schools focus too much on narrative writing and that, in doing so, they fail children in other areas of writing. Stotsky (1995), for example, while admitting that "personal or personalized writing" in the curriculum gives "students opportunities to explore their own lives and to discover things about themselves and others that they might not otherwise have learned" (758), goes on to protest the excessive, sometimes exclusive "emphasis on using the writer's life experience as the chief source of the writer's ideas . . . by means of a 'natural' writing process, that is, by means of a succession of drafts on a topic of the writer's own choosing, with each draft revised in response to peer comments and/or questions by a teacher in a conference" (764). Stotsky lists several researchers and theorists who advocate this approach to teaching writing. But research by Applebee (1981, 1984) and Hillocks (2002) indicates that while it may be advocated by theorists and researchers, very few teachers use it. Most use far more traditional methods of teaching writing, certainly in middle school and high school. They focus on what might be regarded as informational writing linked to subjects of study but almost devoid of any original analysis by the student writers and frequently linked to formulaic writing such as the five-paragraph theme.

The problem is not that teachers spend too much time on narrative, which even Stotsky regards as valuable. Rather, the problem is that teachers do not spend time teaching the *strategies* that enable writers to generate the kinds of concrete detail that make writing effective. They tend to begin with examples of the kinds of writing to be produced or prescriptions for the form the writing is to take and then ask students to write, devoting little or no time to helping them learn *how* to produce the content.

Without question students should become proficient in many kinds of writing. But there are many reasons for including narrative throughout the curriculum. Knowing how to write narratives can become a base for other kinds of writing and for studying literature.

Using Concrete Details

First, effective narrative depends on concrete detail. In my early years of teaching, I found myself writing quick notes in the margins of student papers. One of the most frequent, whatever the kind of writing my students were doing, was "Be more specific." It didn't take me long to conclude that either students did not know what *specific* meant or they did not know how to generate the requisite detail. In narrative writing we can teach students what specificity is and how to achieve it. Once students have learned to generate such concrete details for personal writing, it is easier for them to learn to generate details for other kinds of writing, even though the details serve different functions. Though the function of details in personal writing is primarily to arouse an empathic response from the reader, they also provide a sense of reality and immediacy, both of which are important in other kinds of writing.

Selecting Appropriate Details

Second, effective narrative depends on thoughtfully selecting what to include and what to exclude. Graves (1983) has commented on the tendency of neophyte writers to do bed-to-bed stories, which begin with arising and having breakfast, even though the incident of interest does not take place until late afternoon; perhaps they assume that including whatever comes to mind is fair game because it lets them fill up the required number of pages. On the other hand, students frequently don't think to include the details that will help produce an overall effect. Nor does it occur to them that they might stop and ask themselves what details could make a picture clearer or more compelling.

Learning how to select the appropriate details when writing a narrative is fairly easy. While the principles of selection differ in other genres of writing, the need to select toward a purpose carries over. It is not so great a shift from asking, "What details can I include to convey more forcefully and clearly how I felt in this situation?" to asking, "What specific details will provide more convincing evidence in making this case?"

Developing Audience Awareness

Third, neophyte writers tend to write without much concern for audience response. Their concern is to get a story down on paper in general terms. Because the stories are theirs, these general terms resonate with all the details they experienced, but, of course, their readers will not have the benefit of that resonance. Sound instruction in writing narrative should help students be more aware of writing for an audience, a requisite for all kinds of writing, even alphabetical directory listings. Once learned, the consideration of audience is readily carried over to other kinds of writing.

For the carryover to occur, however, we must design our instruction so that students become metacognitively aware of what they are doing. That is, students should learn to talk about specificity, selection, and audience response in meaningful ways as they discuss their own and others' efforts.

Becoming Better Readers

Finally, the work on writing narrative should contribute to students' reading of literature and do so in specific ways. For one thing, learning to write narrative helps students attend to the details in the literature they read. Having learned to select, they can attend to the selection of other writers. Having learned to write for special effects on audiences, they can think about the effects other writers hope to achieve with their audiences.

More important, once students have a sound understanding of how to write personal narrative, they can bring that knowledge to bear in conceptualizing the literature they read. Making these multiple and layered connections explicit is one of the features identified by Langer (2001) in schools that beat the odds, schools whose students perform well above what might be predicted from their socioeconomic status.

For example, in a unit on courage in which students might work to define courage before reading several works of literature exemplifying different concepts of courage, both teacher and students might write about an incident in which they felt they displayed or failed to display courage. These stories can be used as the basis for a discussion of the essential characteristics of courage—for example, being able to control one's fear in the face of significant danger or threat in order to be able to act for the greater good. (The best discussion of the nature of courage and a far more complete definition appear in Aristotle's *Nichomachean Ethics*, Book III, Chapters 6–9 [1947].)

Here's another example. In a unit on the concept of the outcast that all ninth-grade teachers in my department taught from 1959 to 1965, students were asked to write a story about an experience in which they had felt ostracized. (The original version of this unit appears in *Concepts of Man: A Curriculum for Average Students* [Western Reserve University 1964].) We learned that every student, no matter how popular or "in," had felt ostracized at one time or another. Writing and sharing the stories seemed not only to alleviate tendencies toward ostracism in our classes but also to contribute to a better understanding of the causes and effects of social exclusion. The stories helped students develop tentative answers to questions like *Why do some people ostracize others? What effects does ostracism have on those who are ostracized? On those who perpetrate the exclusion?*

The History of This Book: Learning How to Teach Narrative

During my first fifteen years in the classroom, I tried to teach my students to be specific in their writing by exhorting them to do so, citing examples in stories and essays we read and praising specifics on the rare occasions they appeared in my students' writing. Not surprisingly, these techniques had little or no effect. The writers who were already specific flourished. Most of the others made little or no progress.

In the last class I taught at Bowling Green State University, a writing class for upperclassmen required (in addition to freshman English) for graduation, I had the same problem. In search of a solution, I began to bring unusual natural objects to class so that students would have something specific to observe and write about. After discussing the objects in small groups to help them zero in on characteristics and appropriate specific language, they wrote about them. The level of specificity was terrific. After only three such classes, the exercises began to carry over to other writing: these students used far more specific language in whatever they wrote.

When I moved to the University of Chicago that fall, I became the director of the Master of Arts in Teaching (MAT) program for the English department. In 1972, I instituted a composition workshop for eleven- to fifteen-year-olds whom we recruited from neighboring schools. The goal of the workshop (which met for one hour five days a week) was to provide learning opportunities for the MAT students and for the young people who enrolled. I wanted the MAT students to learn how to structure effective lessons, how to evaluate their success or failure, how to generate discussion, how to operate several productive small-group discussions in a class while monitoring progress in each of the several groups, and so forth. Four days each week we used the kinds of structured activities presented in this book. The fifth day was devoted to elective projects—writing and producing a puppet play, a two-minute movie, a cookbook.

The youngsters enjoyed the workshop. (Two of them recently told me that after more than thirty years, they still have the puppets and scripts for their play.) The problem was that nearly all of our students came from the University of Chicago Laboratory School, were interested in writing, and were fairly proficient at it. Even when the neophyte MAT teachers made errors (forgot an important part of a sequenced lesson, rushed through a discussion, gave faulty directions), our young students, who were very bright to begin with, compensated for the problems and produced fairly good writing. I decided my MAT students needed a more challenging audience to better prepare them for the students they would likely encounter after their graduation.

That spring I visited the principal of a Chicago public school down the street from my office and asked her if it might be possible for my students and me to take over a class of seventh or eighth graders for four or five weeks in the fall in order to teach writing. She seemed pleased and gave me a choice of available classes. I requested what she called "the low-level seventh-grade language arts class." The class was being taught by a science teacher. He was happy to have us, as he did not relish teaching writing. The students in the class were all African Americans except for two Vietnamese boys who spoke very little English. My students and I taught writing to a comparable class every year for fifteen years until that principal retired.

We then found a new school with a different population, nearly all receiving reduced-price or free lunches: about 35 percent African American, 40 percent Hispanic, the remainder Asian and white. Here we worked with sixth-, seventh-, and eighth-grade classes. When this principal left for a suburban school three years later, we moved to a Chicago high school with an 89 percent poverty level and a similar racial mixture.

The MAT students were learning to be English teachers. The great majority had no experience teaching, although some had experience as counselors in summer camps and some had done volunteer work in schools. They were neophyte teachers in every sense. By the time we began the workshop, they had been with me for a course on teaching writing and had planned or examined many of the lessons we replanned for use in our classes. For about eighteen years we taught seventh graders. For a few years, groups of MAT students taught sixth, seventh, and eighth graders, and for about seven years we taught ninth graders. On any given day in the workshop, one of us would be the teacher while everyone else acted as observers using different observational techniques.

The approaches to teaching the writing of narrative presented in this book have been developed and vetted in more than thirty inner-city classrooms in a period of more than twenty years and have been found to be effective with racially diverse student populations, nearly all of whom lived in poverty. Given the current grim reports of African American and Hispanic students' writing ability, this is important, because it demonstrates that significant gains are achievable among students who have "suffered the slings and arrows of outrageous fortune" and for whom little in the way of achievement is expected.

The National Assessment of Educational Progress' *Nation's Report Card* for writing for 2002, for example, indicates that while only 10 percent of white eighth graders score at the lowest level of writing skill, 23 percent of blacks and 23 percent of Hispanics do. Conversely, while 34 percent of white eighth graders score at the proficient level, only 14 percent of black and 17 percent of Hispanic eighth graders do. Hedges and Nowell (1998) argue that while the test score gap has narrowed, it remains large. In examining the data from NAEP writing tests from 1984 to 1994, they found that the standard deviation between blacks and whites in writing ranged from .86 to .67. This is a very large difference, and the differences between low and high socioeconomic groups and between males and females are comparable. According to Hedges and Nowell (1995), "The large sex differences in writing ability suggested by the NAEP trend data are alarming. . . . The data imply that males are, on average, at a rather profound disadvantage in the performance of this basic skill" (45). They believe that the larger number of males who perform near the bottom of the distribution in reading comprehension and writing has policy implications. "It seems likely that individuals with such poor literacy skills will have difficulty finding employment in an increasingly information-driven economy. Thus, some intervention may be required to enable them to participate constructively in the workplace" (45). (For a more comprehensive review of the test score gaps in writing, see Hillocks 2006.)

We know that the traditional approaches to teaching writing described in Applebee (1981, 1984) and Hillocks (2002)—using models and focusing on form—are largely ineffective (Hillocks 1986). One alternative is the focus on writing as process. However, while it is intuitively obvious that students need to learn that writing is a process, that revision is more than cosmetic, and that several drafts may be necessary, that knowledge alone seems inadequate. Lisa Delpit (1995) has commented on the writing process model described by Stotsky (1995), especially in regard to minority children and children raised in poverty. She explains that in her first years of teaching she was a process-oriented teacher in a predominantly African American school. She comments:

> My white students zoomed ahead. They worked hard at the learning stations. They did amazing things with books and writing. My black students played the games; they learned how to weave; and they threw the books around the learning stations. They practiced karate moves on the new carpets. Some of them even learned how to read, but none of them as quickly as my white students. (13)

She argues that this discrepancy is the result of her neglecting to provide explicit instruction in "skills," by which she means not simply grammar and usage and spelling but other kinds of skills as well, which she defines as useful and useable knowledge which contributes to children's ability to communicate effectively in standard, generally acceptable literary forms. . . . I believe that skills are best taught through meaningful communication, best learned in meaningful contexts. . . . Skills are a necessary but insufficient aspect of black and minority students' education. Students need technical skills to open doors, but they need to be able to think critically and creatively to participate in meaningful and potentially liberating work within those doors. (19)

This book concentrates on explicit skills that depend on procedural knowledge, on learning *how* to do things rather than simply being told what is required; the declarative knowledge of traditional teaching. In effect, this book presents a new model of teaching, demonstrating how to engage students in thinking creatively and critically in meaningful contexts. Specifically, this book is about the pedagogical content knowledge (Shulman 1986) necessary to teach the procedural knowledge basic to writing effective personal narrative. Procedural knowledge is the kind of knowledge that 71 percent of English teachers in a recent survey (Dudley-Marling et al, 2006) chose as being the "most, second [most,] or third most important for becoming a 'highly qualified' English teacher" (174). Of the twenty other qualities and qualifications surveyed, no other comes close to this level of selection.

Crucial to procedural knowledge involved in the effective teaching of narrative is knowledge of how to create activities:

- that provide concrete phenomena for students to work with (e.g., sea shells, scenarios, recorded sounds),
- that are nearly instantly enticing and engaging for students,
- that inherently involve using strategies important to generating and shaping the content of writing,
- and that are so designed that what each student says and/or does has the potential for becoming the learning material for everyone in the group.

When activities are designed to meet these criteria, you and your students will be in a flow of activity that appears to jump time. Csikszentmihalyi and Larson (1984) studied affective states of adolescents who volunteered to carry pagers as they went about their daily routines. When the pagers beeped at random times during the day, students would respond by indicating what they were thinking and doing and to indicate their mood by responding to a series of scales and questions. The authors analyze several thousand of these reports and conclude that "the average student is usually bored, apathetic, and unfriendly" (205) in school situations. In fact, they state that "schools are essentially machines for providing negative feedback. They are supposed to reduce deviance, to constrain the behavior and the minds of adolescents within straight and narrow channels" (198–99).

Schools do not provide what the authors call *flow* experience, the kind that results in high levels of pleasure, confidence, and absorption by the tasks at hand. They argue that intrinsic motivation is "relatively high in informal activities like group work and discussions. This is also when students are most happy and active" (206–7). My students and I would argue that the kinds of activities described in the ensuing chapters results in *flow experience* for teacher and students alike and result in gains in writing for our minority students, which the study in Appendix A demonstrates are among the largest for any groups in studies of the teaching of writing. This book wants to help you put your students in the *flow* and help them achieve comparable gains.

2

What Makes a Good Personal Narrative?

Although many teachers teach narrative because it appears on the state assessment, most state scoring guides do not reveal much about what constitutes quality. Many merely reiterate the criteria in the *Nation's Report Card* for writing, developed by the National Assessment of Educational Progress. The 2002 edition lists the following as necessary for a rating of excellent on an eighth-grade narrative response:

1. Tells a clear story that is well developed and shaped with well-chosen details across the response.
2. Is well organized with strong transitions.
3. Sustains variety in sentence structure and exhibits good word choice.
4. Errors in grammar, punctuation, and spelling are few and do not interfere with understanding. (89)

The criteria for an excellent response by twelfth graders are quite similar. For example, the first twelfth-grade criterion is "Tells a clear story that is consistently well developed and detailed; details enhance the story being told" (92). What exactly is the difference here between an excellent response in eighth grade and one in twelfth grade? What does "well developed" mean? The NAEP criteria do not make it clear. Indeed most rubrics for judging narrative do not even specify what counts as detail.

A guide for scoring autobiographical incidents prepared by the California Department of Education (1994, no page numbers) is much more helpful.

The best writers use many strategies, selecting those appropriate to the writing situation. Those strategies include the following:

- Narrating specific action (movements, gestures, postures, expressions).
- Describing visual details of scenes, objects, or people (size, colors, shapes, features, dress).
- Describing sounds or smells of the scene.
- Creating dialogues or interior monologues.
- Expressing remembered feelings or insights at the time of the incident.
- Pacing: accelerating the pace to accommodate time or mood changes or slowing the pace to elaborate the central moment in the incident.

- Creating suspense, tension, or surprise.
- Comparing or contrasting with other scenes or people.

Specificity, Style, and Elaboration

Most of the strategies in the previous list have to do with what I call *specificity*. Only two—pacing and creating suspense—have more to do with selecting and arranging details than with generating them. I would include those two along with effective openings and endings, voice, and similar qualities and characteristics in what I call *style*. The third area determining quality is episodic *elaboration*. Good stories nearly always recount at least one episode that takes place in a particular setting. Even in the simplest story, a character engaged in some activity in a setting encounters something that causes her to take some action, usually an attempt to accomplish or avoid something. The attempt has some result, and there is a response on the part of the character to the result. More complex stories will recount more than one episode and may even introduce interlocking episodes as characters interact.

Rating Scales

Using a rubric to evaluate student writing before, during, and after a unit on writing makes it possible to determine average or mean class gains. More important, *it guides our teaching*, helping us plan what lessons to include from day to day, set the objectives for each lesson, develop a concrete notion of what we need to teach toward in each lesson, and reflect upon the effects of each lesson.

If quality in narrative writing depends largely on episodic elaboration, specificity, and style, we need first to determine what *counts* as effective episodic elaboration, specificity, and style. Without concrete criteria for measuring these elements, teachers often accept and/or praise the ineffective. They are not motivated to help students achieve the most they can, and the students themselves accept a lowered standard for success. The table at the end of this chapter is the rubric my MAT students and I developed over the course of twenty-five years to rate student narratives. We have used it with very high levels of agreement. (If you wish to do a formal evaluation of student progress, it will be best to use the procedures outlined in Appendix A.)

Let's apply this rubric to a number of student-written narratives.

Episodic Elaboration

The idea of elaboration is based on story grammar theory (Stein and Trabasso 1982), which argues that good stories, at a minimum, include a statement of setting or ongoing action and an episode consisting of the following elements:

- an initiating event indicating a change in the protagonist's environment and usually evoking some goal or reaction on the part of the protagonist
- an internal response, which may be implied and which may include an emotional response to the change and the formation of a goal

- some attempt by the protagonist to achieve the goal
- a consequence indicating whether the goal was achieved and in more complex stories giving rise to a second episode
- a reaction to the consequence(s), which might include the character's emotional response to the events that have gone on before, the formation of a new goal, or a statement of what the character has learned

The following text, "The Thrilling Soccer Game," written by an eighth-grade boy, illustrates all of these episodic features. This piece is a revision of an earlier story about the game, written to the following prompt: "Write a story about an event that is meaningful to you in some way. Write about it so specifically that another person reading it will see what you saw and feel what you felt."

The Thrilling Soccer Game

There was a minute in the thrilling soccer game left. Our team, the Vikings, were tied with Hammond 1 to 1. I was dribbling the ball at a fast pace down the field. I could hear the other team's feet trembling against the hard, dry ground. The light-weighted soccer ball was gliding over the hard surface every time I gave it a soft tap. My heart started pumping faster as I closed up on the other goalie. My teammate Charlie was following me on my right side. My feet felt like two humming birds flying to their nests. The fullback on the other team was pushing my shoulder trying to lure the ball away. I passed the ball to Charlie who was just a few feet ahead of me. He dribbled the ball to the goalies box then he centered it to me. I started shaking like a leaf as I kicked the ball past the darting goalie and into the big goal net. I started jumping for joy as my teammates came around me to share my happiness.

The first several sentences provide the setting and ongoing action. The initiating event is the tied score, and the response to that, the goal, is implied in the narrator's dribbling the ball toward the opponent's net. A second initiating action is the opposing fullback's attempt to "lure" the ball away. The speaker responds by passing the ball to his teammate. We must again infer the goal of that pass, but even a little knowledge of the game makes it fairly apparent. Centering the ball to the narrator is another initiating event that sets up the winning score, the goal of the story established at the beginning. Although certain elements of this story are implied, none is far from the surface, given the context. Certain initiating events and responses are compounded—that is, they appear more than once within a single episodic structure—a relatively sophisticated variation because not many students use it.

In contrast, look at this first draft written by a ninth-grade girl to the same prompt:

The Ski Trip

The event that I am writing about is the ski trip. I looked forward to this event. I had fun during this time & enjoyed it a lot. The consequences it brought was this: I came home tired & sore with bruises & pain. I am glad I went but sorry I had all the pain. I have gone skiing before but I have never had the pain like I did with this ski trip. I would want to do this again but don't want pain.

What is missing in this "story"? There is no specific action on the part of the main character, although we can infer the general action of skiing. There is no goal that can be inferred, except perhaps trying to remain upright on the skis. There is a consequence (pain) and an often reiterated response to it (the writer does not want it again). This may have a germ of a story in it, but the writer will have to answer several questions: What precisely did you try to do during the ski trip? What did you do that resulted in pain? What were the various incidents that resulted in pain?

The following example is from a pretest written to the same prompt by Maurice, a seventh grader at a different school:

> Last night when I left school I went home and talked on the phone for about one hour and then I went out front and talked to friends and then came back upstairs and talked on the phone again and then we went to the store and bout some candy and we went home to my house and watch tv for a couple of hours and played around a while then my mother came home from work we went to my grandmother's house for a party it was my mother's birthday we had pizza, lasayna and cake and ice cream and pop and my mother's sister she came over and they went out to party and then we went home and we got to watch movies on tv until really late like 2 in the morning.

This is obviously not a story either. The piece presents a series of actions but no specific goals, no consequences, and therefore no responses to the consequences. Perhaps there is a real story hidden in the comment about staying up "really late" but we cannot infer what it is from the text provided. Both this untitled piece and "The Ski Trip" would be scored 1 on the scale for episode elaboration because there are no parts of an episode and the setting is virtually nonexistent.

At level 2, pieces tend to present settings and episodes in skeletal form with nothing elaborated beyond the bare statement of what happened. Often the skeletal episode appears only after considerable preliminary material that is not directly related either to the setting or to the main episode. These frequently begin as accounts of trips. They do exhibit a fairly clear line of events both in the preliminary material and in the episode, but they have a very expository ring. Here's an example:

The Night I Went to Wisconsin Dells
by Ronakea

This summer 1988 on Friday night at 9:30 P.M. my parents decided to go on a trip to Wisconsin Dells. We packed our bags and loaded the car. We headed out to the highway and the first time my father paid the toll was $1.20 and the next toll was 40 cents. My father drove for 3 hours, but we didn't make it to Wisconsin Dells because my father made a wrong turn and we were heading our way back to Chicago! So my father turned around and said "we'll go to lake Geneva because it was a shorter ride. I fell asleep and my mother did to, finally I woke up and we were at a Motel.

It was $60.00 for one night and all it was a little cottage and all of us couldn't sleep in one bed so father slept on a cot me and my mother slept in the bed. I was so excited because my Grandfather work down in lake Geneva he owned a barbecue pit called Gino's. He sold ribs, chicken, fish, bread pudding, salad, and all the drinks you want. We went there for a little while then I went shopping with my mother to by some biking shorts, Gym Shoes, and a T-Shirt.

Then we kept riding and went to Wisconsin dells. We found a hotel at Wisconsin dells 6:00 A.M. in the morning. So then we all took showers put on our new clothes and headed out to explore Wisconsin. We got on the boat ride call the upper dells at 2:00 P.M. and I saw a lot interesting that God made and nature did together it was beautiful! I [saw] rock formation trees that were growing out of the rocks it was a extrodinary. Then after all that we had a 17 year old captain it was fun. Then it was time to go back home to Chicago and we made it home at 12:00 P.M.

Primarily, Ronakea has listed events that make up her trip. She makes a real attempt to be specific, but the details do not have to do with the episode. I would argue that she includes one skeletal episode beginning "So then we all took showers put on our new clothes and headed out to explore Wisconsin." Her goal is to see something of Wisconsin. She does and presents her reactions. She might have focused on what she saw and made a solid episode of it. That is something she can learn.

The following piece, "My Best Track Meet," does include a fully developed episode. It is a first draft, written as a posttest following instruction.

My Best Track Meet
by Andreanna

In the middle of July, 1994, I was stretching out for a big track race. I was very nervous and I had butterflies in my stomach. There was a lot more teams getting ready to race. Me and my teammates were ready to race. It was almost time to start. We had shirts that said "Independence Park." That was where we were at. The coaches split all of us into groups with other kids. My friends wished me good luck, and I wished them good luck too. It was my group that was going first. We all lined up at the starting line. It was hot and sunny and I was sweating to death. It was very dusty through the track field. All you could hear was people talking, and see kids stretching.

Well, we were all ready, and next thing you know, "On your mark, get set, go!" He blew the whistle. I was sweating so much and running so fast. The field was so dusty I couldn't see much. All I saw was the track field way across the other side of the park. The field was like a snake shriveled up around the whole park. All the dust was going in my mouth. And my sides where my ribs are started to hurt. It felt like my lungs were dying. I could hardly breathe, but I said to myself, "I'm gonna try." So I started running faster and faster. I heard the sound of trees blowing up against each other and the sound of people roaring far away. My body felt hot inside my ankles were hurting like if someone stuck a nail inside of them. My thighs were getting tired and my heart was beating like three or four times a second. I noticed that I passed up about ten or twelve people. There was about four or five or six people in front of me. I saw the red ribbons and the coaches standing there with pens and notepads. I tried to go faster to beat them, but they beat me to it. I passed the red ribbons and they took down my tag number that was on my back.

When I stopped I was dizzy and almost fainted. All I saw was the whole park going round and round. The coaches told me to keep moving and walking around, and get some water. Everybody came through the red ribbons a few seconds after me.

After a while, my body temperature went back to its normal temperature, and my heart was beating normal again. My nerves went back to their normal selves, and the butterflies in my stomach flew out.

Well, it was time to give the medals. My group was the first to call out. I wasn't first or second or third or fourth, but when it came to fifth they called my name. I was so surprised and happy that I jumped up so fast and ran to the coach and got my medal. Well, it wasn't a medal, but it was a fifth place green ribbon. I went by my coach and thanked her for her support, and everything she taught me. She told me, "You're welcome, and congratulations." That night when I went home I was very proud of myself.

This is quite an accomplished piece of writing for a first draft. The opening paragraph presents a fairly elaborate setting and establishes the narrator's goal, to win the race or do her best to win. The second long paragraph narrates several attempts to win as the race progresses so as to include further statements about the setting that become obstacles to overcome. The final three sentences of the paragraph constitute an episode of their own. She sees competitors in front of her, turns on the steam, and attempts to catch them. The final three paragraphs provide her reactions to the race and her winning fifth place. Because the attempts to win are compounded, as in "The Thrilling Soccer Game," this piece scores a 4 (without the compounding, it would score a 3, still respectable).

The following piece, written to the same prompt by a ninth-grade girl from a suburban school after instruction as a posttest, is one of the strongest I have encountered. It includes complex, interacting episodes based on the interactions of different characters.

Cheating
by Casey

"Jenny, come up here and bring your test," the teacher suddenly said. All heads in the class turned to stare at the blonde girl sitting next to me.

"You too, Casey." My whole body stiffened. "What could she want me for?" my mind cried out in panic. Wide-eyed and blushing because now all eyes were fixed on me, I slowly stood up and, test in hand, slid up to my teachers metal-gray desk where Jenny was already standing. My science teacher beckoned us with her perfectly manicured finger to follow her outside while the student teacher stayed to watch the rest of the kids take their mid-terms. Once outside the stuffy classroom, my teacher calmly shut the door. I glanced over at my friend Jenny and, with my eyes, asked her what was going on. She didn't see my mental message because her eyes were glued to an imaginary piece of lint on her angora sweater which she was trying to pick off.

"All right now." I bit my lip in anticipation.

"Why were you two cheating?" she spoke with a hint of exasperation. I couldn't believe my ears. I pinched myself. My head reeled at her accusation. All of a sudden, realization shot through me. Jenny! I shot a murderous yet questioning look at her. She saw my expression and burst into tears.

We had been taking our mid-term science exams. Our teacher, Mrs. Cramer, had asked us to cover our test papers with something. I'd taken a sheet of paper out to cover my test with but when we'd gotten started, I'd forgotten to use it. My lab partner Jenny and I were not the best of friends but we had fun. She had a loud, flirtatious personality while I was quiet and more reserved. Sitting next to her before the test started, I'd noticed that she seemed worried and anxious. That was no big news though because so was everyone else in the class including me.

In the principals office later that day she had broken down and told everything. Jenny had also added, to my cardiovascular relief, that I had no part in it. My emotions were raging intensely against each other. Sympathy fought rage. Relief fought anger. I was allowed to retake my test the next day. Whoopee. I never did find out what happened to Jenny, other than the fact that she'd been suspended and gotten an F for her semester grade, or why she'd done it. From that day on I always covered my tests, but I learned more than that. Whatever motivates people to do such things, it must blind the person from thinking about the consequences.

This story consists of three interlocking episodes, one for the teacher, one for Jenny, and one for Casey, the narrator. The setting for each is taking the test. The initiating event for the teacher is noticing the cheating; her goal is to uncover who is cheating and punish the cheaters. The result is successful punishment of Jenny, but we do not learn the teacher's response to it. For Jenny, the initiating event is the test itself. Her goal is to pass the test by copying answers. The result is being caught and punished. We learn her responses in front of the teacher and in the principal's office. For the narrator, the initiating event is being called to the front of the room; her attempt to deal with the situation is the "murderous look" she gives Jenny. The result is Jenny's confession, and the narrator's response is relief and speculation about what gives rise to cheating.

Such complexity is unusual for stories by middle and high school students. If characters appear other than the narrator, most often they cooperate with or block the narrator, but they do not instigate action that results in a new episode. Note the secondary characters in "The Thrilling Soccer Game." In a sense, they serve as part of the setting. On our scale, we score interlocking episodes of the kind in "Cheating" at the highest level, 5.

Specificity

There is a myth prevalent among many teachers of English that concrete sensory detail is evidenced by many adjectives, a myth widely accepted by writers of textbooks and other authorities. Ladson-Billings, in her book *The Dreamkeepers*, presents the following vignette of a teacher she regards as outstanding:

> To encourage the students to use more descriptive, colorful language in their writing, she has developed an activity to get them to reach for unusual adjectives. This class is held in October and so she benefits from a Halloween atmosphere. She writes a noun on the chalkboard and asks the children to think of as many words as they can to describe it. The first noun is "witch." Tentatively at first, students begin to offer some modifiers. "Old witch," says one student. "Mean witch," says another. "Black witch," offers a third. All of a sudden, Peggy grasps her chest as if she were having a heart attack and rolls her eyes back in their sockets. "Black witch, old witch, mean witch—give me a break! You guys are killin' me! I need some great, fantastic, outstanding, stupendous, magnificent adjectives. I'll even take some compound adjectives. Can anybody save me?" After a few snickers, one boy ventures, "How about a green-faced, hook-nose, evil witch?" "Yes!" shouts Peggy Valentine. "Now you're cookin' with gas. Give me more, more!" The lesson proceeds with students shouting out a variety of compound and complex adjective phrases to revive the "dying" Valentine. The lesson goes on for almost forty minutes. (1994, 43)

The important question is whether or not such listing of adjectives carries over into writing and benefits the writing. Perhaps in Ms. Valentine's class of fourth graders it does, but in several classes of sixth and seventh graders I observed as part of a study I conducted recently, it did not have the salutary effects predicted for it by the teachers who used it. In fact, none of the classes showed positive, let alone significant, gains in writing (Hillocks, in progress).

One reason is that a high level of specificity is not synonymous with "lots of juicy adjectives." Let's take a look at a powerful passage from Toni Morrison's *Beloved*, a passage in which Denver considers Sethe's state of mind in regard to Beloved near the end of the novel.

> Yet she knew Sethe's greatest fear was the same one Denver had in the beginning—that Beloved might leave. That before Sethe could make her understand what it meant—what it took to drag the teeth of that saw under the little chin; to feel the baby blood pump like oil in her hands; to hold her face so her head would stay on; to squeeze her so she could absorb, still, the death spasms that shot through that adored body, plump and sweet with life—Beloved might leave. Leave before Sethe could make her realize that worse than that—far

worse—was what Baby Suggs died of, what Ella knew, what Stamp saw, and what made Paul D tremble. That anybody white could take your whole self for anything that came to mind. Not just work, kill, or maim you, but dirty you. Dirty you so bad you couldn't like yourself anymore. Dirty you so bad you forgot who you were and couldn't think it up. And though she and others lived through and got over it, she could never let it happen to her own. The best thing she was, was her children. Whites might dirty *her* all right, but not her best thing, her beautiful, magical best thing—the part of her that was clean. No undreamable dreams about whether the headless, feetless torso hanging in the tree with a sign on it was her husband or Paul A; whether the bubbling-hot girls in the colored-school fire set by patriots included her daughter; whether a gang of whites invaded her daughter's private parts, soiled her daughter's thighs, and threw her daughter out of the wagon. *She* might have to work the slaughterhouse yard, but not her daughter. (1987)

This passage is 284 words long, but I count only sixteen true adjectives, a mere 5.6 percent. Yet the passage seems quite concrete. The truth is that the quality of concreteness, or specificity, derives from the imagery produced largely by nouns and verbs and the function words that hold them together.

Now examine the following passage from Charles Dickens' *David Copperfield*, the passage in which, when his mother does not appear, David fears that she might be dead and Peggotty tells him that his fragile mother has married Mr. Murdstone:

"Not dead, too! Oh, she's not dead, Peggotty?" Peggotty cried out No! with an astonishing volume of voice; and then sat down, and began to pant, and said I had given her a turn.

I gave her a hug to take away the turn, or to give her another turn in the right direction, and then stood before her, looking at her in anxious inquiry.

"You see, dear, I should have told you before now," said Peggotty, "but I hadn't an opportunity. I ought to have made it, perhaps, but I couldn't azackly"—that was always the substitute for exactly, in Peggotty's militia of words—"bring my mind to it."

"Go on, Peggotty," said I, more frightened than before. "Master Davy," said Peggotty, untying her bonnet with a shaking hand, and speaking in a breathless sort of way. "What do you think? You have got a Pa!"

I trembled, and turned white. Something—I don't know what, or how—connected with the grave in the churchyard, and the raising of the dead, seemed to strike me like an unwholesome wind.

"A new one," said Peggotty. "A new one?" I repeated.

Peggotty gave a gasp, as if she were swallowing something that was very hard, and, putting out her hand, said: "Come and see him."

"I don't want to see him."

"And your mama," said Peggotty.

I ceased to draw back, and we went straight to the best parlour, where she left me. On one side of the fire, sat my mother; on the other, Mr. Murdstone. My mother dropped her work, and arose hurriedly, but timidly I thought.

"Now, Clara my dear," said Mr. Murdstone. "Recollect! Control yourself, always control yourself! Davy boy, how do you do?"

I gave him my hand. After a moment of suspense, I went and kissed my mother: she kissed me, patted me gently on the shoulder and sat down again to her work. I could not look at her, I could not look at him, I knew quite well he was looking at us both; and I turned to the window and looked out there at some shrubs that were drooping their heads in the cold. (1970, 50–51)

This passage has 359 words, of which only 10 are adjectives by my count. Yet it is very specific, providing insight into both Peggotty's and David's attitudes toward Mr. Murdstone. The final three sentences, all of which are simple or compound simple sentences with no adjectives, provide a concrete picture. The poignancy and sadness of the scene are conveyed through pronouns, nouns, and verbs, none of which are unusual, all of which are in the vocabulary range of middle school and high school students.

Consider some of the most powerful images from "Cheating," which appear near the beginning of the story:

My science teacher beckoned us with her perfectly manicured finger to follow her outside while the student teacher stayed to watch the rest of the kids take their mid-terms. Once outside the stuffy classroom, my teacher calmly shut the door. I glanced over at my friend Jenny and, with my eyes, asked her what was going on. She didn't see my mental message because her eyes were glued to an imaginary piece of lint on her angora sweater which she was trying to pick off.

In this passage the words in adjective positions include *science, manicured, student, stuffy, mental, imaginary,* and *angora*—seven words (of which three are nouns being used as adjectives), just under 5 percent. What makes the passage so effective is not the quantity of adjectives or their juiciness, but the details, which are composed mainly of nouns, verbs, and pronouns. The detail of Jenny pretending to focus on an imaginary piece of lint that she is trying to remove characterizes both Jenny and the tension of the situation. It is a wonderful detail but includes only one important adjective: *imaginary*. What counts in specificity is not the adjectives but the kind and quality of the details included. A writer with less talent might have said, "Jenny stood looking down."

Now consider Andreanna's description of running her race:

The field was like a snake shriveled up around the whole park. All the dust was going in my mouth. And my sides where my ribs are started to hurt. It felt like my lungs were dying. I could hardly breathe, but I said to myself, "I'm gonna try." So I started running faster and faster. I heard the sound of trees blowing up against each other and the sound of people roaring far away. My body felt hot inside and my ankles were hurting like if someone stuck a nail inside of them. My thighs were getting tired and my heart was beating like three or four times a second. I noticed that I passed up about ten or twelve people. There was about four or five or six people in front of me. I saw the red ribbons and the coaches standing there with pens and notepads. I tried to go faster to beat them, but they beat me to it.

The passage includes only 163 words, of which 8 can be counted as adjectives, five numbers and three real adjectives: *whole, hot,* and *red*—again, not very juicy specimens. The power of the passage comes from the varied impressions that the writer records as she runs the race in her imagination—the dust in her mouth, her hopes, her pains, her attempts to go faster, the sounds she hears, and the simile of the "field [track] like a snake shriveled up around the whole park."

Let me challenge you. Choose a prose passage of three hundred words from your favorite author. Count the words in adjective positions, between a noun determiner and a noun, after a linking verb, or appended to sentences in absolute modifier positions. My guess is that you will not find above 10 percent.

Mark Twain, known as a great prose stylist, had some comments on the use of adjectives. In "Pudd'nhead Wilson's Calendar," Chapter 11 of *The Tragedy of Pudd'nhead Wilson*, he wrote, "As to the Adjective: when in doubt, strike it out" (1962, 57). In the same vein, in a letter to D. W. Bowser (1880), he wrote:

> I notice that you use plain, simple language, short words and brief sentences. That is the way to write English—it is the modern way and the best way. Stick to it; don't let fluff and flowers and verbosity creep in. When you catch an adjective, kill it. No, I don't mean utterly, but kill most of them—then the rest will be valuable. They weaken when they are close together. They give strength when they are wide apart. An adjective habit, or a wordy, diffuse, flowery habit, once fastened upon a person, is as hard to get rid of as any other vice.

Accordingly, the scale for specificity that my students and I have used for many years is concerned with the presence, elaboration, and focus of details of action, of sensory impression, of internal responses of the body and emotions, of imagery and figurative language, and dialogue both internal and between characters.

At a score of 1 on our scale, the writing is nearly void of such detail. It deals in general abstractions rather than in the specifics necessary to strong narrative. "The Ski Trip" and Maurice's composition are such pieces. Note the abstraction of the language even in speaking of what is supposed to have been an enjoyable experience: "I had fun during this time & enjoyed it a lot. The consequences it brought was this: I came home tired & sore with bruises & pain."

"Graduation," which follows, is a bit more specific. It has one fairly strong image, but the rest is quite general and vague.

Graduation

We were waiting for this day for a long time. Finally we were going to graduate from San Miguel School and go on to high school. We were all waiting patiently behind the sanctuary. Father Jessup came to line us up. We lined up. Then Miss Jensen led us to the front of the church. We walked in and started down the ile. The organ was playing. I didn't know the music but it was loud. The pews looked like bookcases that were turned on their backs. Finally we were on stage. And sat down. There were a lot of speakers. They all said congratulations to the recent class to graduate. Finally it ended. We walked back down the ile to the outside. It was raining and we all got wet.

The image of pews as bookcases, though intriguing, is not enough to raise the score on specificity.

The following story about a little sister going in deep water is the culmination of a story about a trip to Wisconsin. Though the incident selected has potential for detail, it musters nothing very concrete.

> All of a sudden when I wasn't looking, my little sister jumped in about 3 feet of water (it was over her head) and I turned around and started screaming for my brother to get her. He didn't hear me at first so I jumped in as fast as I could and tried to get her head to stay above the water. By that time my brother was over by me trying to help me get her out and my mom and dad ran down to the pier from our cottage, so I handed my little sister to my dad and she couldn't stop coughing because she got so much water in her body.

The action is laid out in broad strokes with little or no detail. It is arguably more specific than "The Ski Trip," but we decided to let score 1 papers be defined by this range.

Pieces scoring a 2 tend to have few highly specific images and little dialogue but are more concrete about actions, context, and what might be called specific information.

Pieces about trips frequently fall into this level. They tend to provide a general account-
ing of the days and how they were spent along with specific information about the names
of places and tours and activities. But the papers do not become specific in the use of sensory detail, dialogue, physical and emotional response, or imagery. Ronakea's composition
quoted earlier is an example of writing at this level of specificity.

Level 3 pieces include some details of various kinds, but they tend to be sporadic
and thin. They may include lines of dialogue and some sensory details, but they are not
consistent or chosen for effect. "The Car Wash," following, is a good example. Some of
the early details about the birds singing and dogs barking are clichés. Others stand alone
("a dented tin box"). The water fight is the most specific section of the writing. At this
point the writer manages to capture some of the details of the action. However, the details remain unfocused and are not precise.

The Car Wash

It was a warm and sunny day in the spring. Today was a day I've been looking forward to
for a month. Our Lady of Heaven was having their car wash and I was going to work at it. I
hurried and got ready and called my girlfriend Colleen. As I walked out her door I heard
the birds singing and dogs barking. I could smell the sweet odor of a new spring day. I saw
young kids outside playing ball and jumping rope already. As we neared the school, we could
begin to hear explosion of laughter and shouting. We finally got there and cars were already
there. I was the cashier and had to kept all the money in a dented tin box. I got rather board
just watching the money so I asked if I could do something else. Then I got sent to the corner store about three times. Soon I just picked up an old torn rag and start washing and
drying any car I saw. When we closed, people start squirting each other with the stringy
hoses. After awhile everyone was in the act and we had buckets and cups flying. People got
thrown in barrels and someone got them with soap. Everyone was completely saturated from
head to toe. We finally slowed down and sat on the church steps. We counted the money
and tried to get a little dryer there. We all decided to hold a dance with the money we made
and finally sped up and returned home. We all had a blast that day and even planned another car wash for the future.

At a score of 4, details are more concentrated and more precise. They show signs of
having been chosen for effect. They may still not be of consistent quality throughout, but
there is a greater density of detail than in 3 papers. The next piece, about finding a raccoon, is a good example:

As I was coming home from a roadrace on July 4th, the best thing in my life came to me. I
was on my bike heading down Old Porter Road from Chesterton. It was sticky hot already,
and it was only 10:30 in the morning. I stopped to get off my t-shirt. There was a train about
100 yards away, and it was closing pretty fast at the crossing. It didn't matter to me at that
moment, but in one split second, a mother raccoon and five baby kits were seen crossing
the road and over the tracks, and this engine and all was only about 20 yards away now.
They all scampered across the tracks. Except one! It lost its footing at the top of the ditch
and fell backwards into the ditch. I saw the mother raccoon stop on the other side, count
four kits and take off over into the woods. As I ran over to the ditch, the baby coon got up
wearily and looked at me with his little blinking eyes. He let a little chatter and walked right
up to me. I said, "Looks like we're stuck together." I put him in my front baggage bag, and
we went off. From then on I knew this was going to be a very different summer.

The opening sentences are the kind of detached reporting of detail found in some 2
papers. But the sequence of action about the raccoons is very concrete. Most writers would

not comment on the mother "counting" her kits and so forth. The details about the baby raccoon coming to the narrator are effective, but the details don't have enough impact to warrant a 5 rating. At level 5, details of setting, action, and response appear consistently over much of the writing. Most details are chosen for effect and contribute to implied meanings that enrich the text. "Cheating," "My Best Track Meet," and "The Thrilling Soccer Game" all receive ratings of 5.

Style

Our ratings of style focus on the forcefulness of language and syntax and control over various stylistic devices, including arresting openings and endings and the effective use of humor, suspense, foreshadowing, and so forth—aspects of writing that reveal the writer's voice. At the lowest level (1), the style conveys little awareness that a person will read the writing. It is flat and unconcerned with affecting the reader. The content and syntax may be unclear and word choice may be awkward or inappropriate. There is no indication of a writer's voice coming through. "The Ski Trip" is a good example.

At level 2 the content and syntax are relatively clear, suggesting the writer's awareness of a possible reader. The content is more specific, but it tends to consist of a list of events, sights, food, and so forth without providing much detail about them. The net effect is matter-of-fact, with little apparent attempt to engage an audience in the experience recounted. A few sentences from Ronakea's composition illustrate this listing technique:

> I was so excited because my Grandfather work down in lake Geneva he owned a barbecue pit called Gino's. He sold ribs, chicken, fish, bread pudding, salad, and all the drinks you want. We went there for a little while then I went shopping with my mother to by some biking shorts, Gym Shoes, and a T-Shirt.

At the midpoint (3), papers move beyond a matter-of-fact presentation of information and show clear signs of attempts to engage a reader. These may show up as interesting syntax or vocabulary or in devices such as in medias res openings, humor, irony, and figurative language. At this level these attempts are sporadic and may misfire; attempts at figurative language may be little more than clichés. "Car Wash" is at the low end of this level with its attempt to convey the writer's excitement in looking forward to the car wash and in the description of the water fight. However, the style throughout is erratic. Note the generalized language and clichés in the first several sentences.

The piece about finding the raccoon is stronger, with the writer developing some suspense in the way he describes the raccoons crossing the tracks and the train approaching, and therefore earns a 4. Voice is clear in a number of spots, including the word *chatter* and the opening and closing sentences. There appears to be a relatively consistent awareness of a reader and an attempt to speak to that reader. At this level inconsistencies and infelicities may still be present, but they are not overwhelming.

At level 5 the voice of the writer is strong and very consistent. Some inconsistencies may appear, but the overall impression of a strong voice is clear. "Cheating" is a good example of this level. The writer is highly consistent in showing the situation's inherent excitement and anxiety. The relationship of the three characters is set up quickly and skillfully. It is especially strong for its in medias res opening and reader awareness. Pieces do not have to be this strong to receive the highest score.

"My Best Track Meet" also scores a 5 but at the low end of the range. The voice and focus are both consistent. There is a constant attention to the difficulties of the race. The writer uses some effective figures of speech. There is an attempt to develop suspense as the race comes to an end. The distraction is the occasionally clumsy syntax. But the piece is a first draft, and we have not established consistently smooth syntax a requisite for a rating of 5.

Episodic Elaboration

Level 1
- The piece merely presents a series of actions, with no specific goals, no consequences, and therefore no responses to the consequences.
- There may be a real story hidden in the piece, but we cannot infer what it is from the text provided.
- The setting is virtually nonexistent.

Level 2
- Settings and episodes are presented in skeletal form with nothing elaborated beyond the bare statement of what happened.
- Often the skeletal episode appears only after considerable preliminary material that is not directly related to either the setting or the main episode.
- There is a fairly clear line of events both in the preliminary material and in the episode.
- The narrative has a very expository ring.

Level 3
- The setting and episode are both present with some elaboration of most parts so that some emotion is conveyed beyond the exposition of level 2.
- An initiating event indicates a change in the protagonist's environment and usually evokes some goal or reaction on the part of the protagonist.
- There is an internal response, which may be implied and which may include an emotional response to the change and the formation of a goal.
- The protagonist makes some attempt to achieve the goal.
- A consequence is indicated in some form.
- The protagonist's response to the consequence is usually indicated.
- One or more parts of the episode may be missing or skeletal (e.g., the response to a consequence), but most are present.

Level 4
- An initiating event indicates a change in the protagonist's environment and usually evokes some goal or reaction on the part of the protagonist.
- There is an internal response, which may be implied and which may include an emotional response to the change and the formation of a goal.
- The protagonist makes one or more attempts to achieve the goal.
- A consequence indicates whether the goal was achieved.
- There is a reaction to the consequence, which may include the character's emotional response to the events that have gone on before, the formation of a new goal, or a statement of what the character has learned.
- The formation of a new goal or the restatement of the first goal may lead to the development of a second episode.

Level 5
- All of the characteristics for level 4.
- There are at least two interacting episodes, one for each of two interacting characters.

SPECIFICITY OF DETAIL

Level 1
- The writing contains almost no specific detail. It simply uses the barest language to tell what happens.
- It deals in general abstractions.
- There is no evocative detail.

Level 2
- The writing contains few highly specific images and little dialogue but is more concrete with regard to actions, context, and bits of specific information.
- It is a general account of broad actions, especially when the writing is about a trip. However, specificity tends to be confined to naming places and times rather than evocative detail.

Level 3
- Includes details of various kinds, but they tend to be sporadic and thin.
- Lines of dialogue, sensory detail, and so on may be included but they are not consistent or chosen for effect.
- Some of the details may be clichés. Others may stand alone.
- The writer manages to capture some details of the action; however, the details remain unfocused and imprecise.

Level 4
- Details are consistent across much of the writing.
- Some details are elaborated to provide a very close look at the object of the description.
- Many details are chosen for effect.

Level 5
- Writing is highly specific and details are chosen for effect.
- The level of detail is consistent over a considerable amount of the writing.
- Nearly all details contribute to a central focus or effect.

STYLE

Level 1
- The style conveys little awareness that a person will read the writing. It is flat and unconcerned with affecting the reader.
- The content and syntax may be unclear and word choice may be awkward or inappropriate.
- There is no indication of a writer's voice coming through.

Level 2
- The content and syntax are relatively clear, suggesting the writer's awareness of a possible reader.
- The content is more specific, but tends to consist of a list of events, sights, food, and so forth, without providing much detail about them.
- The net effect is matter-of-fact, with little apparent attempt to engage an audience in the experience recounted.

Level 3
- Composition shows clear signs of attempts to engage a reader. These may show up as interesting syntax or vocabulary or in devices such as an in medias res opening, humor, irony, and figurative language. However, these attempts are sporadic and may misfire.
- Attempts at figurative language may be little more than clichés.

Level 4
- Composition shows relatively consistent awareness of readers and includes attempts to surprise or impress.
- The paper attempts to use foreshadowing, develop suspense, or use an in medias res opening or other major devices.
- Inconsistencies and infelicities may still be present, but they are not overwhelming.

Level 5
- The voice of the writer is strong and very consistent. The overall impression of a strong voice is clear.
- Pieces at this level maintain the emotional character of the piece consistently.
- Special devices such as an in medias res opening are used effectively.

3

GETTING STARTED

When my MAT students and I work in schools, we begin with narrative writing because it serves both as a basis for later writing in other genres and as a foundation for the study of literature. Our initial goals are these:

- We want to know where our students already are as writers of narrative; that is, how well they use detail, develop episodes, and let their voices or style come through in their writing.
- We want to know how well they are able to use conventions and whether or not they use certain syntactic structures.
- We want to frame the work they are about to undertake, to help them understand it.
- Perhaps most important, we want them to see that they have stories to tell about their own lives, stories that are worth telling because they will be of interest to others.

Learning Where Students Are

If we are going to teach narrative writing, it is important to first find out what our students can *already do without any special help*. At the beginning of a narrative unit, we use the following assignment (each student receives a copy) to help determine just that:

> Write a story about an event that is important to you for some reason. Write about it in as much detail as you can so that someone reading it will be able to see what you saw and feel what you felt.

If students have questions, we answer them, but without coaching them on particulars. We give them a class period to write a first draft, and many finish before the time is up. If we want to see what they can do in revision, we give students red pens to revise their original drafts on a second day. (The red ink makes determining the kinds of revisions they have made easier.) At the conclusion of the unit, we follow the same procedures for the posttest.

As students write, it is useful to observe them systematically. Working as a team, we can each observe a small group of students in some detail. If you are working alone, you will naturally make fewer observations of each student. Even so, the observations are still useful. After we have given the prompt, we observe each student, in sequence, for approximately three seconds. If the student appears to be on task, we enter a plus sign on a chart, if not, a minus sign. The three-second observations allow a single observer to monitor thirty students in ninety seconds. In thirty minutes, that's twenty observations of each student. These rapid observations provide a good estimate of time on task for the class as a whole. The intent is not to supply in-depth information about individual students but simply to estimate who tries to do the writing and for how long.

Whenever we can, we also record the time the student begins writing (followed by a *B*) as well as the time she finishes (followed by an *F*). We cannot differentiate between jotting ideas and writing a composition during the observation, but by collecting all pages the students have written on, we're able to tell whether a student spent any time on written planning.

Conducting an Inventory

Although the compositions written to this prompt are pretests, they are also (and this is more important) the basis for an inventory of what students can already do on their own without help—to use Vygotsky's phrase, their zone of actual development. When my students and I inventory the resulting compositions, we work together. I recommend that, if possible, you work with a colleague when you inventory your own students' writing.

We use the rubric provided in Chapter 2 as a guide, but we do not formally *score* the compositions yet. (That is better left until the end of the unit when we want to measure progress. For that purpose we want to establish rater reliability and mix the pretest and posttest papers together to try to ensure that the pieces of writing receive comparable rating regardless of the time of writing.) At this point, we simply read the pretests and, using the rubric as a guide, make a general rank ordering of the papers to discover who the stronger writers appear to be, what kinds of detail they include in their writing, what mechanical problems appear to be most common, and so forth. Inventorying the work of every student is very time-consuming. Fortunately, it is not necessary to make a detailed analysis of every piece of writing from the class—just choosing three or four of the poorest and three or four of the best gives us a clear sense of what needs to be accomplished, a kind of terrain map for the teaching we'll want to do (although not the order in which to do it).

Maurice's and Ronakea's compositions (see Chapter 2) are two of the pretests my MAT students and I collected one year. When we rank-ordered the compositions for the class, Maurice's appeared at the bottom, Ronakea's at the top. Ronakea's paper (including the title) is 333 words long, and her vocabulary is fairly strong, as is her spelling. (She will be able to learn *extraordinary* with no trouble at all.) She includes some specific details—the cost of tolls and the cottage, the time of the voyage into the Dells, and so forth. Though they are not chosen for effect, they indicate an awareness of specificity. She makes an attempt to use direct quotation but does not quite know how to punctuate it. She does not include figurative language, interior monologue to reveal thoughts and feelings, or highly specific sensory detail. Yet it seems she is excited about writing (note her use of exclamation marks) and on the verge of learning all we have to teach. The fact that this is the best paper in the class indicates what the whole class has to learn.

Sometimes when teachers hear about the kind of teaching presented in the ensuing chapters, they are concerned that there is no talk of grammar. When schools and districts are concerned with syntax and usage, it is useful to examine the usage and syntax of students' writing. Ronakea has reasonable mastery of syntax and usage for a seventh grader. She compounds verb phrases and nouns, punctuating the noun lists correctly in two sentences. Many of her sentences are correctly punctuated, but she has a problem identifying sentence boundaries and includes several run-on sentences. On the other hand, she uses subordinate clauses correctly. Taking a closer look at her syntax, I have marked her t-units (minimal *terminable units*: a main clause and all of its appended modifiers [Hunt 1965]; the length of t-units is said to indicate syntactic maturity) with slash marks and underlined her subordinate clauses.

> This summer 1988 on Friday night at 9:30 p.m. my parents decided to go on a trip to Wisconsin Dells./ We packed our bags and loaded the car./ We headed out to the highway/ and the first time my father paid the toll was $1.20/ and the next toll was 40 cents./ My father drove for 3 hours,/ but we didn't make it to Wisconsin Dells because my father made a wrong turn /and we were heading our way back to Chicago!/ So my father turned around and said "we'll go to lake Geneva because it was a shorter ride./ I fell asleep/ and my mother did to,/ finally I woke up/ and we were at a Motel./

> It was $60.00 for one night/ and all it was a little cottage/ and all of us couldn't sleep in one bed/ so father slept on a cot/ me and my mother slept in the bed./ I was so excited because my Grandfather work down in lake Geneva/ he owned a barbecue pit called Gino's./ He sold ribs, chicken, fish, bread pudding, salad, and all the drinks you want./ We went there for a little while/ then I went shopping with my mother to by some biking shorts, Gym Shoes, and a T-Shirt./

> Then we kept riding and went to Wisconsin dells./ We found a hotel at Wisconsin dells 6:00 a.m. in the morning./ So then we all took showers put on our new clothes and headed out to explore Wisconsin./ We got on the boat ride call the upper dells at 2:00 p.m./ and I saw a lot interesting that God made and nature did together/ it was beautiful!/ I [saw] rock formation trees that were growing out of the rocks/ it was extrodinary./ Then after all that we had a 17 year old captain/ it was fun./ Then it was time to go back home to Chicago/ and we made it home at 12:00 p.m./

Ronakea has thirty-five t-units with an average of 9.5 words each. She includes nine subordinate clauses and a number of compound structures. She writes *and* sixteen times (4.8 percent of the total number of words). The compound structures lead to several errors. Fourteen times clauses should end with a period or be separated from the next with a comma, but six main clauses are punctuated correctly, as are two series of nouns.

Maurice's paper does not hold such promise. On the rubric (see Chapter 2), he scores only 3 points total on the three sections combined. He does not write an episode, he includes no specific detail, and the style remains flat. He has written 136 words arranged in simple syntactic patterns (again, slash marks divide his prose into t-units).

> Last night when I left school I went home and talked on the phone for about one hour/ and then I went out front and talked to friends and then came back upstairs and talked on the phone again/ and then we went to the store and bout some candy/ and we went home to my house and watch tv for a couple of hours and played around a while/ then my mother came home from work/ we went to my grandmother's house for a party/ it was my mother's birthday/ we had pizza, lasanya and cake and ice cream and pop/ and my mother's sister she came over/ and they went out to party/ and then we went home/ and we got to watch movies on tv until really late like 2 in the morning/

Maurice has written twelve t-units with an average of 11.3 words per unit, longer than Ronakea's. But Maurice has only one dependent clause. His t-units are longer because of all of the compounding he has used—one set of nouns in a series and seven instances of compounded verbs. He writes the word *and* seventeen times for 12.5 percent of the total number of words, more than twice the percentage for Ronakea. Maurice does not include a single period. His content is expressed in very vague terms. He includes no figurative language and no detail. There is no hint of excitement and no attempt to focus. But as he wrote, we observed that Maurice seemed intent on his writing. He never appeared to be off task. We know he has a lot to learn, and we predict that he will. If he comes at least close to the level of Ronakea's writing in the next few weeks, we will be pleased.

We often encounter the use of dialect in contexts where we hope for Standard English. In the case of both Maurice's and Ronakea's writing there is virtually no non-Standard English. However, that is never true across the board. Take the following pretest by Shaquita:

The day We went Skateing

It was a Sunday afternoon about 2:20/ we left for skateing./ So we were rideing in the van/ it was about ten of us./ So we got there/ we paid for our own skates and went to go put them on/ and everybody was there./ I seen people from school ther./ So we started skateing and having fun/ so we skated for about an hour or so/ and then we got something to eat/ so then we just sat there./ Then we got up and started skating/ there were a lot of cute boys there/ but all of them acted coseedet [conceited] like they were all that or something/ the girls acted like that to./ They were dance/ they could dance to./ The session we went to was over./ Then my friend call here dad and told him that we were going to stay for the next session/ and her father said ok./ So my friend pays for us to stay./ So we started to skat again/ and then I got off the rink again/ then I told this girl excuse me/ and she would not move some/ I pushed her a little bit and got throug./ And then my cousin told me the gril called me a B/ then I was like I didn't hear/ so I am not about to argue about it./ And then my cosin was like let somebody call me out/ my am bet the B/ but and I was like I hear her/ so I an't going to worry about it./ So my cosin was stady talking/ so then she stop taking and finshed skating./ So we are just skating./ Then we get off the rink/ and the gril was right their/ so me and my cousin and her friend was like excuse me/ and she wouldn't move/ so we just kept on walking/ so I went into the game room with my other two friends./ My cousin was still talking./ So the gril came over their/ and they were argueing./ So then the friends was tell her to bus on her/ so the gril did./ The gril hit her with a skate in her mouth/ and now she has a deep cut on her lip./ So then she ran to the front/ and my friend came and told us what happen/ we were so mad that we want to fight./ They kept her there/ they took the gril to jail/ so then we were just talking to this jamcin boy untile my friend father come to pick us up and asked what happen/ and we told him/ and he go to see how she is doing/ and then we left./ the end

This piece contains 440 words and fifty-nine t-units, with an average t-unit length of 7.5 words, shorter than either Maurice's or Ronakea's. There is also a decided dialect influence. Although the piece generally uses past-tense verb forms, a few *-ed* endings are omitted and occasionally present-tense forms are used instead ("father come to pick us up and asked what happen"). Vernacular expressions are used occasionally ("my cosin was stady talking," meaning talking continuously, and "to bus," meaning to abuse someone verbally or physically). There are also examples of possession by adjacency ("my friend father"). Certainly there are many examples of the widespread teen approach to quotation, using *like* to replace the verb *saying* ("my cosin was like let somebody call me out").

The spelling is erratic. Several words are spelled both correctly and incorrectly (*there/their*, *skateing/skating*). And some are spelled more or less phonetically but miss by a fairly large margin (*coseedet*). The pronoun references lead to confusion with too many references to too many different *shes*.

At the same time, in spite of many mechanical errors, there is a dramatic sense that is probably worth nurturing. The story suggests a kind of social clash between those who go to the rink often and those who perhaps go only occasionally, between the conceited who think they are "all that" and the newcomers. The episodic structure is strong, with two attempts on the part of one particular girl to block the progress of the protagonist and her friends, which lead to the girl's hitting the cousin with a skate. This writer has strengths that are hidden by the rather weak syntax and spelling problems.

Setting Up Collaborative Groups

There are many ways to set up small groups for work in the classroom. At every level I have ever taught, I have preferred groups of no more than five (preferably, four) people. A group of four can sit close enough together that they can hear each other without raising their voices too much. Some teachers set up groups by letting students choose with whom they will work. I allow that in graduate classes but not in high school and below. Some teachers assign students randomly to groups. My MAT students and I use our inventory as a guide to building our writing groups. We want a relatively strong writer in each group. The results of the inventory, while not conclusive, are a guide for setting up these groups.

The class from which I have been drawing examples comprised twenty-eight seventh graders, not all of whom attended every day. We set up seven groups of four, chaired by Ronakea and six other relatively strong writers, who in the early sessions made sure that everyone contributed and the work was covered. We also assigned Maurice and six of the other weakest writers one to each group. The rest of the students were distributed among the groups so as to balance the number of boys and girls in each. (Seventh graders do not like to be the only boy or girl in a group.) Initial group memberships will very likely undergo many changes. Students sometimes do not like one another and refuse to cooperate. Sometimes fights erupt. In this class, for example, during one of the first group meetings, I spotted Ronald kicking a girl across from him under the table. The girl complained very loudly, telling this relatively little boy what she would do to him. I told Ronald that his action was inappropriate and put him in a different group, across from Maurice, who was the tallest and heaviest boy I have ever seen in seventh grade (he was taller than I am and must have weighed more than two hundred pounds). Maurice eyed Ronald with something approaching disdain, and Ronald settled down immediately. No one messed with Maurice.

In a seventh-grade class some years before, John came to school every day with a dirty face and very dirty hands. He was in the habit of writing things (including homework assignments) on his hands and arms. I placed him in various groups, but every group voiced some level of disgust and drew their chairs physically away from him. John usually sat near the group, head down, staring at his lap, never smiling or interacting. One day I approached the members of one of my most productive groups and asked them for a favor—to include John in their group without moving away from him and working to help him respond to whatever problem we were discussing. Linda and Karen quickly agreed and the two boys followed suit. The same day, I noticed John smiling and interacting with the other group members.

Framing the Work

It is always good practice to share learning goals with students. We could say simply that we are going to work on narrative, but many of our seventh graders, even ninth graders, might not know what that means. At inner-city schools I frequently use a piece from *Black Boy*, Richard Wright's autobiography, because it is an example of the kind of personal experience writing I hope the students will produce (I have also used a selection from Sandra Cisneros' *House on Mango Street* [1991]).

The Night I Won the Right to the Streets of Memphis
by Richard Wright

One evening my mother told me that thereafter I would have to do the shopping for food. She took me to the corner store to show me the way. I was proud; I felt like a grownup. The next afternoon I looped the basket over my arm and went down the pavement toward the store. When I reached the corner, a gang of boys grabbed me, knocked me down, snatched the basket, took the money, and sent me running home in panic. That evening I told my mother what had happened, but she made no comment; she sat down at once, wrote another note, gave me more money, and sent me out to the grocery again. I crept down the steps and saw the same gang of boys playing down the street. I ran back into the house.

"What's the matter?" my mother asked.

"It's those same boys," I said. "They'll beat me."

"You've got to get over that," she said. "Now, go on."

"I'm scared," I said.

"Go on and don't pay any attention to them," she said.

I went out of the door and walked briskly down the sidewalk, praying that the gang would not molest me. But when I came abreast of them someone shouted. "There he is!" They came toward me and I broke into a wild run toward home. They overtook me and flung me to the pavement. I yelled, pleaded, kicked, but they wrenched the money out of my hand. They yanked me to my feet, gave me a few slaps, and sent me home sobbing. My mother met me at the door.

"They b-beat m-me," I gasped. "They t-t-took the m-money." I started up the steps, seeking the shelter of the house.

"Don't you come in here," my mother warned me.

I froze in my tracks and stared at her. "But they're coming after me," I said.

"You just stay right where you are," she said in a deadly tone. "I'm going to teach you this night to stand up and fight for yourself." She went into the house and I waited, terrified, wondering what she was about. Presently she returned with more money and another note; she also had a long heavy stick. "Take this money, this note, and this stick," she said. "Go to the store and buy those groceries. If those boys bother you, then fight."

I was baffled. My mother was telling me to fight, a thing that she had never done before. "But I'm scared," I said.

"Don't you come into this house until you've gotten those groceries," she said.

"They'll beat me; they'll beat me," I said.

"Then stay in the streets; don't come back here!"

I ran up the steps and tried to force my way past her into the house. A stinging-slap came on my jaw. I stood on the sidewalk, crying. "Please, let me wait until tomorrow," I begged.

"No," she said. "Go now! If you come back into this house without those groceries, I'll whip you!" She slammed the door and I heard the key turn in the lock. I shook with fright. I was alone upon the dark, hostile streets and gangs were after me. I had the choice of being beaten at home or away from home. I clutched the stick, crying, trying to reason. If I were beaten at home, there was absolutely nothing that I could do about it; but if I were beaten in the streets, I had a chance to fight and defend myself. I walked slowly down the sidewalk, coming closer to the gang of boys, holding the stick tightly. I was so full of fear that I could scarcely breathe. I was almost upon them now.

"There he is again!" the cry went up. They surrounded me quickly and began to grab for my hand.

"I'll kill you!" I threatened.

They closed in. In blind fear I let the stick fly, feeling it crack against a boy's skull. I swung again, lamming another skull, then another. Realizing that they would retaliate if I let up for but a second, I fought to lay them low, to knock them cold, to kill them so that they could not strike back at me. I flayed with tears in my eyes, teeth clenched, stark fear making me throw every ounce of my strength behind each blow. I hit again and again, dropping the money and the grocery list. The boys scattered, yelling, nursing their heads, staring at me in utter disbelief. They had never seen such frenzy. I stood panting, egging them on, taunting them to come on and fight. When they refused, I ran after them and they tore out for their homes, screaming. The parents of the boys rushed into the streets and threatened me, and for the first time in my life I shouted at grownups, telling them that I would give them the same if they bothered me. I finally found my grocery list and the money and went to the store. On my way back I kept my stick poised for instant use, but there was not a single boy in sight. That night I won the right to the streets of Memphis. (1951, 23–25)

The first time my MAT students and I used the piece, we led a fairly conventional discussion of it, which I realized in retrospect was no more than a recitation. We knew how we would answer our questions, and we wanted to know whether the students would provide those same answers. That was unexciting. But it was also clear that our students liked the story. I still remember a little boy standing up in the back row and pretending to brandish a stick at imaginary bullies.

Now we use drama to help our students get into the story: *If you were making a movie of this story, how would you set up the scenes for the camera?* We ask students to make those decisions in small groups, drawing lines through the text to mark off each scene. They usually divide the story into seven or eight scenes.

Once the scenes are divided, small groups pick scenes to act out, or we assign scenes. We talk about what the mother would wear, what Richard would wear, how the mother would stand, how she would hold her head, how Richard would act in different scenes, and so forth. We have found it very useful to talk about why Richard is so fearful, because it helps boys realize how the part must be played. (Seventh-grade girls know how to play the mama figure, but boys are more reluctant to play a sobbing Richard.) Then we let students plan what exactly they will do, what props they might use, where in the classroom they will present the scene, and rehearse if there is time.

Following the dramatization, we outline the events of the story:

- What initiates Richard's actions in the story?
- What is Richard attempting to do?
- How many attempts does he make? What is the result of each attempt?
- What is Richard's response to the results?

This is the introduction to episode structure. (We usually do this from Richard's perspective, but it could be done from his mother's as well. The episodes are interlocking.) Next we look at the specific details to focus attention on the impact of the detail:

- What details do you think are most effective in showing Richard's fear?
- What details are most effective in showing his final resolution to fight?
- What details are strongest in revealing what his mother is like?
- What details best show Richard's actions in the fight against the boys?
- How do all of these details help you in knowing how to act out the story?

These questions are fairly simple, but they help students see the importance in shaping how they see the story taking place. As Wilhelm (2003) points out, "Reading is seeing."

Finding Story Ideas

Most students in the classes I have taught have trouble identifying things in their own experience to write about: they are not movie heroes, after all. We need to help them see that although their adventures may be small, even the smallest can be worth writing about. I knew that students think they have nothing to write about because they say it so often, but it took me some years to figure out what to do about it. Finally it occurred to me that I could give students a sample list of ideas for writing from my own life and ask them to develop similar lists.

Some people believe that writing about personal experience has no place in schools. They argue that assignments that require writing about personal experience allow strangers to pry into private family life and that teachers have no right to meddle in the private lives of children. In the more than thirty years that my MAT students and I have taught such writing in schools, we have never been charged with such meddling. It doesn't seem a problem to me, especially when we all respect each other's rights to privacy.

Figure 3.1 is a list I developed to use with my MAT students in a summer course on teaching writing. That fall, we used it with seventh graders and later with ninth graders. I did not make the list anonymous because I wanted students to know that I was willing to share my experience with them. After all, I was asking them to share theirs with me and their classmates.

Examining Story Ideas

Whenever I use my list of story ideas, I read them to the students and ask which they might like to hear more about. The most frequently nominated are 3, 6, 7, and 8. These are boy stories obviously. But girls are interested in the story about hiding from my

1. Mrs. Minich was my favorite teacher. A few days after her husband died, a group of fifth graders came into our room with a flowering plant for Mrs. Minich. She indicated that we should applaud the fifth graders. We did, but the boy next to me booed loudly. Mrs. Minich began to cry, turned, and left the room. After school, we caught the boy and beat him up pretty well.

2. One summer, I found a painted turtle early in the summer and later I caught a snapping turtle. I kept them in a large tub in the backyard. When school started, my father said that I had to return them to a park. I liked having the turtles, but he insisted, predicting they would die. I was very upset. We let them go in a pond and watched them swim away.

3. On a hike with my Boy Scout troop, I went along a narrow path on the face of a shale cliff to get a better view of a waterfall that dropped a hundred feet or so to the bottom of a ravine. My leader shouted for me to get off the path, but I ignored him and continued until I was at the waterfall. I had a great view of the falls all the way to the bottom, about 150 feet below me. When I moved forward and peered around the bend in the face of the cliff, I realized that the path ended at the bend. When I looked back, I saw that the path I had come along had crumbled from my weight. I was trapped.

4. I liked cooking outdoors. But I was not very skilled at it. When I tried cooking a dinner for my cooking merit badge in Scouting, I flunked the first time. A year later I tried again with a dinner for ten adult leaders complete with meat, vegetables, potatoes, bread, gingerbread for dessert, and coffee, all over an open fire.

5. In the first grade I was whistling one day and was sent to the principal's office to explain.

6. In elementary school, the biggest bully was a boy named Mars (the god of war). He had failed a few times, and we thought he was about fifteen even though he was in the sixth grade. He would follow me home and punch me for no reason. I tried to hide from him. One day he took our stuff at recess and would not give it back. I ended up in a fight with him and was beaten in no uncertain terms. I felt terrible.

7. When I was seven or eight, I was captured by teenagers playing war. They had built large dugouts and a trench in a field I usually crossed to get to the grocery store. One day when Grandma sent me to the store, they caught me, tied me up, and held me prisoner in one of the dugouts for several hours. Grandma was in a state when I finally got home. But I got revenge.

8. When I was about twelve, my grandma took me shopping. We traveled on a streetcar to stores that were about three or four miles from home. While she was busy, I hid from her and made her think I was lost. Grandma looked and looked for me, and after some time she went home alone on the streetcar. I was in big trouble with my mother and father. Grandma was hurt, which was much worse than angry. I have been sorry about doing that ever since.

Figure 3.1 *Stories I Could Tell*

grandmother and about my cooking exploits. They usually want to know what happened and how. We do not discuss my ideas for very long—just long enough to arouse curiosity and let them see that everyone has such ideas. I tell them I will write about one of the stories. (My story about my encounter with Mars, in Chapter 1, is the result of one of these sessions.)

Then I remind my students that they have good ideas for stories too. I ask if my ideas remind them of events or happenings they might write about. I prompt them to suggest a few. Perhaps a boy tells about having a bicycle stolen because he left his lock at home. A girl suggests that she could maybe write about the first time she tried to make dinner for her mother and little sisters; after burning the macaroni and cheese, she was so afraid of burning the hot dogs that she served them almost cold. A girls tells about a gymnastics meet that she tried hard to win but didn't. A boy tells of seeing a near drowning on Lake Michigan during the summer. After several contributions, I ask students to list as many ideas for stories as they can. I point to a set of questions on the board (we had real blackboards in those days) and read them aloud.

- What experiences have made you feel really happy or very sad?
- What experiences have been very alarming or really frightening?
- What experiences have made you feel proud of yourself?
- What have been the most difficult tasks you have had to undertake?
- What contests or games have you tried hard to win?
- What experiences have made you feel ashamed of yourself?
- What experiences have made you realize that you truly care about someone?
- What experiences have made you laugh a lot?

The students then spend the rest of the hour listing ideas. Some write constantly, others only sporadically. Some seem to have major writer's block even at this stage. I go to those who seem stuck and prompt them: *Can you think of a time you were afraid? Can you think of a game that you tried hard to win or maybe just make a score or catch a crucial fly ball? What is your most exciting experience? What is the funniest event you ever saw?* By the end of the hour, all students have at least two ideas on their sheet. I repeat the prompt questions displayed on the board and ask students to continue thinking about story ideas. They will have a chance to continue their list tomorrow. I collect the papers to hold for the next day. (It is not a good idea to allow seventh graders to take important project papers out of the room.)

I look over the efforts. One student has written nine ideas. One has eight. Three have seven. Most have four or five. Two boys have only two. The next day I give them fifteen minutes at the beginning of the period to add to their lists. The boys who had only two ideas now have at least four. It looks as though everyone has added at least two ideas. I decide that is good enough for now.

Now I redistribute my own idea sheet and remind them that they have nominated numbers 3, 6, 7, and 8 to hear more about. I read number 7 aloud:

> When I was seven or eight, I was captured by teenagers playing war. They had built large dugouts and a trench in a field I usually crossed to get to the grocery store. One day when Grandma sent me to the store, they caught me, tied me up, and held me prisoner in one of the dugouts for several hours. Grandma was in a state when I finally got home. But I got revenge.

Setting
Where does the story take place? How is the place important to the story? What needs to be explained? What is going on?

Characters
Who are the characters? Which are important to the action of the story? What do we need to know about them?

Initiating Action
What initiates or begins the action? What causes a character to do something?

Attempts
What attempts does the main character make? To do what? Why?

Results
What are the results of the character's attempts? Does the result initiate a new action?

Responses
How does the character respond to or feel about the initiating action, the attempts, and the results?

Dialogue
What do the characters say to one another?

Figure 3.2 *Questions for Story Ideas*

I ask what they would like to know about this adventure. Anthony wants to know what the revenge was. I explain that I went to the house of some big boys who lived on the street behind ours. I knew them because our fathers, both Scots, were friends. They were tall and looked strong to me. They knew the boys who had made the dugouts, and after I had told my story, they found two other big boys, and we launched an invasion. I got on the crossbar of Donald's bike and we rode to the field where the dugouts were. The boys hid their bikes behind some bushes while we reconnoitered. Then we attacked, running across the field to the dugouts, yelling, "Death to the Nazis."

"Do you have any questions about that?" I ask. They have plenty. *What's a dugout? Why did you yell those things? What's* reconnoiter *mean? What did you do beside yell? Where were the dugouts? How do you make a dugout? What happened to the guys who kept you prisoner? Did they fight back? Did you guys fight? How did you get captured in the first place? How did they tie you up? What did you do? Why did they let you go?*

I explain that these are the kinds of questions I will have to answer in writing about that experience and that it will help if I first separate them into important types. I distribute a sheet with seven spaced headings, each followed by brief prototypical questions for the category (see Figure 3.2).

Then I give students their assignment: look over their story ideas and decide on two that they are willing to share with their classmates. In their small groups, they are to read their two story ideas aloud to the group. The group members get to ask whatever questions they have about the story ideas, decide which one they would like to hear more about, and then decide which of the questions on the handout need to be answered to make the story a good one. (These directions are on the board for ready reference.) Every person in the group must receive advice from the group on at least one story idea.

I visit the groups to monitor progress and see if they understand the directions. In each group I note that one student is reading an idea while the others are listening attentively. I return to the first group I watched, listening to what the kids have to say about one of Hank's story ideas, which is this:

> Last summer my friends and me was walking down 63rd under the el. We was going to get some food at MacDonald's on Cottage Grove. We hear a siren and we go out into the street to see what's up. All a sudden this car whip out of Drexel and it come toward us. But its like going all over the street. The next thing is a cop car with lights blinking. Siren going. The car running away going all over the place. We jump back on the sidewalk because it looks like it's coming at us. Then it slam into one of them posts that hold up the el. Blam! Big crash. A cop jump out with his gun out and he go up to the crashed car, but the guy, he bleeding and leaning forward over the wheel. He look dead to us.

By the time I arrive, students are asking questions: *So what did the cop do? Did the driver live? How much blood was there? Did an ambulance come?* After several more questions, the group considers the question sheet. They decide they need more information about the setting, because the el tracks are important to the story and what happens. The students work through each category on the list, suggesting what they think needs to be added: more about the cop, the driver, and the kids themselves; more about the driver's attempt to get away; more about responses of the characters and more of what people said.

It is evident that this group is going to be fine. It is also evident that I have stayed too long. I move to the next groups. All are doing pretty well, though one or two are bogged down on one story idea. I encourage them to move along, because they need to cover one idea for each of them. The groups stay pretty much on task until the end of the period. From my visits I am fairly certain that all students have read one story idea aloud. But I ask anyway: "How many of you have read at least one story idea to your group and received feedback?" All hands go up. "How many have read two?" About two-thirds of the hands go up. "Great," I say and collect the story idea sheets. The bell rings. "See you tomorrow. We'll have some good things to do tomorrow."

I am happy with the progress the class has made. The students are invested and are learning about story structure. They enjoyed listening to each other's experiences and, I believe, feel positive about the class. We are going to have fun. The students are off to an excellent start. I hope this is the beginning of *flow experience*.

4

Incorporating Detail and Figurative Language

Perhaps the most important quality of effective stories is concrete detail. Specific details allow readers to see scenes in their own minds as they read. But effective specific detail may be the most difficult quality to achieve. Writers have to remember or imagine what it is they want to portray, search their memories for words to do it, arrange the words in effective syntax, evaluate the effort by comparing it with the vision in their mind, perhaps search for additional or different words or different ways to use them, write those down, and evaluate the effort again. Ernest Hemingway wrote only five hundred words a day, a testament, at least in part, to how difficult it is to be specific.

Just before I left Bowling Green State University for Chicago, I taught an advanced composition course for juniors and seniors. Their major problem was a lack of specificity regardless of what they wrote. I thought if I brought something to class for them to examine and talk about in detail, they might learn to be specific. I had a pinecone collection that included sugar and Jeffrey pinecones, both of which are large. The sugar pinecones are between eighteen and twenty inches long; the Jeffrey is eight or nine inches long and about five inches in diameter at its widest point. These Midwestern students had never seen such large cones and were suitably impressed. When each student had a cone, I asked them to write a specific description. Most wrote about the approximate dimensions of the cone, noted the color as brownish, and described the general shape. I was struck by the term *brownish*, because the cones were brown only in a fairly vague sense. I asked them to look at the Jeffrey pinecones again and identify what other colors they could see. In a few minutes they found colors that are not much like brown: silver, yellow, dark red, ochre. The end of each scale on a Jeffrey pinecone has a large prickle scalloped in silver, as though someone had taken the time to paint each one. The side of the scale where the seeds lie is dark yellow and dark red. Several of the scales on each of my Jeffrey pinecones had at least one of their two seeds remaining, seeds with a little silvery translucent wing attached. In short, there were plenty of details that belied the initial decision to call the shell brownish. A few more experiments like this and these twenty- and twenty-one-year-olds were able to transfer the idea of specificity to most of their writing.

I continued my quest for ways to teach specificity when I moved to Chicago and began working as director of the MAT program. As part of program requirements for the MAT students, in the summer of 1972, I instituted a composition workshop for eleven- to fifteen-year-old students in connection with my course on teaching writing. In that summer, my MAT students and I began a tradition of inventing and testing activities that we hoped would teach strategies for writing effective narrative and later argument. I taught a seventh-grade class of my own for a year to check the efficacy of the activities. But many of the activities were developed by collaborative teams of four to six MAT students working with an adviser as they prepared for and taught these workshops.

Examining and Writing About Seashells

I have always been fascinated by seashells, particularly univalves. I love the colors, the shapes, the Fibonaccian proportions in the growth whorls, their occasional translucence. It occurred to me that shells might be much more interesting to students than pinecones. But the activity needed to be more meaningful than simply looking at seashells—it needed a rhetorical frame, writing for a purpose and an audience. I had an idea: Could students write about a shell so specifically that someone reading their piece would be able to identify the shell? But they would need some help in doing the writing. I could do that with a shell that the entire class could help describe with my prompting. This would be the teacher-led, scaffolded part of the lesson.

The first time my MAT students and I used this activity was in a workshop of eleven-to fifteen-year-olds, all of whom were fairly competent writers. I held up a shell as I walked about the room. The children suggested details, commenting on the color, the protrusions, the different colors of the inside and outside, the color patterns, and the patterns made by the protrusions. A few used similes, comparing it to some otherwise unlike object with one salient common feature. I realized that I should have been asking for similes all along. So I asked for more and got them.

In the summer workshops, our eleven- to fifteen-year-old students were all volunteers, which meant they liked writing, were interested, and were probably pretty good at it. After working with one shell with my help, each student received a different shell. I asked students to describe their shells as specifically as they could so that another student would be able to read what they had written and pick the shell described from among the nearly forty shells used. Students wrote silently for almost twenty-five minutes. Reading over their shoulders, I was happy to discover that most students had the idea. When nearly all thought they were finished, I collected and redistributed the papers. We had a little more than ten minutes remaining.

We had planned in advance how to redistribute the papers so that no students sitting in the vicinity of another would receive a paper from that student. Papers from the outer rows went to the inner rows and vice versa. After students had an opportunity to read the paper they had received, we sent the two outer rows to the table holding the shells, then the next two opposite rows, and finally the two inner rows. They didn't remove the shells when they found them, so all forty shells remained on the table all the time. When all the students had returned to their seats, everyone—all at once—went back to claim a shell. As expected, some students had identified the same shell, some could not identify any shell, but most found the shell described.

We also wanted the writers to receive feedback from the readers (which details helped the most, which one was the best and why), but the logistics were formidable. Readers could not find their writers, and each student had to meet with two different people, giving feedback to one and receiving feedback from the other. Nearly fifteen minutes of the activity were lost to management tasks. The solution was simple: we asked writers to exchange papers with someone at least a couple of rows away.

Refining the Seashell Game with Less Skilled Writers

In the fall quarter the composition workshop moved to the Chicago public school down the street. There we worked with what the school designated as the seventh-grade low-level language arts class. Writing samples revealed that the class did not have the writing skills of our summer group. The class was nearly all African American. I decided that a group activity would be imperative. This has become another principle of sequencing for us, moving from teacher-led support to peer-group support with the teacher coaching as the groups work, and finally to individual work

Introducing the Shells

I told our class of seventh graders that they would be writing about a shell as specifically as they could and that another student would read what they had written and try to pick out the shell from the total collection of shells. First, for practice, I had the class as a whole describe my prize helmet shell, which is about eight inches long and nearly six inches in diameter at the widest point. It tapers down gradually from the widest point for a couple of inches and then drops precipitously to a curlicue-like tail. At the opposite end, the whorls gradually increase in size from the tiny innermost ones to the large, most recent growths. The outside is covered with smooth wrinkles, and there are regular protrusions around the top of the outer whorl. I asked them what they thought it looked like. "If I hold it this way [*closed side out*], you may see one thing, but if I hold it this way [*opening out*], you may see another." There were no responses.

I had already talked to my MAT students about waiting for responses. So I walked about the room offering a close-up view to each youngster. Still there were no responses. Out of the corner of my eye I could see my MAT students begin to squirm in their seats, pens poised above their note paper, waiting. Minutes passed. I was beginning to squirm. I was beginning to think I might need to give an example of a simile, but the seventh graders needed to see for themselves that they could do it. I was holding the shell by the curlicue, closed side out, when a boy raised his hand. "When you hold it like that," he said, "it looks like an athletic trophy."

"But when you hold it by the other end," another boy said, "it looks like an elf's hat with that little curly thing." Suddenly, the responses seemed to pour out: *like an ear* (with the opening perpendicular to the floor), *like a shark's mouth with teeth showing* (the opening parallel to the floor), *like a ball gown* (broad end down), *like vanilla ice cream with chocolate fudge swirls* (the outside color). A boy who had stroked the shell said, "It's all wrinkly, like an old person's skin."

Then we talked about details of shape and color: the brown and white dabs in rows on the outside, the tapering down, the curly end. One girl described the top of the shell as a "tiny road spiraling up to a tiny point at the top of the shell." Another pointed out that the road became narrower and narrower as it neared the top. Someone mentioned the peach color on the inside of the shell; someone else said the inside surface was as smooth as glass. I praised each response as I wrote it on the overhead. It was time for group work.

Setting Up Student Groups

Many students don't know how to work collaboratively in groups; they sit next to each other and talk, but they work independently. I strongly recommend not allowing students to choose their own groups. Already having identified the strongest writers and most

Chair: Your job is to make sure the writing assignment is completed.
Whip: Your job is to ensure that everyone in your group contributes.
Writer: Your job is to write down your group's work.
Reviewer: Your job is to review your group's work to make sure enough detail has been included.

Figure 4.1   *Roles for Student Groups*

responsive students in the class, my MAT students and I assigned one of these students to chair each group (we wanted to take advantage of the Vygotskian concept that children learn from more skilled peers). Then we distributed seven students with the weakest writing samples one to each group, and so on until each group had four students. Besides the chair, each group had a whip (a Congressional term for the person who makes sure everyone in his party votes), whose job was to ensure that everyone contributed; the writer; and the reviewer, whose job was to review the writing to make sure that enough detail had been included. (See Figure 4.1.)

We assigned classroom spots for each group to meet, putting a diagram on the board with the names of each student in each group. I explained how to move the desks into a square so that four students could sit facing each other, two on each side. I also told the students not to move their regular desks, but go to their assigned location and use the desks there. This may seem trivial, but I remember too well observing a new seventh-grade teacher. When she asked her students to get into their groups, the boy with the desk nearest the door stood up and ferociously pushed his desk and chair to the far corner of the room, ramming at least two girls on the way. Other boys did the same, to shouts of recrimination and general chaos. The teacher lost control of the class for nearly ten minutes. Some teachers resort to numbered commands: "One, stand up. Two, push your chair under the desk. Three, go to your group position. Four, find a desk and chair nearby. Five, move it into your group square. Six, take a seat." Whenever I have done this in a class, I have never had to do it again.

Group Assignment 1

Each group received two shells in a bag. The students were to inspect the shells and choose one to write about. (The general shapes and colors were comparable, but the shells were of different species.) Here's what I said: "Once you have chosen the shell you want to describe, talk about what language to use to describe it. Talk about what it looks like, its shape, its colors, any textures that you notice, and its special features, just as we did with the helmet shell. One person in the group will write out the description, but each of you should make contributions. When you're finished, I will collect your work and your shells and pass them to another group. That group will decide which of the two shells you have described. So write as specifically as you can. Any questions?"

The first question, of course, was "Who's gonna do the writing?"

"You decide," I said. I looked at my watch. Thirty minutes of class were gone, but we still had twenty minutes left.

Observing and Coaching

I had an MAT student observing each group, but I wanted to demonstrate that one teacher could supervise all of the groups. I visited each group, listening to each for a few moments to determine if the kids were on track, asking questions and making suggestions if not. This is hard work. It is also essential. Success in group work leads to success in the independent work that follows. I have observed many classes in which teachers set up groups, give the assignment, and retire to their desks. This is a recipe for disaster, even when students are highly motivated. Especially when group work is at a fairly early stage, the students are bound to hit a snag, and they are more likely to ask for help when a teacher is circulating and coaching. Another fatal error is concentrating on one group to the exclusion of the others. A few weeks ago, I observed a tenth-grade teacher who had asked groups to discuss color symbolism in *The Scarlet Letter*, a not very well-defined task. She sat with the first group and stayed with it for the thirty remaining minutes of class time. It was clear that the other groups were off task that whole time.

In the first two groups I visited, students were talking about who was going to write. I told the chair to assign someone and moved on. The third group was examining one of the shells and describing it but not writing anything down. I suggested they at least make a list of their ideas, since they would then be able to use these details to write a several-sentence description of the shell. The next group had written down phrases about the color and shape and some similes:

> It has fudge brown stripes and white stripes going around the shell. It has little white sharp spikes going around the edge of the top. The top look like a little spiral road going higher and higher to the top. The point at the top could be a castle, the kind you see in fairy tales. It is very tiny.

As I approached, one boy was saying the shell could be a weapon: "See, you could hold it like this and use these little spikes to cut somebody."

A girl responded, "That's stupid. Put it down so we can see it." He made a little sort of warrior cry but returned it promptly to the desk. It was one of my favorite shells, but I had never noticed the possibility of weaponry.

The other girl in the group said, "I think the top is a tiny crown." A metaphor, I thought. The first girl agreed.

One of the boys said, "Let me see." He picked it up and said, "Oh yeah!" I told the group that the shell was native to Florida and that its common name is king's crown. This group was doing fine.

The next group was having trouble. They had written nothing and were somberly looking at the shell, afraid to venture any ideas. I squatted beside their square of desks and asked about the shape. One boy said, "It is kind of round." I looked at the group expectantly.

A girl said, "It has these smooth ridges. There are lots of them." I waited for more. Another girl said, "It is sort of brown . . . and white."

"That's a start," I said, "but try to be more specific about the shape. Is it really round like a ball? What is the roundness like? Is it really brown? I think I see other colors. What do you think it looks like?"

A boy turned the shell over. "This has a really big opening," he said. "It sort of reminds me of a cup."

A girl said, "You know that fountain on the wall at the back of the school. This [*pointing to the lip of the opening*] reminds me of that. It has the same shape. Like the same kind of curve."

"What do you call that curve?" I asked.

"It's like an oval," said a boy. "Well, half an oval."

Just then, in another group across the room, I saw Ronald kicking Shaquita, who was about twice his size. Then I saw Shaquita's foot kick Ronald in the shin, hard. Ronald let out a yell and grabbed his leg with both hands. As I was hurrying over, Ronald called Shaquita a name with five parts, each one of which would be regarded as inappropriate by the principal. Shaquita obviously did not appreciate the sobriquet. She had her arm pulled back, ready to slap Ronald silly. "Hold on!" I said. "I saw what happened."

Ronald turned to me. "She kicked me," he said. "Really hard. I think she prolly broke my leg. I think it's bleeding."

"Is that so? Let me take a look." I pulled his chair back and asked him to pull up his trouser leg. Of course there was no wound, but Ronald winced in pain anyway to impress me. "I saw you kicking Shaquita and then she kicked you back. Do you know the school policy about fighting?" Both of their heads were hanging. They murmured that they did. "What happens when you go to the office for fighting?" I asked.

Shaquita said, "Principal calls yo' mama, and she has to come in an' drag you butt home." Obviously neither one of them thought this a pleasant prospect.

"OK," I said, "today I am not going to send you to the office. But if I catch either one of you fighting again, you will go straight to Ms. Sparrows. Understand?" They nodded. "But I am going to change seats. Shaquita, you and Maurice change seats so that Maurice is sitting across from Ronald." (And I have already told the rest of this story.)

I looked at my watch—only seven or eight minutes left. Aloud, I said, "How many groups need more time?" Only three raised their hands. "Good. Try to finish up now. I'll collect what you've done. Please put both shells in your bag."

Group Assignment 2

I began collecting the shells and the writing, redistributing the compositions as I went: "You have to read the composition and find the shell described. Then underline the best parts, the words or phrases that helped you identify the shell. Write a note about the best detail and why you liked it. When you finish, you'll report to the writers."

After a minute or two, the groups began talking about the writing they had received. I was standing at the front, attending to the group on my right. They thought they had identified the shell described and were in the process of underlining the best details. Behind me I heard a male voice say, "Hey, they sayin' our stuff is stupid. You can't say that. You the ones that be stupid." I turned.

Ronakea, the leader of the group under fire, stood and, a shell in each hand, stomped across to her accuser. She held out the two shells for the group to see. "Look!" she said. "They both kind of brownish, they both kind of small, and they both kind of bumpity. We can't tell which one you talking about. And that stupid." She turned on her heel and walked back to her group, seated herself, and said to her group, "I'm just gonna write that because they ain't no good details to underline." I stood there, mouth agape—wow, unfortunate, but what a good lesson, efficiently dispatched. I never could have delivered such a comment; I would have had to do it in some other way.

I looked at my watch; less than a minute to go. "Let's finish up now. The bell is going to ring. When you've completed your comments, please put the desks back where they belong."

Reflecting on the Shell Game Lesson

Back at the university, sitting around a large table in the commons, we had a little more than two hours to examine what happened in the class, what the students had produced, and to plan for the next day. My students confessed they thought the lesson would flop altogether when students seemed so reluctant at the beginning. A few students thought perhaps I should have made specific prompts earlier. I confessed that I had been considering more specific questions or perhaps outlining shapes with my finger, but that I had never had a class that wasn't able to generate some similes eventually. "When your prompts are too concrete, you deprive the kids of a chance to do the real work of seeing and inventing for themselves." We decided that the timing of that first episode was not bad. There was no wasted time.

Did I waste time on setting up the group work? We decided I had not. It was a necessary bit of management that would save time on other days. We would see the following day.

Then the students reported on the progress of each group. The first two I had visited only long enough to urge them to decide who would do the writing. I did not return. One of them had been the group criticized by Ronakea. Both groups had needed coaching, and I had not managed to give it.

We also talked about the kicking incident. Perhaps there was some preexisting animosity between Ronald and Shaquita, or perhaps Ronald just liked her and wanted her attention. Jane, who had observed that group, said that afterward Ronald claimed he had not tried to kick Shaquita but had only been swinging his feet. But according to Roger, who had also seen the incident, Ronald had been kicking for some time, and Shaquita had moved her chair to avoid his feet. "He had to stretch out to kick her," Roger said.

"Should I have tossed them?" I asked.

"It's a school rule," Jane said.

"Yeah," said Sarah, "but you can give a warning or two before sending kids out."

Roger agreed. "It wasn't much of a fight anyway," he said.

"But it disrupted the class, and George didn't get back to the first two groups," Jane insisted.

I explained my rationale. "If I'd taken them to the office, that would have been the end of the class. I thought it was better to give a warning and save the time. In some cases, it would be better to act on the rule. But remember, when you're student teaching, administrators often frown on sending a kid to the office on a first offense. If you can't handle a situation, then it's probably best to get help from the administration. But we didn't have any more problems from Ronald, did we?"

"Are you kidding? Did you see that look Maurice gave him? He's scared to death of Maurice," someone said. Everyone chuckled.

"But you're right, Jane, I did miss the coaching, and it showed up in Ronakea's comment."

"Well, maybe the coaching wouldn't have helped that group much," Roger said.

"I don't know," Sandy said. "The group I was observing made a lot of progress with just the little coaching you did. They ended up with three or four similes and a lot of detail."

"Let's see what they wrote," I said. Sandy found the piece of writing and read it aloud:

> Our shell is brown and white, sort of. It has a lot of ridges. They are very smooth. They are also even. It has a big opening. It looks like a cup also the curve of the outside of the opening is like a half oval. It looks kind of like the basin of the drinking fountain outside school. If you look at the top of the shell the ridges swirl around. It looks like a whirlpool, a little. If you stare at it. You might get dizzy.

"So, what do you think? Are we happy with this?" A fairly lengthy conversation followed. We decided that it did contain some similes, was largely punctuated correctly, and included a number of details. However, nearly all sentences were simple and limited to a single detail. It might have been better to pull all the material about the ridges together, to expand on the color, and to use the similes more strategically, perhaps to frame the other material.

I suggested that we look at the descriptions the other groups had written. Most of the writing had similar characteristics. My assignment had really asked students to do no more than list their observations. My asking them to use those details in a description had obviously not been meaningful to them. We needed to show them how to do that.

Finally I asked, "What do you think? Should we go to individual work in describing a shell independently or should we provide a model of how to write it up?" We agreed on the modeling. I asked Alan if he wanted to do that, since he was scheduled to teach the next session, or if I should. He said, "Are we going to plan it first?"

"Absolutely."

Planning for Day 2

"Does everyone have notes on the talk about the helmet shell?" My MAT students nodded. "Good. Let's work from that. Why don't you each try to write a description of that shell using what the class came up with?"

"Only what the class said?"

"Well, I suppose it would be OK to add some of your own details, especially about the color. We mainly want to see what kind of syntax we come up with."

Everyone went to work. Here is what I wrote:

> I like the helmet shell very much, partly because we can see so many different things in it. At the small end is a curlicue. If you hold the little curlicue with the large end up, it looks like an athletic trophy from the closed side. If you turn the shell to see its opening, it looks like a human ear. If you put the curlicue on top, it looks like an elf's cap and perhaps a ball gown. If you hold the shell so that the opening is level with the top of your desk, it looks like a gaping shark's mouth ready to scoop up everything through its teeth. And that is not all. If you look at the broad top, you will see a roof slowly rising to a peak. Or you can see a road slowly spiraling up to the peak, a peak that might be a tiny castle. The outside of the shell is smooth but pockmarked and wrinkled, like an old person's skin. But the inside is as smooth as glass. The outside of the shell is a cream color with tiny light caramel marks in regularly spaced indentations. The shell also has larger spots of a deeper caramel brown

at regular intervals around its body and around the outside of the opening. Inside the mouth of the shell the color is a soft peach. The helmet shell is an amazing treasure of images.

In writing this I was constantly tempted to go beyond what the seventh graders had suggested. And I did with the color. But I made myself exclude words like *stippled, diameter, ascending,* and *ratio.* However, I did allow myself *images* and *indentations.*

The seventh graders would not see any of what we had written. The point was to find out what syntactic structures we used so that we could be prepared to guide them in a class discussion that would lead to building a description of the shell together. We compared what we had written. Nearly everyone had included general framing statements such as my first and last statements. Several had used the same if . . . then structures I had. Most had expanded the descriptions of the color, noting the regular patterns. We decided that Alan would include all of these elements, asking our students to generate possible sentences for him to write on the overhead. He would first ask for a general statement about the shell. If necessary, he would ask leading questions, but only as a last resort. Together we imagined a kind of script as Alan asked the questions and we responded as we thought seventh graders might. (It has always seemed to me that this kind of imaginative activity is essential to planning, and I wanted my students to try using it. The caveat is that you have to think hard about the questions you imagine in an effort to avoid stupid ones.)

"So, Alan, what do you think you might do tomorrow?"

"Well, I guess I should begin by reviewing what they said about the shell today. Don't you think?" He looked around the table.

"We could make copies of all of their details to pass out and you could review that way," said Sarah.

"Good idea," he said. "I was just wondering if they would remember what they said. OK, I'll do that. And then I'll ask for a general statement." There was a pause.

"How will you do that?" I asked. "What do the rest of you think?" Another pause.

Sarah said, "I think we need to have them think about the audience, people who may not have seen the shell before or are seeing it for the first time, like in a museum." I looked at her expectantly. She continued, "So you'd tell them that and ask for a statement to introduce the shell, something general that would get their attention, I mean the reader's attention. Like you could ask, 'What might we say in the first sentence to get the reader's attention?'"

"What do you do if there's no response right away?" I asked.

"Wait," Alan said. "But what if I have to wait even longer than you did today?"

"Good question," I said.

Jane chimed in almost immediately. "You could ask, 'What did you all think about the shell in a word?' or 'What's a word that tells what you felt about the shell?'"

Roger looked skeptical. "What if Ronald decides that he wants to be a pain and says, 'It sucks,' or 'It's bogus,' or maybe just 'Stupid'?"

"I don't think they'll say that. They liked the shell today," Jane said.

"Someone might," I said. "Last year we had a kid who claimed that the shell he received for the individual writing was so ugly that he did not want to describe it."

"What did you do?" someone asked.

"I told him he could tell about how ugly the shell was as long as he described it so someone would be able to pick it out."

"Did he do it?"

"No, he didn't even mention ugly," I said. "He must have changed his mind. But this is a little different. This is Ronald issuing a challenge to you as the teacher. What can you do? Other than throw him out."

They were all silent. Then Sarah cleared her throat. "The class is writing this together. So you could ask if the class agrees. And then just ask for another opinion."

"I am not being difficult, but assume that they do agree that it is bogus or ugly or putrid or whatever. What would you do?"

Alan said, "We could just go with that. That would be the framing statement we talked about: *The helmet shell is one of the ugliest shells I have ever seen.* And then still ask them to describe it, showing why it's so ugly. Writers make and support negative judgments all the time—well, often anyway."

"Right," I said, "if you go with the negative, it tends to dissipate. If you fight it, it will get stronger. But let's get back to our discussion. What if the kids say it is really a nice shell and they all agree. Will you go with that?"

Sandy said, "I think I would write that down and ask for other words that the kids like better. Try to make a list, and then have them choose the one they like the best."

"That would work," Jane said. "Or you could ask, 'What did you think when you heard all the things the shell looked like?' You know, maybe you'll get something like *amazing*, or *magic*, or maybe even *phantasmagoric*."

Everyone laughed. "Yeah, right," someone muttered.

"Well, you might!" said Jane.

"Right," I said. "We want to start with what they know. But we don't want to underestimate them. That's important."

"So what do we do next?" Alan asked. "After I get an opening sentence, do I just ask them, 'What detail do you want to put next?'"

Roger said, "I think you could. But what if you get 'It looks like an athletic trophy,' and 'It looks like an ear,' and 'It looks like a shark's mouth'? I mean, what would you do with all those?"

Sarah jumped in. "You could use those sentences and then ask if they could think of how to avoid repeating *it looks like* so many times. Then if they do not know, you could show them how to do a parallel structure. Right?" She looked at me.

"Sounds good to me," I said, "especially if you have an opening sentence that calls the shell something like *amazing*."

"What do we do then, forget the if . . . then structure?" Jane asked.

"No," Sarah said. "Then they have to explain the *if* part. Like 'If you hold it by the little curlicue and turn to the opening, the shape of an ear appears.' Do you see what I mean?"

"I like that," Alan said. "But it will depend on what the kids say."

"What about the grammar? Should we teach them what an introductory clause is?" asked Jane. "Or how to punctuate it?"

"I think we should," I said. "I don't remember seeing many in their pretest writing. They may have a chance to use if . . . then several times tomorrow, which means good practice. But I'd advise keeping it simple. After they produce several examples, then tell them they have been writing introductory adverbial clauses and that a comma separates it from the rest of the sentence. With any luck, after writing four or five, they will have a feel for the pattern. I don't think it will be useful to spend a week trying to teach subject and predicate and then teaching the difference between main and subordinate clauses. I had some success using that pattern approach with what we used to call remedial ninth graders."

Next we talked about how we might teach the pattern with the sentences that the students constructed. If students suggested using the similes from the discussion, we could simply list them: *you see an athletic trophy*, *the shape of an ear appears*. Alan would help the kids write the first if clause and then ask students to write an if . . . then clause for each of the remaining similes individually. He would do over-the-shoulder observations as they worked, coaching when necessary, and, when they finished, call on successful students to read their complete sentences aloud. I suggested calling on as many students as possible for different versions. They would then develop details about color and a closing sentence. We talked about some other possibilities—the general shape of the shell, the ratio of the length of the shell to the width at the greatest diameter—but we decided we had enough to go on. If students did not bring these possibilities up, we would let them go.

We estimated that this would take anywhere from twenty-five to thirty-five minutes, leaving at least twenty-five minutes remaining. Sandy suggested that the seventh graders, in their groups, could revise their compositions using what they had learned from the whole-class activity. But should they revise their first draft or simply rewrite it using some of what they had written along with additional content and introductory clauses? We decided to have them write a new version. Teaching the techniques of revision with numbers and carets would require more modeling and double-spaced writing. All of the groups had written single-spaced descriptions, and there was only one copy of each to work with. We decided to ask that they include at least two introductory adverbial clauses in their new version. If there were time, we would have each group read their writing to the class.

The Shell Game: Day 2

The next day, Alan did a fine job. He finished with twenty-three minutes remaining for the group work. He distributed the shells and the first drafts along with a note telling the common name of each shell. The groups finished with nearly three minutes left, so two groups were able to read their rewrites aloud. When we read all of the group papers, we decided the lesson had worked well. All groups showed significant improvement over the initial drafts, and the changes were both substantive and syntactic. Here are the first and second drafts from one group. (Spelling is corrected.)

First Draft

This shell looks like a tiny tornado. It has a long tail. The tail gets wider as it gets closer to the top of the funnel. The opening begins near the top of the shell. It goes to the end of the tail. It is kind of grayish brown. It also has cream color.

Second Draft

Believe it or not, the whelk is a tiny tornado. If you hold it by the tail, you can imagine it on a street. It is tearing up trees and throwing houses around. People run away from it screaming. If you look closer at it, you will notice that the funnel has a kind of roof. The roof is made of wedge-shaped pieces. The biggest wedge is at the opening of the shell. They become smaller as they go around the shell to the top. They are in a spiral that goes to a point. The whelk is a gray-brown. There are some cream marks on it. At the end of each wedge in the outside of the funnel roof, there is a piece sticking out that looks like a thorn. It is cream-color. If you see a whelk coming down the street, you should run. It might be a tornado.

It would be easy to find fault with this piece of writing. But we were very pleased with the signs of positive growth. The MAT student who observed the group reported that the level of collaboration was very high, with one student proposing a detail, another proposing a way to put it in a sentence, and another adding still another detail. Her observation notes included this transcript:

ROSCOE: You know it has a kind of roof.

DARLENE: You could say, "If you look close, comma, you will see it has a roof."
TWILA: [*Writing*] "You will notice it has a roof."
JEFFERSON: The top has wedges.
ROSCOE: How about "The roof is made of wedge-shaped pieces."
TWILA: That sounds good.
JEFFERSON: And they get smaller as they go around.
ROSCOE: The biggest at the opening of the shell.
TWILA: Do you want me to put that first?
DARLENE: Yeah, and then put "They become smaller as they go around the shell to the top."
TWILA: Well give me a chance. You going too fast.
JEFFERSON: This gonna to be pretty good.
ROSCOE: Yeah.

I was particularly pleased that the boys recognized their progress. That is a good sign. My MAT students reported this level of collaboration in five of the seven groups. Two were less effective but worked together nonetheless.

The Shell Game: Days 3 and 4

The following day each student received a shell to write about. They knew that another student would receive what they wrote and be asked to pick out the shell from among all of the shells. We were satisfied with the results. All students used at least one simile or metaphor. All used considerable detail about shape and color and some detail about texture. The readers of all but four papers were able to find their shell based on the description. When we evaluated the papers, we commented on each, trying to point out something positive (which in nearly all cases was not difficult) and making several specific suggestions about possible revisions. The next day students had an opportunity to revise their papers after we had spent about fifteen minutes showing them how to revise using numbers and carets. Across the board, the revisions increased the quality of the writing to a considerable extent.

In the last few years, my daughter, Marjorie, has had her fifth and sixth graders make various class museums featuring their writing. These museums are always a hit among her students, other teachers, their students, and parents on parent night. Had I thought of it at the time, I would have suggested that the students use their writing and the shells to make a shell museum along the windowsills of the classroom.

The Power of the Shell Game

My students and I used the shell game for the first time in 1972. It remains one of my favorite, sure-fire lessons. It has all the characteristics we believe are necessary for successful learning. First, it's based on concrete phenomena that students have immediate contact with. Second, it has the power to engage students in generating the kinds of language that will be effective in personal narrative writing, in effect, allowing them to practice or rehearse the production of such language. Third, this rehearsal carries over to personal writing. Fourth, the language students produce in the activity becomes instructive for everyone in the group including, and perhaps especially, the teacher.

Over the years, some of my MAT students have researched the effect the shell game has on the students' ensuing work. They have found that on pretests most students did not use figurative language. In writing about the individual seashells, all students used at least one simile, and some used metaphors. Checking all the other major writing the students produced during the remainder of the workshop with us, they found that about 70 percent continued to use figurative language and used it on the posttests several weeks later. This might not have happened if we had not continued to reinforce the use of figurative language, but I credit the power of the shell lesson.

Some of my friends and colleagues have tried other objects for the lesson. One has used decorative buttons. One has used inkblots. One even claims to have used potatoes. Perhaps they were successful lessons, but if your goal is the recurrence of simile and metaphor in student writing, I would bet on the shells.

Tips for Using the Shell Game in Your Own Classroom

What You Need
- one shell that is large enough for all students to see
- six to eight pairs of shells similar in coloring, size, and shape
- enough different shells for each of your students to write about one independently

Choosing Good Shells
- For group work and independent writing, I like to use shells that are at least two inches long.
- Avoid colors such as green and purple, which are uncommon among seashells. A unique color is too easy a clue.
- It is best to buy the shells individually or collect them yourself. I have collected some of my own shells, but I've bought most in shops, from catalogs, or online. If you are beginning, avoid buying shells in bulk or by the basket, quart, or pound. In bulk, many of the shells you buy will be bivalves—clam shells—which are not nearly as interesting to examine or write about. And despite the large number of shells, the variety will not be extensive enough for the lesson.
- Probably the best place to find the assortment you need is on the Web. Three sites I recommend are Shell World (www.shellworld.com), Sea Shell City (www.seashellcity.com), and Einsteins Emporium (www.einsteinsemporium.com). All three sell individual shells, some for under a dollar. You can see pictures of the shells, and the sites indicate the size of the shells.

Lessons Learned

My MAT students and I learned a number of lessons from this experience:

1. If we hope to see meaningful student progress, thoughtful planning is mandatory. Some educators believe that planning is harmful, that it limits what students are allowed to learn and imposes the teacher's values. I argue that teachers have a responsibility to help students develop skills and values such as seeing writing as valuable and interesting.

2. Meaningful planning has to be based on a careful analysis of the tasks to be taught and knowledge of the students, particularly what they know and can already do.

3. Even when our planning is as careful as we can make it, we may have overlooked something that will make the lesson less successful than we hope. We have to be alert to that possibility and be prepared to make the necessary adjustments as the lesson progresses.

4. Effective learning begins with a concrete experience in which students can participate directly, as in observing the shells. It is developed with teacher support and leads to independent work.

5. Something almost always happens that we cannot control, like Ronald's kicking and Shaquita's revenge.

6. We must be reflective at all times: we have to know what we hope to accomplish and question the extent to which it is being accomplished.

Five General Principles for Planning and Teaching

Our experience with the shell game can be generalized to all teaching:

1. Analyze the task to be taught.

2. Develop criteria for judging the work produced by students in order to assess your teaching. This is more important than assessing the students.

3. Invent activities that will help students learn the procedural knowledge necessary to the task being taught.

4. Sequence activities from teacher-led to group work and finally to independent work and from simple to complex.

5. Use teaching strategies that allow students to interpret data for themselves, strategies they can apply to a wide variety of materials that become more and more complex.

5

CREATING DIALOGUE

The first narratives our inner-city students write include virtually no dialogue. The closest most come is indirect dialogue, statements such as "He told me to go to the door." The result is that they fail to capture some of the things in their own stories that might be most interesting to readers. Yet anyone with teaching experience knows very well that excited students can recount lengthy conversations, sometimes with more than two speakers. We've heard them do it. They use *I go*, *he goes*, and *she goes* or *I'm like*, *he's like*, and *she's like* as introductions to what they quote. It is relatively easy to harness this propensity for relating conversation by suggesting scenarios for which students are asked to invent dialogue. The problem is that they often cannot remember the rules about where the commas and quotation marks go. Many African American students do not use the Standard English form of the third-person singular. They drop the *s* because in Black English vernacular (BEV) it is not required; indeed, according to Labov (1972) it "does not exist" (33).

The activities in this chapter and Chapter 6 help students develop dialogue between two or more speakers, first in dramatic form (the name of a speaker followed by a colon) and then in narrative style. The materials include a few simple rules for teaching, practicing, and learning how to punctuate dialogue. In addition, they include strategies for helping students learn to add details about the speaker's stance, actions, facial expressions, and so forth. Again, these activities move from teacher-led to group and finally to independent work in which students write dialogue appropriate to one of their own stories.

Day 1: Examining Dialogue with Students

Introducing the Concept

In the class I'm using as an example, Roger presented the lesson. He asked the seventh graders to take the Richard Wright piece (see Chapter 3) out of their portfolios and find examples of what the characters in the story say and underline them. After a moment or two, he asked them to read some examples aloud.

"What do you think? Do you think the story could do without the dialogue?" There was a chorus of nos. "Why do you think the dialogue is important?"

Ronald said, "Because you need it."

"Ronald says it is important because you need it. Do you all agree with Ronald?" Students nodded yes. "Now, the question is why do you need it?" Ronakea was waving her hand, but Roger waited for a few more hands and called on Jefferson.

"It tell what his mother want him to do."

"Does anyone want to add anything to what Jefferson says?" Ronakea was still aggressively waving her hand, but Roger called on Celine.

"It tell that his mother be mean to him. She make him get in a fight."

Ronakea could no longer contain herself. She blurted out, "She not mean. She want him to learn how to take care of hisself. If he don't do it now, he'll get hisself beat all the time." She stopped, looked at her copy of the story, and then continued. "Look at this here." She read from the story:

> "What's the matter?" my mother asked.
>
> "It's those same boys," I said. "They'll beat me."
>
> "You've got to get over that," she said. "Now, go on."
>
> "I'm scared," I said.
>
> "Go on and don't pay any attention to them," she said.

"See, that show that she want to help him learn how to stand up for hisself."

I tried not to smile too broadly. I wanted to see what Roger would do. My MAT students and I had talked about discussion patterns and how positive reactions can cut off discussion, as though a positive response to a student's comment means the student has given the right answer and there is no need to say anything further. To my delight, Roger did not simply approve; he set up a problem. "Well, we have two different points of view here. Celine says Richard's mother is mean for making him fight, and Ronakea thinks she is not mean but that she is trying to help him learn to stand up for himself. What do the rest of you think about this difference?" Roger had pulled it off. This is what Nystrand (Nystrand et al. 1997) calls "up-take," making what students have to say the subject of further talk in the classroom. It honors student ideas and makes those ideas the center of discussion, a very important means of prompting and continuing student talk.

There were several hands up. Roger called on Alicia. "I agree with Celine. Richard a little boy and there a whole bunch of boys after him. So it be mean to send him out like that." There were still hands in the air, among them Maurice's. Roger called on him.

"He ain't that little. He pretty big," said Maurice, "on account of he bust a lot of heads with the stick."

Roger said, "Can you explain why that's true, Maurice?"

"Well, ya know, if he little, he couldn't reach their heads."

Alicia said, "Well maybe he ain't that little, but it still mean to send him."

Ernest said, "Tha's just your opinion, Alicia. I don't think she mean. She just want him to learn that he can protect hisself. An' he do."

Ronakea jumped back in. "Right. The dialogue there to let you know how he feel, what his mother want, an' why he has to fight. Like he ain't got no choice. 'Cause it say right here, 'If I were beaten at home, there was absolutely nothing that I could do about it; but if I were beaten in the streets, I had a chance to fight and defend myself.' So, see, he kind of figure out that he has to fight. Tha's what his mother want. She just don't want him to get beat up, noway." Ronakea looked at Roger. "Is that stuff dialogue?"

"Why do you ask?" Roger said.

"'Cause it what he sayin', but it ain't in them quote marks."

Roger addressed the class. "Does anyone know what that's called?" Seeing the blank looks, he continued, "That's called *internal monologue.*" He wrote the phrase on the board.

"It tells what the character is thinking, but since he does not say it aloud, it does not appear in quotation marks. Does anyone know what the word *dialogue* means?"

Ernest said, "It like people talking."

"Does anyone know what the first part of *dialogue* means, just the *d* and *i*?" No one appeared to know, so Roger explained. "It means two. And the second part, *logue*, means words. So *dialogue* has come to mean the words of two or more people talking." He underlined *mono* on the board. "Does anyone know what *mono* means?"

Ernest raised his hand tentatively, and Roger called on him.

"I think it mean like one, like in monorail, it mean one rail."

"Very good," said Roger. This was specific information there was no need to discuss. "So this phrase [*pointing to* interior monologue] means one person speaking or thinking to himself or herself. Does anyone know what *interior* means?"

Jefferson said, "Tha's easy. It means inside."

"Right, it means *the* inside." Roger asked for examples and got several: the interior of a car, the interior of this school, the interior of my house. Pointing to *interior monologue*, he asked, "Can anyone explain this phrase again?"

Verita said, "It means someone talking to herself."

Alicia added, "Or talking on the inside of herself."

"OK," Roger said. "I'm glad we made that distinction between dialogue and interior monologue. That is important. We'll come back to it. Now, I want you to try to invent a dialogue in your groups. I am going to distribute a sheet of possible scenes in which two or more people are having a disagreement of some kind. We will read and talk about one together. Then I'll assign one for each group to work on." He distributed a sheet containing eight scenarios (see Figure 5.1). Fifteen minutes had passed since the class had begun.

Creating Dialogue with the Whole Class

Roger directed the class to the eighth scenario on the sheet. He read it aloud and then told the students that he would like them to make up the dialogue for it. "How many characters will we have?" The students said three. "OK, let's name them." The students assumed the borrower was a boy and named him Lester. Someone suggested naming the sister Vampira because she was going to be so angry. But not many agreed. They finally picked the name Helen. Roger said, "Let's give Helen the first line as she comes up to Lester." He wrote the name *Helen* on the overhead and put a colon after it. "This is the way the scripts for plays are written, the name of the character followed by a colon and the lines that the character is to say."

Hank suggested a line: "Give me my Discman back right now. You said you would give it back yesterday. I still don' got it."

Roger wrote the line on the overhead. "I forgot to ask. Where do you want this scene to take place, where in the house?"

Ronakea volunteered, without raising her hand, "Let's have it in the kitchen. He there drinking a pop."

Jefferson said, "Yeah, after school in the afternoon."

"Is that OK with everybody?" Hearing no objections, Roger wrote the stage directions on the overhead: *The scene is the afternoon after school. Lester is drinking pop in the kitchen. Helen enters.* Then he asked, "What will Lester say?"

Hands went up. Roger called on Hank. "I lost it, bitch! What are you gonna do about it?"

1. Roberto tells his sister, Clareese, that it's her turn to wash the dishes. He says that he has washed them three times in a row and that they had agreed to wash every other night. She says that he owes her three nights because he missed washing for a whole week when he went to visit their aunt. He denies it and gives his reasons. Clareese becomes angry with him. Develop this dialogue beginning with Roberto's opening demand. Grandmother comes into the kitchen. What does she say after listening for a minute?

2. Your mother has decided to take a few days off work and take you and your sister on a weekend car trip to Wisconsin. You and your sister have been sitting in the backseat of the station wagon all morning, and for the last three hours your sister has been putting her feet on your side of the seat while you have been ignoring her completely. Finally, after she grabs your magazine with her toes, you can't take it anymore. What do you and your sister say to each other? How does your mother intervene?

3. The bell rang a few minutes ago and you are late to your English class. As you try to sneak into the class unnoticed, hoping to avoid your sixth tardy, you trip on your shoelace and you and the large stack of books and papers you are carrying fly across the room and fall directly in front of the teacher. A student laughs and makes an insulting remark. You begin to make up an excuse, but your teacher makes a comment about your dramatic entrance. What do you, the other student, and the teacher say to one another?

4. Shawn has been sitting quietly in class, minding his own business. Clarence, the boy sitting next to him, shoots a paper wad at Cherise two rows away. The wad hits her in the cheek. She assumes that Shawn did it. The wad stings and makes her cry out. The teacher looks up and asks what happened. Cherise is very angry. What do Cherise, the teacher, and Shawn say?

5. It's Friday night and your friend is having a party and has invited you. You have been grounded because you failed two math tests in a row. You cannot go out until you pass the next test with a C or better. You had a test today and passed it with a D. You decide to try to talk your mother into letting you go. After a few words with you, she calls your father into the room. What do the three of you say to one another?

6. There is an R-rated action movie showing at the local theater. You and your friends would love to see it, but you will have to have a parent with you. You and your friend try to talk one of your mothers into taking you. What do you three say to one another?

7. Leslie has just learned that she is failing in English because she missed several homework assignments. She cannot believe it, since she received a B on three tests. If she fails English she will not be eligible for the seventh-grade basketball team, her very favorite activity and one at which she excels. She goes to the teacher to protest, claiming that the teacher never told the class about this homework policy. When she talks to the teacher, she is very angry but tries to control her anger. What do they say to each other?

8. The other day, you borrowed your older sister's Discman, which she loves and cannot be without. It was a special present for her good report card last semester. Now, two days later, she wants to have it back. The problem is that you took it outside to the park and lost it. She approaches you to demand it back because you said you would return it yesterday, and you have not. She does not know that you lost it—yet. What do you say to each other? What do you both say to your mother when she comes into the room after hearing you shouting?

Figure 5.1 *Scenarios for Writing Dialogue*

Roger said, "Well, that's a thought, but we have to keep it clean. We may be showing this to the principal or your parents. You're going to have an audience."

Ronakea's hand was up. "He wouldn't say that anyway. Helen older. She probably bigger. He wouldn't say that."

Roger asked, "Do you think he would admit right away that he lost it?"

Alicia said, "No. He probably try not to tell, 'cause he gonna get in trouble from his mom, too."

"Anybody have an idea?"

Jefferson suggested he might say he took it to his friend's house and he forgot it there. "'Cause he gonna try to buy time."

"Who can make that into an actual line of dialogue?"

Jefferson said, "He would say, 'I took it to my friend's house yesterday, and I forgot it there.'"

"Any other suggestions?"

Jefferson was miffed. "What's the matter with that? That's OK, what I said."

Since there were no other suggestions, Roger wrote down Jefferson's contribution and continued to help build the dialogue for several more minutes. Here's the dialogue the class developed:

The scene is the afternoon after school. Lester is drinking pop in the kitchen. Helen enters.

HELEN: Give me my Discman back right now. You said you would give it back yesterday. I still don't got it.

LESTER: I took it to my friend's house yesterday, and I forgot it there.

HELEN: Oh yeah? What friend is that?

LESTER: Danny.

HELEN: Well, you call Danny right this minute and tell him to bring that Discman here to me.

LESTER: He can't just be runnin' around for you. He got stuff to do.

HELEN: Then you call him and tell him that I am comin' to get it. Now do it now!

LESTER: I can't just be callin' him up any time. He busy.

HELEN You lying to me about something? You sure makin' a lot of excuses.

Mother enters.

MOTHER: What on earth you two shoutin' about? I hear you shouting from the front porch. What is going on here?

HELEN: He borrowed my Discman two days ago. He promised it back yesterday, and I still don't have it. He say he took it to Danny's house and forgot it there.

MOTHER: You didn't tell me you went to Danny's house. That fifteen blocks from here. You told me you went to the park just down the street. You in big trouble for one thing or another.

Roger said, "We'll stop here."

Ronald didn't want to stop. He wanted Lester to get in big trouble.

"We can get him in big trouble later," Roger said.

Another fourteen minutes of class time had passed.

Creating Dialogue in Small Groups

Roger then said, "I want you to develop a dialogue in your group." He assigned each group one of the remaining seven scenarios. "You have about twenty minutes for this, not a lot of time. I want each one of you to make a copy for yourself. Use the form we used for the Discman scenario. The character's name followed by a colon and the line that he or she says. So get to work. Try to finish by the bell."

The kids moved into groups. In a little over a minute, they were all working. Roger walked around the room, listening and coaching. Just before the bell, he said, "I am going to collect your copies of the dialogue. If you think you need more time tomorrow, write *more time* at the bottom of your sheet."

Reflecting on the Dialogue Lesson

Returning to the university, my teacher education students and I read the dialogues eagerly, hoping that these seventh graders had done a thorough job. We decided that, for the most part, they had. A few students were behind the rest of their group, Maurice about two exchanges. But in general the dialogues looked pretty strong. We remarked that the students had seemed to stay on task, working up to the end of class. It also appeared they had not quite finished. Many had written *more time* at the bottom of their sheets.

Ronakea's group, which included Maurice, Dashonda, and Hank, had been assigned scenario 4, in which Clarence hits Cherise with a paper wad and Cherise assumes Shawn did it.

Here is what they wrote, with spelling corrected:

The scene is in a class. The teacher is in front of the room explaining stuff. Clarence has a large rubber band. He makes a paper wad to fire with the rubber band. He aim it at Cherise and fires. It hit her in the face.

CHERISE: Eeeeeh!

TEACHER: What is going on here?

CHERISE: Shawn shot a paper wad at me. He hit me in the face. It really hurt.

TEACHER: Shawn, why are you carrying on like that? You know that's not allowed in this room.

SHAWN: I didn't do nothing. I'm just sitting here.

CHERISE: Yes he did. I got the paper wad right here.

SHAWN: You might got the paper wad, but that don't mean I shot it. There a lot of other people in this room.

TEACHER: Let me see that wad. Hmmm. Looks like a spelling test paper to me. (*She unfolds the paper.*) Well, well. Looks like it's got a name on it. Now whose name do you think it is?

CHERISE: It be Shawn's name. I know he done it.

TEACHER: No, it is not. I am going to give the person who did this a chance to confess. Raise your hand now. Don't be a liar and a sneak. Okay, so nobody wants to confess. Clarence stand up.

CLARENCE: I did not do it. Probably somebody got my spelling test. They framing me. I did not do it.

More time.

This was good dialogue. It went beyond the scenario. "Whose idea was the spelling test paper?" Roger wondered. "That's a neat idea. Was it Ronakea?"

"I am pretty sure it was. I think she mentioned it first. But they were going so fast, I couldn't get everything down," said Sandy, who had been observing that group. We decided that the dialogue, while it was strong, still needed some work. For one thing, it didn't include all of the stage directions: how the teacher got the paper wad, for example, or that she waited for answers. My MAT students thought it needed a pause after *sneak*, a direction for Cherise after she had been hit, directions for Clarence throughout, and so forth.

After examining all of the dialogues, we decided that all groups needed to work on directions for the actors. Roger pointed out that he hadn't really covered that, only general scene directions. We also noted that two groups needed to try to add a few more exchanges.

Sandy asked what we should do about the verb forms. Ronakea's dialogue was pretty sound, but there were some nonstandard forms. "Sometimes they omit the verb *be*. Shawn says, 'There a lot,' and sometimes they drop the *s* for third-person singular, especially *don't* for *doesn't*." We had talked briefly about this problem during our preparation for the workshop. I had explained that we would see a difference between the dialect of the students and our Standard English, particularly in verbs. In what Labov (1972) calls Black English vernacular, the third-person singular is not inflected (*s* does not appear), and linking verbs do not often appear before predicate nouns and adjectives. For example, in BEV a speaker is not likely to say, "He is a man," but rather "He a man." Likewise, a speaker of BEV would not be likely to say, "She is good," but rather "She good"; not "She is in the room," but rather "She in the room"; not "He is drinking pop," but rather "He drinkin' pop"; and so forth (see Labov 1972, 67–69, for other examples).

We had talked about the BEV use of *be* in verb phrases to indicate habitual action: "He be eatin'." Shirley Brice Heath (1983) gives the following example of a black child being misinterpreted by a teacher:

TEACHER: Where is Susan? Isn't she here today?
  LEM: She ain't ride the bus.
TEACHER: She *doesn't* ride the bus, Lem.
  LEM: She *do* be ridin' the bus.

Heath reports that the teacher "frowned at Lem and turned away" (277). In Lem's system of BEV, *ain't* is equivalent to *didn't*, thus indicating that on this particular day, Susan did not ride the bus. The teacher assumed that Lem used it mistakenly for *doesn't* and "corrected" him, having erroneously derived the meaning that Susan never rode the bus. Lem's response attempted to tell the teacher that Susan did ride the bus regularly. But she lost the information that Lem tried to convey because she did not understand the use of *be* to indicate habitual action.

We had also talked about the use of *been* to indicate a distant action completed in the past (as in "He been had that house") and perfect progressive (as in "He been talking in class") and about double negatives and the indication of possession through adjacency, with no *s* (as in "Her friend brother").

Because of these and other differences, Labov argues that BEV is "best seen as a distinct subsystem within the larger grammar of English." He continues, "But the gears and axles of English grammatical machinery are available to all speakers of all dialects, whether or not they use all of them in everyday speech" (1972, 63–64). (Many other BEV studies are available, including *African American Vernacular English: Features, Evolution, Educational Implications*, by Rickford [1999].)

The implication I draw from Labov's work is that these dialect features are part of BEV in oral language and can be changed only when students want to change them. However, our concern was written language. As the Richard Wright piece indicates, writers can and do change their dialects when it comes to writing. Many of my African American friends are fluent in both Standard English and BEV. However, my own experience in seventh and eighth grades with a teacher who was bent on correcting my oral language was and still is memorable. She corrected our usage and pronunciation in class as we asked questions or responded to her questions, and as a result no one said much of anything for fear of coming under her scrutiny. She shut the class down completely. I had a problem: I did not want my students trying to change the way these children spoke, but I was interested in changing their writing (or at least trying to).

To what extent should we make this effort? I believed we should accept all oral language, incorporate it into the dialogues as we developed them in class, and by and large, write them on the overhead as dictated by the students. After all, we were helping them write out their dialogues, not ours. But when we were not quoting characters, we should help students learn standard forms in stage directions and in the transformations of the directions into narrative. But I also believed that we could not make such changes through constant correction. We needed to do it by modeling. Our work on narrative shouldn't turn into grammar and usage lessons. Doubtless, some readers will say we were remiss in not teaching and drilling the usage directly; others will say that we should have left the language of the students alone. In this debate, I side with Delpit:

> Skills are a necessary but insufficient aspect of black and minority students' education. Students need technical skills to open doors, but they need to be able to think critically and creatively to participate in meaningful and potentially liberating work within those doors. (1995, 19)

My MAT students and I decided that we would try to teach skills, but only in the context of meaningful communication. But we would not disrupt that communication to correct their talk, nor discourage their writing by spilling red ink on their pages. (For a summary of the research on the impact of teacher corrections, see Hillocks 1986.)

Planning Day 2

Sandy would be teaching the following day and would lead students through the Discman dialogue, helping them add stage and actor directions. We estimated this would take between twelve and fifteen minutes. Students would then work on the directions for their own dialogues for another fifteen minutes. Sandy would work with the two groups that needed additional help. That should leave at least twenty minutes for the groups to act out their dialogues.

We read the dialogue from Ronakea's group aloud. It took less than two minutes. We estimated that if it took a minute to set up each scene, two minutes to read it, and two minutes for comments from the class, at least four groups should be able to present their dialogues. (I did warn them that our estimates might be pretty far off.) We discussed which group should read first. I suggested that we wanted strong readers who would act their parts well and therefore be good role models. We thought Ronakea's and Ronald's groups were the best candidates. The next day in class, Sandy would decide which one to ask to go first.

Day 2: Creating Dialogue with Students

Creating Stage Directions with the Whole Class

Sandy called the class to order. "We are going to return to the Discman dialogue now," she said, putting the dialogue on the overhead. "I want you to think about stage directions. All we have is the general scene directions and entrances of Helen and Mother. But if you want the scene to be performed in a certain way, you have to give some directions to the actors. We can do that by adding some indications about how the actors speak and move. For example, how should Helen say her first line? Is she going to say it in a calm way, or is she going to be angry? What do you think?"

Shaquita said, "She angry. She gonna shout."

Jefferson added, "She so angry, she gonna hit him or bus him with a bat."

Sandy asked, "Do you all agree with that?"

"No, she wouldn't hit him right away, 'cause she wants her Discman back," said Alicia.

No one had anything to add, and Sandy said, "OK, the key words are *angry* and *shout*. So we can insert them before the colon, in parentheses, right before the line she is to speak." She used a caret to insert (Shouting angrily) after *Helen* and before the colon. "Do you want to say anything about the way she enters? Would she run in? Saunter calmly? How do you think she would enter?"

Jefferson said, "I think she would sneak up on him and shout in his ear."

Ronakea was out of her seat. "Yeah, here the way I'd do it." Picking her feet high off the floor in an exaggerated tiptoe, hands stretched out as though to strangle, she pretended to sneak behind Ronald, who, of course, was watching her every move. She bent down to his ear and shouted, "I want my Discman back now, you li'l thief!" Ronald jumped from his seat, hands up as if to fend off blows. The whole class cracked up.

Jefferson said, "She ain't say the line right."

"That's OK, she was giving us a demonstration of how to play the scene. Great demonstration, Ronakea." Some of the students applauded. Ronakea returned to her seat, but Ronald took a formal little bow.

"OK," Sandy said. "How will we put that into stage directions?"

Several hands went up, Verita's among them. Verita was quiet and shy, and my MAT students and I had talked about how to include her. Sandy called on her, and Verita said, "Up where it says *Helen enters*, put it there. Like 'Helen enters on tiptoe with her hands like she's gonna strangle Ronald,' I mean Lester."

"Anybody want to add to that?"

"You gotta say she sneak up behind him," said Jefferson, who's original suggestion had been altered a bit in Ronakea's enactment.

"Any other suggestions?"

"You could say he jump up scared, for Lester," Ronald said.

Sandy waited for other suggestions. Then she turned to the overhead and added (after *Helen enters*) *on tiptoe, sneaking up behind Lester, hands out like she's about to strangle him.* Then she asked, "What did you want to add for Lester?"

Ronald repeated, "Jumping out of his chair scared." Sandy used a caret to add that in parentheses after *Lester*.

"Do you want to add *hands in the air*?"

Ronald nodded, and Sandy added it with a caret.

Sandy led the class through adding stage directions for the remaining lines. Several more students contributed. "Good job," Sandy said. "Now I would like you to add the stage directions and acting directions for your own dialogues." The session had taken a little more than twelve minutes.

Creating Stage Directions in Small Groups

Student groups began working on their own directions. We had thirty-seven minutes left. Sandy first worked with the two needy groups and then checked in with the others. After about ten minutes, Sandy told the groups to assign parts and rehearse reading their dialogues, so they'd be prepared to read them to the class. Eight minutes later the groups were ready to go. There were nineteen minutes of class left.

Sandy asked Ronakea's group to read first. Ronakea played the teacher, Dashonda was Cherise, Maurice played Clarence, and Hank was Shawn. They went to the front of the room and borrowed three desks from other students. They took their places. Maurice had a rubber band and a paper wad. (I suddenly realized that we hadn't talked about props, but the groups had taken care of that oversight on their own.) Maurice enjoyed launching the wad at Dashonda. It hit her in the arm. She squealed and then started moaning as though she had received a major injury. Ronakea, playing a no-nonsense teacher, delivered her first line angrily. Dashonda accused Hank vehemently, pointing her accusing finger, punching the air repeatedly with it. Hank played his part well, hands in the air to protest his innocence. Maurice sat looking like Maurice. When Ronakea made a menacing move toward Hank, as if she were going to box his ears, Maurice smiled. Was he amused or playing the part of getting away with something? The scene ended with Ronakea revealing the real name on the spelling test. She went to Maurice, took him by the elbow, pulled him up, and marched him toward the door. "You're going to the office now. The principal going to call you mama, and you outta here." Maurice turned, looked over her head, and smiled. Everyone laughed and applauded.

After the actors had returned to their seats, Sandy asked, "How did you like it?"

Ronald replied, "Gooood," stretching out the vowels. Everyone agreed.

"What did you especially like about the scene?"

It turned out the students liked everything about the scene, from the shooting of the wad to the way Ronakea marched Maurice out the door. They had a compliment for every actor. The students were proud of their classmates.

"OK," Sandy said, "let's move along." She called on Ronald's group to read. Two other groups read as well, but the final group finished their scene just as the bell rang. There was no time for comment. Sandy asked for applause and the class gave it generously. She collected the dialogues and reminded the other three groups that they would read the next day.

Back at the university, we reviewed the class in detail. It was mostly happy self-congratulation about how wonderful the students were, how much they enjoyed the activity, and so forth. Most of the youngsters hadn't used their scripts but had memorized or paraphrased the lines. The few who had to read from their papers had done so a bit clumsily. I told the group that if we were going to teach this class all year, we would be wise to administer an oral reading inventory to those who'd had trouble. I explained an oral reading inventory briefly and said we would deal with that in the other course they were taking with me.

Then we began planning the next day's work, which would be transforming the dramatic scripts into narratives.

6

Transforming Dramatic Scripts into Narratives

Planning Day 3

Our general plan was to finish the group presentations and move to the next stage, changing the scripts into narratives. In our summer course, we had talked about rules for punctuating dialogue and prepared a handout (see Figure 6.1). We decided we would distribute the handout, go over the rules, and apply them to a few lines of the Discman dialogue. Since we wanted everyone to have a copy of the Discman dialogue, Jane volunteered to type it up and make photocopies. We would help the seventh graders add the stage directions to the first two lines as they would appear in a narrative and punctuate the quotations correctly. We came up with examples of those sentences, knowing full well they would likely end up being quite different; we just wanted to get an idea of the appropriate changes. We also discussed whether to put the narrative in past or present tense. We decided on present, because it seemed an easier transition from a dramatic script. Since Jane would be in charge the next day, we asked her to develop a more detailed plan that night and fill us in the next morning.

At eight the next morning we reviewed Jane's lesson. She had decided to lead the class in transforming the first five speeches of the Discman dialogue and then ask students to transform the remaining five speeches individually. We agreed that should work, but how would we check their work before moving on? We decided Jane would ask some students to read their work aloud, indicating the position of the punctuation. Jane said, "I'll have them do the first five speeches one at a time. One student will dictate to me, and I can ask questions of the class. Then for the second five, I'll call on someone, have her or him write it up on the overhead, and ask for corrections. If that goes well, I'll ask each student to do three or four speeches from his or her group dialogue."

Roger asked, "Is that going to take up the whole class?"

Jane wasn't sure.

"If there are several minutes left, you could ask students to write one speech on the board," I suggested. "If you have more time, improvise."

"Today's not going to be as much fun as yesterday," Jane said, looking a bit down.

"Probably not," I agreed, "but it's important. Remember how much trouble the kids had with sentence boundaries? It's not our main point in this lesson, but each time we punctuate a line of dialogue, we'll be putting in the terminal punctuation. We'll be reinforcing that convention."

Follow these rules when you use dialogue in your narratives:

1. Put quotation marks (" ") around the words that actually come out of people's mouths. Keep *he said*, *she said*, and other words outside the quotes. For example:

    Karen said, "I love basketball."

2. Capitalize the first word that the speaker says. For example:

    She shouted, "Meet me at the gym tonight!"

3. For variety, you can move *he said/she said* to the end of the sentence. Just make sure you separate the quote with a comma, question mark, or exclamation point positioned to the left of the end quotation mark. For example:

    "Make it five dollars for rent," Joe said.

    "Can I borrow your black bag?" Mike asked.

    "I can't believe that's true!" shouted Susan.

4. Every time a new character talks, indent for a new paragraph, even if he or she says only one word. For example:

    Joe quietly said, "Becky, you aren't going to be happy. I broke your Discman."

    "What?" Becky screamed.

    "You heard me. I broke your Discman. Here are the thirty-seven pieces it broke into," Joe said as he ran out of the room.

Figure 6.1 *Rules for Punctuating Dialogue*

Day 3: Punctuating Dialogue with the Whole Class

Jane had about thirty-five minutes for her lesson. She distributed the Discman dialogue and projected a copy on the overhead:

> *The scene is the afternoon after school. Lester is drinking pop in the kitchen. Helen enters on tiptoe with her hands out as though she's going to strangle Lester. She creeps up behind him.*

"Look at how this scene is set at the beginning. If you were writing this as a story, how might you change it? Would you begin with the same words for a story?"

The students were unsure. After a few moments Verita and Ronakea raised their hands. Jane called on Verita first.

"Wouldn't you say for a story, 'One day after school, Lester was drinking pop in the kitchen'?"

"Yes, you could. If we did, we would have to change all the verbs in the stage directions to past tense," Jane said. I tried not to cringe. Jane continued, "Who can change the next verb to past tense? Helen what?" She waited.

Shaquita said, "Helen enter the kitchen with her hands out as though she gonna strangle Lester."

Jane reddened. She wasn't sure what to say. I thought I saw her take a breath. Then she plunged on. "Well, actually, in formal English, it would be *entered*, with an *-ed* on the end." She paused, looking at the students to see whether they understood. Then she said, "And we would have to change the next verb to *were going to*, because that is the subjunctive required by the conditional *as though*. That is, in, um, in formal English." Just as I was about to raise my hand and draw it across my throat, she said, "That's too complicated for today. Why don't we leave it in present tense. OK?" It was obviously OK with the kids, who almost certainly had no idea what she was talking about. I made a note to discuss the problem in our session after class.

Ronakea had her hand up. "I was gonna say we could just take that stuff and use it as the beginning." She read the description of the scene setting as it was.

"Yes, you could. Or you could say, 'It is afternoon after school and Lester is drinking pop in the kitchen.'" Jane wrote that statement on the overhead. "Ronakea, do you want to add the rest?" Ronakea nodded, and Jane added the remainder. "What would come next?" There was a pause. "Do you remember what Ronakea did when she acted it out?"

Ronald said, "She bend over to my ear."

"So how will we phrase that?"

"She bends over and shouts in Lester's ear," Verita said.

"OK, good. And then comes the line of dialogue." She wrote Verita's statement on the overhead. "Let me distribute these rule sheets now." The kids squirmed a little at the mention of rule sheets, but they took a copy and some even began to read it. "You can mark this up if you want, but you are going to keep the sheet in your portfolio with all the other writing things." Jane read the rules aloud, verbally punctuating each example. She read the final rule twice and called on a different student to read each of the examples, inserting verbal punctuation. Finally she asked, "Who can tell me how to punctuate the first line of dialogue?"

Verita's hand was up. "Put a comma after *ear*, then a quote mark, Give my Discman back right now, period. You said you would give it back yesterday, period. I still don't have it, exclamation point. Then another quote mark." Jane wrote the words and punctuation on the overhead.

"Who can tell us how to do the next one? We have to do his stage directions too."

Several hands were up. Jane looked for someone who hadn't yet responded. She called on Roscoe.

"We could have him say, 'No big deal.' "

"We could. Do you guys want to add some physical description?"

"How about 'He shrugs his shoulders'?"

"Do you want to add anything else? No? Well, then, think about how to put all of that together." Jane paused. "Who can act it out?" She paused again. "Try it at your seats, all of you." She watched as they tried to act it out. "OK, who will do it for the class?" No hands were up. "You did a good job, Hank. Show us all what you did."

The class turned toward Hank. He sat up, then slouched and shrugged his shoulders and said, "No big deal," waving his hand as if to make light of Helen's annoyance. "I took it to my friend's house yesterday, and I forgot it there."

"We all saw that. How would you describe it?"

"He shrug his shoulders and wave his hand," Ronald said.

"It's hard to describe how he waved his hand, but when he waved it, what did it mean?"

Ronakea didn't wait to be called on. "It mean like it don't matter that he took the Discman and forgot it."

"Other suggestions?"

"It mean like it's no big deal, like she gettin' bent up out of shape 'bout nothin'," Ronald said.

"Other suggestions?"

"It mean he think she silly." This came from Jerome, a new source.

"Any others?" Jane paused for a couple of seconds and said, "Try this," and wrote the words *waving his hand as though* on the overhead. "Now I want you to write that on your papers and complete the *as though*. Explain as though what." Jane walked about the room, helping students who seemed puzzled or confused. She waited for nearly three minutes before she asked, "Anyone?" I remembered the relatively simple syntax in these children's pretest writing and wondered if they would be able to deal with this somewhat sophisticated clause. But there was no reason they shouldn't try. "Anyone?" Jane asked again. Three hands were up; the faithful Ronakea, Verita, and Ronald all wanted to offer their ideas. Jane reminded them to read the punctuation marks and called on Ronald first.

"I got this: *He wave his hand as though she gettin' all bent up out of shape over nothing,* period."

Jane said, "OK, good. Let's see what others have. Ronakea?"

"I wrote, *He wave his hand as though she was being silly about something of no importance,* period."

"Verita?"

"*He waves his hand as though her worry is for nothing about something of no importance,* period."

Jane collected several more similar responses. She told the students that all of their suggestions were good and they should write whichever one they liked the best. She reminded them to capitalize the first word of the speaker's actual words. She waited for a moment as the students wrote; then she moved on to the next line. Immediately, the students produced *Helen is standing with her clenched fists on her hips.* Then Jane asked, "What is Helen feeling at this point?"

There was a chorus of the words *angry* and *mad*, among others that Jane ignored. She said, "If she's angry or mad, we want a verb other than *said* or *asks* to indicate the anger." There was a long pause. "Well, think about this: what sounds do various animals make when they're angry?" Wow, I thought, what a good idea. I wondered whether Jane had planned that or thought of it on the spot. But the students seemed puzzled. She asked, "What sounds do angry dogs make?" From the class came *growl*, *bark*, and *howl*.

"Good," Jane said, repeating their words. "Remember describing the shells? We asked you what they looked like. Here you can do the same thing. What does her voice sound like?" She wrote the words they had suggested beside the word *dog* on the board. "How about an angry snake?" The class provided a chorus of hisses. "How about an angry bird?" *Screech* and *squawk* were popular suggestions. A boy in the back volunteered *caw*. Jane had been writing all of these words on the board next to the corresponding animal name. Now she pointed to Helen's first speech and said, "OK, choose one of those words and turn it into a verb that tells us how this line was said." She waited and then called for volunteers to read what they had written, verbalizing the punctuation. Each of the suggested words had been used, along with two new ones, *roar* and *squeal*.

"We have about twelve minutes left. I want you to do the remaining lines of the dialogue by yourselves. Remember to change the stage directions so that they will be appropriate for a story and follow the rules for punctuating dialogue. I'll come around to help you. Raise your hand if you want me." Jane walked around the room. After a couple of minutes, there were several hands in the air, and Jane visited those students. Most just wanted her to check their work. At the end of the hour, just before the bell, she collected their papers.

Reflecting on Day 3 and Planning Day 4

Later, in the university common room, we examined the students' work. There were very few errors in punctuation, since the script format had made it very clear what words each speaker had said. There were, however, many errors in the present-tense verbs introducing the quotations. Each verb should have been third-person singular in Standard English (SE), but these students had often omitted the *s*. (Verita had not omitted the *s*, but, as Jane said, "In class, she put the endings on as well." She had developed standard dialect. How? We never did find out.) We decided to present a little lesson on third-person-singular verb endings and ask students to revise their descriptive clauses to reflect the standard forms. (We felt the vernacular forms were appropriate in the quotations themselves, because the students were representing their own speech.)

We did question whether the students would be able to replicate the punctuation independently. We decided we would monitor this carefully. Roger suggested that we ask them to repeat the exercise using their group dialogues. Jane thought this was unnecessary, that they could move directly to writing a dialogue for one of their own stories. Sandy agreed. Alan suggested a compromise: we could have them write a dramatic script for one of their own story ideas and then turn that into a narrative. He argued that this two-step process would make the task simpler. We all liked this approach. Jane then suggested that we ask them to edit each other's narrative versions of the dialogue. I agreed. It was an opportunity to introduce some editing and revising skills.

I asked Jane why she had decided to drop the work on past tense. She said, "When I found myself trying to explain subjunctive, I realized that if I really wanted to teach it, I might have to devote a whole period to it. And I wasn't sure I knew where the subjunctive matters. Isn't it only in first- and third-person singular in the present tense? I didn't know, and I didn't want to stop and figure it out." She giggled. "I'm not sure I use it myself."

I suggested we take a few minutes to work it out. "We say, 'I was at home,' and 'If I were at home.' So there is a change. But we also say, 'You were at home,' and 'If you were at home.' No change. What about other cases? Or tenses?" We laboriously tested each person and tense but were not really sure about what Standard English practice is with regard to the subjunctive. Clearly, this wasn't something that could be reduced to a simple table. I went to my office to get my 1965 edition of Fowler's *Dictionary of Modern English Usage* and *The Chicago Manual of Style*.

Fowler defines the subjunctive as a "verb-form different from that of the indicative mood in order to 'denote an action or a state as conceived (and not as a fact) and [expressing] a wish, command, exhortation, or a contingent, hypothetical, or prospective event'—OED." He goes on to contend that the "subjunctive is dying" (595) and that the remaining uses may be classified as alives (still natural forms of speech), revivals (antiquated uses for a specific purpose), survivals (formerly natural uses that have fallen out of favor), and arrivals (incorrect uses brought on by a failure to understand the idiom), also suggesting that no one need worry about the second two classes. Our classroom example was one of the alives, one of the "*if . . . were* clauses expressing a hypothesis that is not a fact" (595). However, Fowler does not provide a list of the subjunctive uses for even the *if . . . were* clause. In fact, he indicates that no one has ever made a table of all subjunctive uses. We gave up on that project for the moment.

The Chicago Manual of Style indicates that except for a few formulaic phrases ("be that as it may," for example), the subjunctive mood is confined to the *if . . . were* clause. It notes that if the condition is hypothetical, the subjunctive pertains, but that if the condition is one the speaker or writer believes is or may be factual, then the indicative mood pertains ("If the party is on, I will attend"). It also indicates that with a subjunctive, the ensuing clause requires a modal, for example, "If you were going to throw a party, I would attend."

Roger gave me a quizzical look. "Do you think we should teach all that?"

I asked what the group thought.

"It's way too complicated for our purposes of teaching narrative," Roger said.

"We'd have to spend at least a week on it," Alan said. "I mean, if we were to teach it systematically."

"More than that, I bet," Jane chimed in.

"Let's not do it," said Roger. "We have been planning all along to teach narrative." Everyone not only agreed but seemed relieved.

Alan said, "You know, I think there were two subjunctives in that sentence from Richard Wright that Ronakea read." He opened his folder. "Yeah, here it is: 'If I were beaten at home, there was absolutely nothing that I could do about it; but if I were beaten in the streets, I had a chance to fight and defend myself.' So if it comes up, we could refer to that and show students how to use it individually." We decided to leave it at that.

Day 4: Developing Scripts from Students' Story Ideas

The next day Sandy asked the seventh graders to turn to their story ideas in their folders, pick out one that involved a conversation of at least three speeches per person, and turn it into a script. She helped them recall how a script is set up and the stage and actor directions involved. Then they went to work. Sandy walked around, answering questions. The first questions had to do with which idea to select. I heard Sandy ask, "Well, does this one have talk? You know, did the characters say anything to each other?" She visited with at least six students about their story ideas during the next seven or eight minutes. She also inspected the work of several students who had begun to write. Then she asked for everyone's attention. "One thing I want to remind you about. Remember how we began the dialogue about the Discman?" Most students were paying attention, but only Ronakea and Verita had their hands in the air. Sandy asked everyone to take out the Discman dialogue. After a minute, she asked, "How does it begin?" Roscoe had his hand up now too. Sandy called on him.

Roscoe read, "The scene is the afternoon after school. Lester is drinking pop in the kitchen."

"Good," Sandy said. "Now the key words that I want to see on your papers are *the scene is* or *it is*." She wrote the phrases on the board. "Then go on and describe the scene. Use the word *is* for this kind of formal writing, the present tense, as we did in the Discman dialogue. When I come around, I'll check on that." She continued her rounds for the rest of the period, stopping frequently to coach and answer questions. Most students were on task most of the time. The few who were observed chatting with their neighbors were talking about their story ideas.

Reflecting on Day 4

Back at the university, we sat down to examine the writing Sandy had collected. We looked the pieces over quickly to see how much the students had written. Three ran to three pages. A few were nearly two pages. Only two students, Maurice and Reggie, had written a bit less than a page, but they had two or more speeches for each of two speakers.

We compared what they had written with their story ideas. We noticed several tendencies. First, students used lines from their idea sheet almost verbatim—including personal pronouns—to set the scene or provide stage directions. Someone commented that we hadn't thought to tell them not to use personal pronouns. I asked whether it mattered for what we had in mind. After some debate, we decided it didn't. Our main goals were to have them set the scene, provide stage directions, and write the dialogue as a script. Everyone had done that. Everyone had several lines of dialogue for at least two speakers, and the dialogue was connected—that is, the speakers were responding to each other. There were no major problems with what the students had written. Hank's dialogue was typical (his story idea is presented first):

Hank's Story Idea

Last summer my friends and me was walking down 63rd under the el. We was going to get some food at MacDonald's on Cottage Grove. We hear a siren and we go out into the street to see wha's up. All a sudden this car whip out of Drexel and it come toward us. But it going all over the street. The next thing is a cop car with lights blinking. Siren going. The car running away going all over the place. We jump back on the sidewalk because it look like it coming at us. Then it slam into one of them posts that hold up the el. Blam! Big crash. A cop jump out with his gun out and he go up to the crashed car, but the guy, he bleeding and leaning forward over the wheel. He look dead to us.

Hank's Dialogue (spelling not corrected)

The scene is last sumer 63rd st under the el Friday afternoon. Me and my frinds walk down the street. We here a siren and we go out into the street to see wha's up. All of a suden, a car whip out of Drexel and turn to come at us. But it like going all over the street. The next thang is a cop car with lights blinking. Siren going. The car running away going all over the place.

HANK: Hey, Get out the street. Look out. That driver crazy.

GERARD: Watch you ass. He coming at us.

SNAKE: We outta here.

The first car slam into one of them posts for the el. Blam! Big crash. Cop car stop about 40 feet behind the crash car. A cop jump out with his gun out. He creep near to the crash car. Cop look at us.

COP: You kids, get outta here. This guy got a gun. He ain't afraid to use it.

HANK: He look dead from here.

COP: What he doing.

HANK: Ain't doing nothin except bleeding.

COP: Is he bleeding bad?

HANK: Yeah. Look like his face hit the winshield.

COP: Okay. You keep an eye on him from there. Yell if he move.

The cop creep to the side of the car. He stand slow with his gun at the dude head. We standing like statues. Another cop car come up.

COP: Call an ambalance. This guy went into the winshield.

COP 2:   We got it. Be here in five minutes.

Cop 2 goes over to first cop. They pull open the car door. The driver don't move. We go closer for a better look. The driver look about my brother age, about 16. The first cop reaches in the car and pull out a pistol.

COP 2:   You boys back off. This ain't something you should be looking at.

We walk away to the MacDonald's on Cottage. But we ain't hungry anymore.

Hank added some good details: the comment about the driver's age, the indication that the boys were standing like statues, and the final "we ain't hungry anymore."

Planning Day 5

The following day we planned how we would have the students transform their scripts into narratives complete with punctuated dialogue. Would the kids complain about having to write the dialogue again? We should probably have told them to double-space so that they could use carets to insert the introductory phrases. Then again, simply inserting the needed changes might not be a solid learning experience. In any case, they'd have to re-write everything.

We also wrote comments on the scripts. Each of my MAT students took five or six papers. I told them that in my experience, marking and correcting every error is futile. It probably makes no difference in future writing and it frustrates the students. I told them to mark only what we had taught them so far except for spelling. We found that their spelling errors were phonetic; that is, the spelling approximated the way the word sounded in their dialect. At least it was related to the English sound system. I told them to correct only the one-of-a-kind errors, such as Hank's spellings of *ambulance*, *summer*, *sudden*, and *windshield*. I suggested they circle such words, draw a line to the margin, and print the word, spelled correctly, there.

I also suggested they correct dialect features such as the possessive by adjacency and omitted *be* verbs only in the stage and acting directions. In the dialogue, these features were accurate representations of the dialect of the speakers. We would have to teach these and similar grammar issues as special lessons.

Finally I told them to be sure to include at least one compliment on each paper.

We developed comments for Hank's paper together. Acting as scribe, Sandy wrote *good job* at the top. She underlined the new details that we liked and wrote *good* in the margin beside each. She wrote *good use of the colon* and made the spelling corrections. She also suggested that it might be a good idea to have his two friends say something on the way to McDonald's.

A Digression on Teacher Comments

Research on teacher comments indicates that "students receiving negative criticism [write] less and [develop] negative attitudes about themselves as writers and about writing as an activity" (Hillocks 1986, 164). Sperling and Freedman (1987), using a case study culled from Freedman (1987), examine the question of why even the most promising students misunderstand and/or misconstrue the comments teachers write on their papers even when the comments are accompanied by conferences, peer-group response, and whole-class discussions. In the Sperling and Freedman case study (the responses of a high-achieving ninth grader to her teacher's comments on a character study developed over several drafts), the teacher comments either reflect information previously conveyed explicitly in class or provide new information. Half of the teacher's comments about things previously taught in class are positive reinforcements; the other half point out needed revisions. The student has no problems processing the reinforcements. When the teacher compliments word choice or the use of detail, for example, the student tries to produce similar effects in the next piece of writing. Her attempts to revise, however, are frequently complicated by differences between her and her teacher's values and knowledge. And whenever the teacher refers to information that has not been taught, the student's attempts at revision inevitably fail in some way.

This study helps explain the results of my study (Hillocks 1982) in which three teachers and I tested four sets of instructional conditions: (1) observational activities comparable with those presented in this book (e.g., the shell activity of Chapter 4), writing assignment, teacher comment, revision; (2) observational activities, writing assignment, teacher comment, no revision; (3) writing assignment, teacher comment, revision; and (4) writing assignment, teacher comment, no revision. Students in each of the twelve classes (four for each of three teachers) were divided into two groups using a table of random numbers. One group received short comments (fifteen words or fewer) consisting of at least one compliment and one or more brief suggestions for increasing specificity or focus. Cooperating teachers were asked to keep short comments to ten or fewer words. The short comments actually averaged nine to ten words for two of the teachers and just more than fourteen for the third. The second group received much longer comments (twenty-five words or more) consisting of one or more compliments and very specific suggestions for improvement.

The results of this experiment, using a scale for specificity comparable with that described in Chapter 2, indicate that first, groups with observational activities made significantly greater gains than those with no observational activities; second, focused comments coupled with the assignment and revision produced a significant quality gain, as did short comments coupled with assignment and no revision. Third, the gain for students doing revision (1.57) was nearly twice that for students doing no revision (.89). Fourth, there was a significant interaction between comment length and instructional pattern ($p < .009$). For students engaged in observational activities and writing, the gains for those receiving longer comments were greater, but not significantly. For students who did not engage in observational activities, however, longer comments were less effective than shorter comments. Indeed, for the classes doing the writing assignments only, the short comments were twice as effective as the longer comments (1.12 versus .55, $p < .02$).

I also asked the teachers who participated in this study to record the amount of time they spent commenting on the compositions. Although long comments by all three teachers required approximately twice as much time as short comments, they were never significantly more effective than the short comments. However, long comments not accompanied by observational activities or revision were significantly less effective than short comments. Thus, a teacher who spends ten hours a week making focused comments on matters of specificity and focus on the compositions of seventh and eighth graders might expect to achieve comparable, if not better, results with only five hours of work.

And that is why I always recommend focused, positive, short comments related to previous teaching for these grade levels and for high school students. My experience suggests that the same is true for college and graduate students. If I have not taught the skill or concept related to my comment, I try not to make it. Instead, I go back and try to teach what the students' writing indicates they need to learn.

Day 5: Transforming Dialogue into Narrative

The next day Sarah returned the students' scripts. She allowed a minute or two for questions about the comments. There weren't any, so she made the assignment to transform the dialogues into narratives and reviewed the rules for punctuating dialogue. She asked for a volunteer to read the first line of her dialogue. Several hands were in the air, including Darlene's. This was the first time Darlene had volunteered in class, and Sarah called on her. Darlene said, "This is my first line and Grandma says it: 'What you been doing all day?'"

Sarah wrote it on the overhead and then asked, "Do you have any acting directions for her?" Darlene shook her head no. "How did she ask it?"

"Kind of suspicious like."

"OK, what does she look like when she is suspicious?"

"She kinda squishes her one eye."

"Would you say she squints with one eye?"

"Yeah, like this," said Darlene, squinting her right eye and tipping her head to one side.

Sarah asked, "Who can put all that in a sentence or phrase?" No hands went up. Sarah waited and then repeated the question more specifically. "Who can put 'squinting her right eye and tipping her head to one side' in a sentence or phrase?"

"You could just use that," Ronald said.

"I suppose I could," Sarah said, a bit embarrassed at having been so obvious. She wrote the phrase on the board in parentheses after *Grandma*. "Now let's everyone change this into narrative style using quotation marks. Write it out on your papers." After a pause, she asked, "Anyone?" Ronakea raised her hand immediately. Sarah waited a bit longer, and after more hands had gone up, she called on Jefferson.

"Grandma tip her head to one side and squint her eye. She say, quote, What you been doing all day, question mark, quote." Sarah wrote the words on the board. "Good use of punctuation. Does this look OK to everyone? Does anything need to be changed?"

Ronakea and Verita had their hands up. Sarah called on Verita.

"You should have an *s* on *tip* and *squint*, shouldn't you? I mean, I thought that was what you said."

"Yes, in formal English, you would say *tips* her head and *squints* her eye."

Ronakea added, "You need *s* on *says*, too."

"Right. You need an *s* on all these verbs. Now, let me ask you, can anyone think of another way to phrase this?" There was no response. When it was obvious that there would be no response, she said, "Jefferson put the acting directions into a whole sentence, but it is possible to put them in an introductory phrase using a different form of the verbs, by adding *i n g*." She wrote *tipping* and *squinting* on the board. "Who can construct a phrase using those verbs?"

"You mean like 'Squinting her eye and tipping her head'?" Ronald asked.

"Yes, good. Now who can put that together with what Grandma says, including the punctuation?"

Several hands went up. Sarah called on Darlene. "Squinting her eye and tipping her head to the side, Grandma asks, quote, What you been doing all day, question mark, quote."

"Good." Sarah wrote the line on the overhead.

Sarah asked for a sentence and acting directions from three more students, each time going through the process for transforming the acting directions to narrative. Then she asked the students to begin converting their own dialogue scripts into narratives. The students worked attentively for the next half hour. Sarah circulated, reading over students' shoulders and making suggestions. I overheard her correcting a missing *s* now and then and asking for more acting directions. Just before the bell, she collected the papers.

Reflecting on Day 5

Back at the university, we immediately divided up the papers and began reading. We found that the work was generally strong. There were some common errors in punctuation: a missing final quotation mark or a missing comma after the introductory verb. I suggested we count the total lines of dialogue in all the papers and underline all the punctuation errors. For the class as a whole there were 195 lines of dialogue. Estimating the number of punctuation marks relevant to the quotations at four each, there were 780 possibilities for error. Adding up the total number of errors (only an estimate, given our hasty perusal), we arrived at a total of 63, which meant that 92 percent of the punctuation was correct. "Not bad," I said, "but Sarah was helping." We calculated the error distribution. Six students had none, four had only one, seven had two, four had three, five had four, one had six, and one had seven. We did the same for the *s* ending of verbs. To my surprise, there were only 13 errors in 195 lines of dialogue. Sarah explained that she had been paying particular attention to that because she had reviewed it early in the hour.

Next we discussed the quality of the narratives. Most included several lines of dialogue that were appropriate to the story. Most of the students had chosen an interesting idea on which to base their story. All had set the scene pretty well. Most of the dialogues depicted a character's attempt to do something and another character's response. Some details of what the characters did during the dialogue were strong, but many were vague. On the whole we were pleased, but we were also somewhat disappointed. Some of the dialogues were flat, not well developed. We had a long way to go in helping students learn to be more detailed. Our lessons on writing about character and setting lay ahead.

This is one of the papers we judged to be underdeveloped:

> The dentist's office is very large it is a lot of little rooms with big chairs in them. Every chair has a big light over it. The dentist lady takes me to a little room to sit in the big chair. She says, "Are you comfortable?" I tell her, "I am not." I say, "When is the dentist coming?"
>
> She says, "He will be with you in a moment." She walks away down the little hall to another room. I am watching the clock on the wall. Ten minutes later she come back.
>
> I say, "Where the dentist? You say he be here in a moment. Ten minutes gone by."
>
> She says, "My oh my, aren't you the impashunt one. He will be here shortly." Then she walk away again down the little hall. I stay in the chair and watch the clock. Another ten minutes go by. Finally, he comes in to my chair. He comes up close with his little pick and his little mirror.
>
> He says, "How are we today, Twila?"
>
> I say, "I ain't good, I been here waiting 20 minutes. And it ain't no fun."
>
> He says, "Well open your mouth and let me see the tooth that's bothering you."
>
> I tell him, "You been having a smoke, I can smell it." Then he jams his little mirror in my mouth and I do not get to say any more.

Nevertheless, I suggested that the piece did have some potential. Jane agreed. She made the case that it is about Twila's fear of the dentist and his office and the impersonality of it. "She has just not written about her fear or her impatience, but it is there. I think that this is going to be pretty good. We are going to teach writing about feelings, right?"

"I hope we will get to that later this week," I said. "What else could she write about?" People suggested including more about the dental assistant and the dentist and about Twila herself, who is a little, dainty girl. They thought Twila could tell how old she is and what is going through her mind. For the moment we decided to hold off on those suggestions until after we had taught writing about character. Now we would concentrate on dialogue punctuation, details about the characters' actions, and spelling.

Hank's piece is stronger:

> It is summer and me and my friends are walking down 63rd St under the el on Friday afternoon. We hear a siren and we go out into the street to see what's up. All of a sudden, a car whip out of Drexel and turn to come at us. But it's going all over the street like the driver can't control it. The next thing is a cop car with lights blinking. The siren is going. The car running away is going all over the place.
>
> I say, "Hey, Get out the street. Look out. That driver crazy." I jump back to the curb.

Gerard is yelling "Watch you ass. He coming at us." He ducks behind a car like he is hiding.

Snake jumps back to the curb and runs to the nearest store. "We outta here." I can see him shaking.

The first car slams into one of the posts for the el. Blam! Big crash. The police car stops about 40 feet behind the crashed car. A cop jumps out with his gun out. He creeps near to the crashed car. He looks at us. He is keeping his head down. "You kids, get outta here. This guy got a gun. He ain't afraid to use it."

I tell the cop, "He looks dead from here."

The cop looks at me and aks, "What is he doing? Can you see anything?

I am staring at the man in the car. "Ain't doing nothin' except bleeding," I say. I move over to an el post to hold on to.

The cop asks, "Is he bleeding bad?"

"Yeah. Look like his face hit the windshield."

The cop says, "Okay. You keep an eye on him from there. Yell if he moves." The cop creeps to the side of the car. He stands low with his gun at the dude's head. We standing like statues. Another cop car come up.

The first cop yell to the new cop, "Call an ambulance. This guy went into the windshield. That kid says he bleeding bad."

The second cop says, "We got it. Be here in five minutes."

The second cop goes over to first cop. They pull open the car door. The driver doesn't move. We go closer for a better look. The driver looks about my brother age, about 16. His face is like hamburger meat. The first cop reaches in the car and pulls out a pistol. My stomach is turning. I do not want to throw up.

The second cop says, "You boys back off. This ain't something you should be looking at. We'll take care of it."

We back toward the other side of the street and start to walk away to MacDonald's on Cottage.

Snake says, "Did you see that dude's face? Man, that sickening."

Gerard says, "I'm not hungry anymore."

"Me neither," I say. But we keep walking to MacDonald's. Maybe we will be hungry when we get there.

Several of Hank's details about the characters reveal their feelings. It would be interesting to see what he would include if he chose to continue this piece after our work on character and feelings.

7

WRITING ABOUT INNER THOUGHTS, FEELINGS, AND SENSATIONS

In the earliest days of our teaching narrative writing, my MAT students and I concentrated on helping our students observe and record concrete phenomena: things they could see, feel, hear, smell, and sense. We also included activities that encouraged this kind of observation (and this kind of writing) when we taught them to write dialogue. But at first the activities were largely independent of each other, unified only by our focus on attending to detail (see Hillocks 1975).

As our teaching progressed and we developed more skill and knowledge, we began to use the activities in substantively related clusters. The previous two chapters discuss instruction on setting scenes and providing acting directions, both elements of dramatic scripts, and, later, incorporating these elements as descriptive statements in narrative. Some of our other observational activities were related to character (Chapter 8) and settings or scenes (Chapter 9).

This chapter looks at a variety of activities related to writing about people's inner thoughts, sensations, and feelings. We had already dealt with this a bit in writing the narrative dialogues. But there was much more to do. We began with models of what we hoped the students would write.

Introducing Inner Thoughts and Feelings

To introduce writing about inner thoughts and feelings, we asked our students to examine pieces of writing that show such inner thoughts and feelings. Writers express their inner thoughts and feelings both explicitly and by implication. In the following passage from the Richard Wright story, I have underlined the main character's explicit thoughts. (If Roger had not already introduced this class to the concept of interior monologue, we would have done so here.) This piece also contains direct statements that imply strong feelings but that are not interior monologues ("I shook with fright"; "I clutched the stick"). I have double-underlined those.

> She slammed the door and I heard the key turn in the lock. <u>I shook with fright</u>. I was alone upon the dark, hostile streets and gangs were after me. <u>I had the choice of being beaten at</u>

home or away from home. I clutched the stick, crying, trying to reason. If I were beaten at home, there was absolutely nothing that I could do about it; but if I were beaten in the streets, I had a chance to fight and defend myself. I walked slowly down the sidewalk, coming closer to the gang of boys, holding the stick tightly. I was so full of fear that I could scarcely breathe. I was almost upon them now.

Handing out copies of this paragraph, we asked, "What sentences or phrases or words indicate the internal thoughts of the writer?" Students pointed out the underlined lines. Then we asked what words, phrases, or sentences indicated the feelings of the writer. Generally our students pointed to "I shook with fright," "crying," and the next-to-last sentence. Then we asked, "What do you think those lines do for the story?" Some students thought the lines did nothing for the story. Anticipating this, I had rewritten the passage without the explicit statements of thinking and feeling:

> She slammed the door and I heard the key turn in the lock. I was alone upon the dark, hostile streets and gangs were after me. I clutched the stick, trying to reason. I walked slowly down the sidewalk, coming closer to the gang of boys, holding the stick tightly. I was almost upon them now.

Showing the students this version, I asked, "What do you think of the passage written this way?" More than one boy liked it better stripped down. "It don't beat around the bush so much."

"What do the rest of you think? Do you all agree?"

A girl responded, "I don't agree. You need to know more about the little boy and what he thinks and how he feel."

Another responded, "If you don't know what he think and feel, you won't know why he finally fight at the end. If you didn't know that, the story would be silly."

The boy continued his resistance for a time, joined by a couple of others. But several students in the class made a case for including such statements, their primary reasons being that the statements tell more about the character, his motivation, and his feelings and that such information makes the reading more appealing and more understandable. (Although such debates may seem unnecessary, they provide an opportunity for students on both sides of the issue to develop their critical skills and their understanding of how literature works. I recommend that my students always take advantage of such opportunities.)

After reading and discussing examples from other writing, we asked the students to think about crucial points in their narratives and what they might have been thinking and feeling at those moments. For example, in the following section of Twila's transformation of dialogue into narrative, we asked these questions in the margins next to the appropriate spots: *What were you thinking after the dental assistant left you to wait? What were you thinking as the dentist approached with his pick and mirror? What were you thinking as he jammed his little mirror in your mouth?*

> She says, "My oh my, aren't you the impashunt one. He will be here shortly." Then she walk away again down the little hall. I stay in the chair and watch the clock. Another ten minutes go by. Finally, he comes in to my chair. He comes up close with his little pick and his little mirror.
>
> He says, "How are we today, Twila?"
>
> I say, "I ain't good, I been here waiting 20 minutes. And it ain't no fun."

He says, "Well open your mouth and let me see the tooth that's bothering you."

I tell him, "You been having a smoke, I can smell it." Then he jams his little mirror in my mouth and I do not get to say any more.

Including thoughts and feelings is relatively easy for students. With appropriate activities, many will learn to do it well.

Introducing the Difficult Sensations

Most people are aware that we have five senses: seeing, hearing, smelling, touching, and tasting. Many composition books tell students to infuse their writing with the five senses. That, of course, is easier said than done. Student writing about personal experience seldom includes sensations other than those of sight. When children do include other sensations, the descriptions tend to be very vague (as in "The Ski Trip" in Chapter 2). You may remember that Hank did use an onomatopoetic *blam* in his description of a car crash—a nice touch—but descriptions of sounds, smells, tastes, tactile sensations, and inner bodily sensations are few. I call these the difficult sensations. In the early days of our work on narrative, we developed several lessons to help students learn strategies to write about these difficult sensations.

Sound

Sounds play an important part in many narratives. Sometimes they are used to underscore the importance of an event, sometimes to set a scene, sometimes to make an important point about a character. I considered including sound in the chapter about describing scenes, where it is probably most important. However, it seems reasonable to include it here, along with the other senses.

Writing and Performing Sound Scripts

Perhaps the most famous first-person narrative in which sound is crucial to character is Poe's short story "The Tell-Tale Heart." The first time I taught a lesson about including sounds in writing (to a class of seventh graders), I began by reading "The Tell-Tale Heart" as they followed along in their copies. I put in all the dramatic expression I could muster. They were enthralled. I then directed them to the following passage, in which the officers who have come to investigate a report of a scream are preparing to leave, and asked them to find all the words and phrases that referred directly or indirectly to sound:

> I brought chairs into the room, and desired them here to rest from their fatigues, while I myself, in the wild audacity of my perfect triumph, placed my own seat upon the very spot beneath which reposed the corpse of the victim.
>
> The officers were satisfied. My *manner* had convinced them. I was singularly at ease. They sat, and while I answered cheerily, they chatted of familiar things. But, ere long, I felt myself getting pale and wished them gone. My head ached, and I fancied a ringing in my ears: but still they sat and still chatted. The ringing became more distinct: I talked more freely to get rid of the feeling: but it continued and gained definitiveness—until, at length, I found that the noise was *not* within my ears.
>
> No doubt I now grew very pale; but I talked more fluently, and with a heightened voice. Yet the sound increased—and what could I do? It was *a low dull quick sound—much such a*

sound as a watch makes when enveloped in cotton. I gasped for breath—and yet the officers heard it not. I talked more quickly—more vehemently; but the noise steadily increased. I arose and argued about trifles, in a high key and with violent gesticulations; but the noise steadily increased. Why would they not be gone? I paced the floor to and fro with heavy strides, as if excited to fury by the observations of the men—but the noise steadily increased. Oh God! what could I do? I foamed—I raved—I swore! I swung my chair upon which I had been sitting, and grated it upon the boards, but the noise arose over all and continually increased. It grew louder—louder—louder! And still the men chatted pleasantly, and smiled. Was it possible they heard not? Almighty God!—no, no! They heard!—they suspected! They *knew!*—they were making a mockery of my horror!—this I thought, and this I think. But anything was better than this agony! Anything was more tolerable than this derision! I could bear those hypocritical smiles no longer! I felt that I must scream or die!—and now—again!—hark! louder! louder! louder! *louder!*—

"Villains!" I shrieked, "dissemble no more! I admit the deed!—tear up the planks!—here, here!—it is the beating of his hideous heart!" (1984, 559)

The class compiled the following list: *answered, chatted, ringing, chatted, ringing, talked, noise, talked, heightened voice, sound increased, a low dull quick sound—much such a sound as a watch makes when enveloped in cotton, gasped, talked, argued, in a high key, noise steadily increased, paced the floor, heavy strides, the noise steadily increased, raved, swore, grated, the noise arose over all and continually increased, grew louder—louder—louder, chatted pleasantly, scream, and now—again!—hark! louder! louder! louder! louder!, shrieked, the beating of his hideous heart!*

In addition, some students wanted to include the sounds of the chairs being placed on the floor. Linda thought the sound of the officers' chairs would be muffled by carpeting while the narrator's chair would produce a hollow thump when it came down on the bare floor above the resting place of the victim. I joked, "You're developing a sound script."

Linda came back with, "Oh! Could we?"

Jerry asked, "What's a sound script?"

"It's like a list of sound effects and it tells when to make the sound, for, you know, like a movie or a recording," Linda explained.

Suddenly, they all wanted to make a sound script and use it to accompany a reading of the story. I decided that while these lessons on sensory description were taking longer than I had expected, their enthusiasm was too great to pass up.

"Good idea!" I said. I assigned groups to investigate the sounds associated with different parts of the story, including the scuffle and the dismembering of the body.

Once we had the groups' lists of "necessary sounds," we talked as a class about how to produce them. One boy, a trumpet player, had a metronome to simulate the ticking sound. We decide to muffle it in a blanket and gradually remove the layers of the blanket and bring it closer and closer to the microphone as the heartbeats became louder.

Alexander volunteered to bring his father's bullhorn to amplify the ticking sound when it reached its maximum crescendo. We could borrow a dry cell and a doorbell from the science lab to create the ringing sound. This too would be muffled and gradually unwrapped. Bill suggested dropping lumps of clay into a metal pail to simulate the body being dismembered. Various students volunteered to borrow clay from their younger siblings. We discussed how we might authentically make the sounds of floorboards being removed and put back. Eddie suggested we nail some planks together and use a claw hammer to pull them apart. Nearly all the students wanted the boards to creak until Susan reminded us that the narrator takes the boards up very carefully so that no one will notice they have been disturbed. We decided that Eddie's idea would work.

The footsteps students thought should be scattered throughout the story were a problem. Because we would be using the same microphone for both the reading and the sound effects, we couldn't just follow someone's footsteps with the mike. I explained that in the old radio dramas, sound effects were usually produced on a table near the mike and that if we had a pair of shoes someone could wear them on his hands and bring the shoes down on a board in a walking rhythm.

Each student would be responsible for at least one sound in the script, and some sounds required more than one student (regulating the volume of the ringing and ticking sounds, for example).

A portion of our script looked like this:

I brought chairs into the room, and desired them here to rest from their fatigues, while I myself, in the wild audacity of my perfect triumph, placed my own seat upon the very spot beneath which reposed the corpse of the victim.	Footsteps and moving chairs on carpet. Ivan, Jorge, Bill
The officers were satisfied. My *manner* had convinced them. I was singularly at ease. They sat, and while I answered cheerily, they chatted of familiar things.	Chatter about baseball. Charles, Rick, John
But, ere long, I felt myself getting pale and wished them gone. My head ached, and I fancied a ringing in my ears: but still they sat and still they chatted. The ringing became more distinct:	Soft ringing. Ellen and Sue Louder ringing. Ellen and Sue

The students practiced until everything sounded more or less authentic. The next day we first recorded each sound effect individually to see how well the mike picked it up. Then we had a practice run. It was ragged: there were many missed cues, the dismemberment sounded like a hacksaw cutting wood, and the doorbell failed to sound because the blanket got caught between the hammer and the bell. Each failure generated a good deal of laughter. When I asked how the students thought it went, they said it would be better the next day, and it was. They all brought in cassettes so that I could make a copy for everyone.

Writing About Sounds Using Audio Recordings

The most important tools in this activity are audio recordings of sounds. My favorite is one my son made for me when he was ten of sounds around our house and yard: water dripping into a metal pot, the squeak of our backyard gate, the roar of the clothes dryer, ice cubes clinking in a glass, a tissue being pulled from its box, a kitchen match scraping along the side of the matchbox and bursting into flame, a toilet flushing, a key turning in a lock, a car door slamming, a car engine starting, and a heavy chain being dragged down stairs. I also have commercially produced recordings of sounds, but I like my son's compilation of common household sounds best. Students find them more intriguing and challenging.

I play the sounds one at a time and ask students to identify what produced each and then describe it. Over the years I've broken the process of writing about sounds into smaller parts, focusing on professional writing techniques:

1. Indicate the source of the sound.
2. Use words that imitate the sound.
3. Break complicated sounds into parts.
4. Describe the character of the sound.
5. Use figurative language or analogy to describe the sound, comparing it to something else.
   (Poe uses all of these techniques in the previous passage.)

Writers often indicate the source of sound in the hope that readers will be able to recall that same sound from their own experience. For example, a writer may refer to a "lonely foghorn sounding over the water at night." If you have heard a foghorn at night, even in the movies, that will be meaningful to you. Sounds indicated by their origins will be more or less clear depending on your familiarity with them: a bad muffler on a truck, an automobile engine trying to start in cold weather, rain falling on the roof of a metal shack, a steam locomotive. Often, however, sounds are not so easily identified.

Some of our most common words are onomatopoetic: *ticktock*, *hiss*, *chime*, *ring*, *bong*, *zip*, *bump*, and *crunch*. Many less common words also imitate sounds: *whisper*, *rickety*, *galumph*, *gallop*, *cacophony*. People often make up words to indicate sounds—for example, the *rat-a-tat-tat*, *pow*, *biff*, and *bam* of comic books.

Sometimes what we think of as sounds are not really single sounds. We come to think of them as single sounds because we are so used to hearing them together. For example:

- A bus stopping on a city street may include a high-pitched squeal of brake drums, a discharging sound of air, and the soft rumble of doors opening.
- An automobile starting on a cold winter day may include the throbbing whine of the starter as it attempts to turn the engine over, the initial cough of the engine, and the sputter of cylinders as they come to life.
- The sound of typing on a computer keyboard may include the click of fingernails against keys, the louder click of the keys being depressed, and the soft whir of the computer's fan.

Writers often break these down into their parts to better describe them.

Writers also describe the character of sound in terms of various qualities, particularly rhythm (*irregular*, *rapid*, *erratic*, *sluggish*, *wild*, *pulsating*, *throbbing*, *steady*) and pitch and tone (*high*, *low*, *bass*, *full-bodied*, *thin*, *flat*, *sharp*, *soft*, *crescendoing*, *decrescendoing*). For example:

- Her words came rapidly in irregular bursts, the high, thin voice crescendoing.
- He listened to the steady, dull dripping, low and soft but irrevocable.
- The washer throbbed steadily, churning clothes and water with low full-bodied thuds against the sides of the tank.

Sometimes even when we listen carefully to a sound we cannot tell what has made it. In that sense it is a strange sound, but we can compare it to something that is familiar. One seventh grader wrote: "I hear a series of light, metallic, clicking sounds. They are irregular, several grouped together, followed by silence followed by another group of clicks but in a different pattern, like a spastic alarm clock two rooms away." The comparison to a spastic alarm clock gives us a good idea of what he was hearing.

In other cases, comparisons indicate one's feelings about the sound. For instance, we can add comparisons that convey the impressions of the listener to the first two examples from the previous list (the first indicates both an emotional and a real connection; the second provides emotional impact):

- Her words came rapidly, in irregular bursts, the high, thin voice crescendoing *like the squawking of an excited crow*.
- He listened to the steady, dull dripping, low and soft but irrevocable *as death*.

Let's apply some of these techniques to the sound of a match striking and lighting:

- Make up a word that captures the sound: *ssssssssspiffsss*.
- Break the sound into parts and describe it: "I hear the scrape and puff of a match lighting."
- Describe the character of the sound: "I hear the low, soft scrape and hiss of the match lighting."
- Compare the sound to other sounds: *a gentle explosion, a puff of sound, a snake spitting fire*.

Figure 7.1 is an exercise I often have students work on in groups to develop their ability to describe sounds.

Listening Carefully to Describe Sounds

I have used a variety of assignments for individual work on describing sounds. Sometimes I've asked students to sit down at home at night and write about all the sounds they hear inside and outside. I've also asked them to go to a particular location and write about the sounds they hear there. Here are examples produced by some of my seventh graders:

Sounds of Night
by Johanna Freedman

I am sitting in my room with the door shut. The lights are on but the room does not glow. Three lights are burned out. The sounds of the night drift in softened muted and in passing through the thin wall between the wind and me. A truck goes by, whirring flatly in a hapless voice of its troubles. The wind, lost in the city, catches itself on the corners of buildings in a frenzied attempt to find its way home. Below, my brother bounces a basketball on the shaky wooden floor and the sound bounds up, hard, short and brutal, a club of sound.

The Park
by Linda Skinner

One side of the small park was bordered by the steady traffic of Lake Shore Drive. It was Sunday morning when I went there, and the park was almost deserted when I arrived. Except

Describing Sounds

Think about, take notes on, and compose sentences describing *four* of the following sounds:

1. an automatic dishwasher
2. an automatic ice-cube maker
3. someone taking a shower
4. a basketball player dribbling and shooting baskets alone in a gym
5. late-night sounds from the street near your house
6. a gas-powered lawn mower
7. a diesel locomotive
8. someone sawing a plank in half
9. a screen door slamming
10. a sound of your choice

Remember to do the following:

- Take the sounds apart.
- Think of words or phrases to describe rhythm and tone.
- Think of words that imitate the sound.
- Invent comparisons.

When you are done, share what you have written with others in your group.

Figure 7.1 *Describing Sounds*

for a few people and their children, a couple of squirrels hunting for nuts, and the company of some birds, I was alone to enjoy myself. There was an awkward emptiness about the park, interrupted by an occasional chirping, some anonymous bird gaily singing on a hazy autumn day.

The stillness seemed to be surrounded on all sides by a monotonous hum of distant vehicles. Once in a while I would hear horns honking like bright islands in the grey sea of sound. Within the stillness was a mixture of sounds. As I was listening I could hear leaves skittering across the pavement like rocks skipping on the waves. Infrequently, couples wandered by, rustling and crunching the dry leaves with each step. The murmur of their mingled voices rippled across the stillness.

I've also asked students to write about the "sounds of silence" as they sit writing in the classroom. They include everything from the low buzzing of fluorescent lights to ambulance sirens, from the squeaking and scraping of chairs to the clicking of high heels in the hallway, from the sound of ballpoint pens moving across paper to another student's sneeze.

Adding Sounds to Student Drafts

My MAT students and I asked our seventh graders to add sound details to the conversational narratives they had produced (see Chapter 6). Instead of asking them to rewrite the entire composition yet again, we had them put carets and marginal numbers on their final paper and list the sound descriptions, linked to the numbers, on another sheet. Here are Hank's very effective sound details (now inserted at the appropriate points and underlined):

It is summer and me and my friends are walking down 63rd St under the el on Friday afternoon. We hear a siren <u>shrieking up and down</u> and we go out into the street to see what's up. All of a sudden, a car whip out of Blackstone <u>tires screaming on the pavement</u> and turn to come at us. But it's going all over the street like the driver can't control it. The next thing is a cop car with lights blinking. <u>Its tires scream on the pavement too.</u> The siren <u>still shrieking up and down</u>. The car running away is going all over the place.

I say, "Hey, Get out the street. Look out. That driver crazy." I jump back to the curb.

Gerard is yelling "Watch you ass. He coming at us." He ducks behind a car like he is hiding.

Snake jumps back to the curb and runs to the nearest store. "We outta here." I can see him shaking.

The first car slams into one of the posts for the el. Blam! Big crash. <u>Little pieces of metal and glass tinkle into the street. You can hear a hub cap rolling down 63rd.</u> The police car <u>squeal loud</u> to stop about 40 feet behind the crashed car. A cop jumps out with his gun out.

Here are the sound descriptions Twila added:

The dentist's office is very large it is a lot of little rooms with big chairs in them. Every chair has a big light over it. The dentist lady takes me to a little room to sit in the big chair. She says, "Are you comfortable?" I tell her, "I am not." I say, "When is the dentist coming?"

She says, "He will be with you in a moment." She walks away, <u>rubber soles squeaking on the tile floor</u>, down the little hall to another room. I am watching the clock on the wall.

<u>It make a soft ticking sound. I hear the high pitched whine of the dentist's drill two or three rooms away. A lady say, "Ouch," loud and and angry. I hear soft mumbling, probally the dentist apologizing for wounding the lady.</u> Ten minutes later the lady dentist come back.

Twila's additions are good ones. They add to the tone of dislike that she told us she wanted to convey. Unfortunately, she stopped with these few. She might have added more when the dentist enters the room.

Smell

Perhaps the most difficult of sense impressions to record are those of taste and smell. Scientists tell us that our taste buds detect only certain basic differences: sweet, sour, and salt. The remainder of what we think we taste is really only smell. That is, when we taste a chocolate cake, we really taste the sweetness and smell the chocolate. While we can make thousands of discriminations in smell, we have few words to describe those differences. We convey the distinctions through suggestion and comparison (descriptions of the taste of wine brim with comparisons to fruit other than grapes, for example) and by telling what produces the taste sensation and hoping other people will be able to imagine or recall that sensation.

Sometimes comparisons to other sense impressions help. I think, for example, of the smell of ammonia as being *sharp*, *abrasive*, or *screeching*. The words *sharp* and *abrasive* suggest something we touch. *Screeching* suggests something we hear. Describing one sense in terms of another (smell as sound, sound as touch, touch as sight, and so forth) is called *synaesthesia*.

When my MAT students and I first began to work with the sense of smell, we bought little vials from a drugstore and filled them with small amounts of substances like ammonia, anise, cinnamon, cloves, vanilla, automobile oil, perfume, and talcum powder. We wanted students to smell each odor, describe it using synaesthesia, and tell how it made them feel or of what it reminded them, as Richard Wright does in "the drenching hospitality in the pervading smell of sweet magnolias."

This had to be a group activity, and each group had its own set of ten vials, so the logistics were demanding. We asked students to describe the odors in terms of color, shape, weight, temperature, sound, or other sensory perceptions. Thus, I might describe ammonia as psychedelic chartreuse, screeching, and sharp and say it reminds me of my seventeenth summer when I cleaned all the lockers of the workers who had been emptied out of a local factory for a two-week vacation. I might describe cinnamon as a soft, sweet, welcoming smell that brings to mind the image of my mother baking cookies.

After the group work with vials, we used the individual assignment in Figure 7.2.

Touch

My work with tactile sensations over the years has focused on three activities. The first was inspired by an old party game in which blindfolded guests were escorted along a supposed banquet table in a haunted house. At intervals the escort would tell the guests that the bowl in front of them was a delicacy made of some body organ and guide the hand of a guest into a bowl containing something that felt like that organ (cold gelatin for liver or skinned grapes for eyeballs). I blindfolded the children and let them touch various food products (from raw vegetables to cooked noodles) so they could zero in on the tactile sensations. It was logistically complex (read, a lot of work to set up) and the payoff was not as great as I had thought it would be. But the kids liked the activity.

Crossing Senses

Choose *five* odors from the numbered list below to describe.

1. bacon burning
2. your favorite food, either as it's cooking or when you sit down to eat it
3. exhaust fumes of a bus or truck
4. a beach along the ocean
5. an auto-repair shop
6. a forest
7. a burning garbage dump
8. a locker room
9. the school cafeteria
10. hot grease on machinery
11. carnations or other flowers
12. a dusty, sun-baked field
13. a bakery
14. a shoe store
15. any odor that makes you recall a pleasant experience

Describe each in terms of

- color
- shape
- weight
- temperature
- sound
- what it reminds you of

Write a sentence or two about each of the five odors you choose.

Figure 7.2 *Crossing Senses*

My next attempt was to make up several little bags of various substances that were rough, including pieces of carpet, steel wool, sandpapers of different coarsenesses, unsanded and unfinished wood, and burlap. The problem was to describe the coarseness of the items in the bags. I began by distributing a piece of carpeting with different textures on the front and back. The backing was evenly woven, smooth except for the intersections of the warp and woof, where the threads bristled slightly. One boy described them as feeling like tiny hairs. Someone else suggested fuzzy hairs. Someone else noticed that they were flexible and when pressed down, sprang back up. Students described the front side of the carpet, where the piling was made up of longer threads, as spongy, less firm. Someone said it was softer and deeper than the back. We were making progress, but it was slow. Next, we felt a piece of very coarse sandpaper, which elicited words like *sharp*, *firm*, *cutting*, *scraping*, *cold*, and *unpleasant*. When they described the carpet in contrast with the sandpaper, the carpet became *dull*, *soft*, *comforting*, *spongy*, and *warm*. As we contrasted more items, additional differences in terminology emerged. Although it was a difficult task, students became more and more attuned to detecting the differences.

Bodily Sensations

Descriptions of physical or bodily sensations are important, and writers convey them by focusing on muscular and other internal responses to internal or external stress. They may refer to the affected body part directly or through analogy, metaphor, or simile—or both, as in the following statement from the narrative "My Best Track Meet": "My body felt hot inside and my ankles were hurting like if someone stuck a nail inside of them."

Most young writers do not even mention such sensations except in the vaguest language, as in "The Ski Trip": "I came home tired & sore with bruises & pain." An excellent strategy to move them in the right direction is to have students experience bodily sensations in the classroom, concentrate on them then and there, and describe them.

Using Physical Activities

A sequence of physical activities is a good way to begin. The first year I used jumping jacks in my classroom, but I received immediate complaints from the teacher in the classroom below me. Thereafter, I used more sedate activities: trying to hold a heavy dictionary at arm's length for two or three minutes (most students can't manage more than a minute); picking cherries, an activity we did in high school phys ed that involves holding both arms to the side at shoulder height and moving the thumb and fingers of each hand as rapidly as possible in a picking motion (in high school, I found this little better than torture); and various isometric exercises such as pulling up on the seat of a chair while sitting on it, pushing the fist of one hand into the palm of the other, and hooking the fingers of one hand into those of the other and pulling as hard as possible. Since these are all endurance exercises, it's best to call out the time every five or ten seconds. They can also become contests to see who can continue the longest. After each exercise, talk about the sensations. The goal is to generate responses like these:

Holding the Dictionary

At first it is light and no problem to hold, but after 15 seconds, I know I'm going to drop it, because the weight of the dictionary is increasing by five or ten pounds a second. (Twila)

After 25 seconds, the dictionary was so heavy, I thought like its going to pull my arm out the shoulder. I felt a sharp pain in the joint of my thumb where it was holding the dictionary. Then I couldn't hold it any more and my arm just fell down. (Roscoe)

Picking Cherries

At first, picking cherries was easy. I think nothing to it. But then after about 15 seconds, something seemed to be holding my fingers away from the thumbs. By 30 seconds, it was like a tennis ball that I had to squeeze to bring the tips of my fingers to my hand. Then the ball turn into hard rubber that I could not squeeze any longer. (Ronakea)

After 15 seconds, it was harder to pull my fingers to my thumb. It became more and more harder. After a minute, my shoulders felt like they were going to drop off and my arms felt like I was holding up two or three dictionaries. (Maurice)

Pulling Up on One's Chair

I tried to pull up on my chair hard enough to put it on my desk. But I could not budge it. It would not move, hard as I tried. Then the muscles in my lower arms and elbows got tangled up like tight rubber bands. (Celine)

I pull and pull and pull on the bottom of my chair. My arms soon tire and my shoulders ached. The edge of the bottom was cutting into my hands. I felt tingling in my lower arms. I was holding my breathe to pull harder. After sixty seconds, I stop to take a breathe. Then I out of breath. (Jefferson)

Using Imaginative Leap Assignments

To extend this work beyond the confines of the classroom, we asked students to imagine themselves in precarious positions and write about how they would feel: diving off a high cliff to escape a deadly enemy, moving along the eight-inch ledge below the school's second-story windows in pursuit of a spy, crawling through a dense forest with a lot of undergrowth to escape a crazed shooter with a rifle. These imaginative leaps help students learn not only how to concentrate on bodily sensations but also how to conjure up scenes in their imagination as a basis for their writing.

The Dumpster Assignment

One year a group of my MAT students invented a scenario intended to pull together all of the work we had done on writing about sensations:

Imagine that you are walking home alone after dark in Hyde Park. It is early November and the weather is cold and windy. As you walk down Kenwood Avenue you hear footsteps behind you. You look over your shoulder. You see a man in a heavy jacket and jeans behind you. You begin to walk faster, but the footsteps behind you also pick up speed. You walk faster still, but the footsteps match your pace. You become more and more worried. Your parents have told you how dangerous it is to be out walking alone in Hyde Park. You break into a run and check over your shoulder. To your horror, the man is running now as well. You dash down the first alley you come to. It is darker than the street, and you squeeze up against a brick wall behind the first Dumpster you come to. You crouch down as low as possible to better hide yourself. Write about what you see, smell, hear, and feel as you wait for the man to approach the Dumpster.

We assigned this activity about halfway through our workshop, at the end of the second week. We assumed that the children's responses would tell us what we had accomplished so far that year and what remained to be done. Here is a response by a sixth grader:

> As I was waiting behind the dumpster I felt footsteps getting closer and closer as his footsteps were going clap, clap, boom and then again clap, clap, boom. As he got closer I could feel my stomach going Grr, Grr. I am hungry it felt like it were tying in knots like a chain twisting really hard. While he got closer and closer my heart was pounding like a earthquake like if I was going to dye. When I heared these little voices were are you little brat. As he approached I could see rats approaching me and I was scared like a cat. All I could see was him walking towards me. I could hear water splashes going harder and harder like waves crashing against rocks, like hammers hammering then I heard a car coming through the alley, if only I could scream and I did but he goes here you are so I started running.

The piece goes on for several more lines. Despite the problems in punctuation and spelling, we regarded this paper as successful. We had made some progress, even though we still had a long way to go. The MAT student who commented on the paper wrote, "Wow! What a great job! You've got lots of good details, and you've included sounds, feelings, and great metaphors." She asked a few questions about what the writer might have smelled and other things he might have seen and ended with another compliment. (She didn't make any critical comments about spelling or punctuation because we hadn't yet taught those things.)

The first time we did this activity, we had students crouch behind their desks as the scenario was read aloud so they would have a firsthand sense of the physical discomfort when they wrote. We used the scenario every year thereafter. The assignment is always popular, and most students rank it above average on our rating scales.

Figurative Language and Feelings: Developing a New Lesson

Sometimes personal feelings and sensations are best expressed through figurative language. In the shell game, students had used figurative language to say what the shell looked like, comparing it to something quite different. Is describing an *experience* more difficult than describing a seashell? To me it is, because the experience is more abstract, encompassing many more elements than the relatively concrete seashell. Because the students have already successfully used similes (and a few metaphors) in the seashell lesson, perhaps a more abstract lesson might focus on describing personal experiences using figurative language. The following is a description of how we might go about developing such a new lesson.

Eight Steps in Developing and Refining Lessons

Whenever my MAT students and I developed lessons we followed these eight steps:

1. We identified or created a specific writing strategy.
2. We tried to use that strategy ourselves.
3. We analyzed what tasks were involved in using the strategy.
4. We came up with a *gateway activity* (one with simple parameters and materials) to introduce the strategy. (The shell game lesson in Chapter 4 is a gateway activity for using detail and using figurative language in writing, as are the various sense lessons in this chapter.)
5. We found or created a writing sample in which the strategy was used.
6. We tested the activity in imagination.

7. We tested it in a real classroom.
8. We evaluated the success or failure of the activity, revising it or scrapping it as necessary.

Identifying the Strategy

For developing our new lesson, the first step has already been accomplished. To express feelings and emotional responses more effectively, one possible strategy is using figurative language.

Using the Strategy Ourselves

Could and did we use the strategy? If not, it would be foolish to try to teach it. So, could we think of similes or metaphors to convey some of the feelings of a given personal experience? What is the emotional experience of waiting in a dental chair like?

- like being handcuffed and unable to move
- like being hogtied
- like waiting for a lethal injection on death row
- like lying in a coffin
- like sitting in a torture chamber with all the gadgets of torture in view near our heads

What is it like to witness a bad accident or, more generally, a horrific scene of any kind? Hank used the simile *standing like statues*. Could we think of others?

- My eyes were riveted to the scene.
- I was hypnotized.
- I was engulfed (or suffocated) by the horror.
- I watched with tunnel vision.
- The crash roared in my ears.
- The sight of the man's face shredded my thinking.

OK. Because we could think of some similes and metaphors, it might be worth a try to develop a more elaborate lesson. (We still do not know if it will work.)

Analyzing the Tasks

What was involved in producing such similes and metaphors? To produce our examples, we had to focus on parts of the scene as well on the scene as a whole. Until we imagined sitting in the dental chair, we had no ideas. But as soon as we focused on the chair, we developed several workable similes. We first focused on seeing the accident, then on the sound of the crash and the sight of the face. All of our metaphors involved some particular aspect of the scene and our own physical or mental responses.

Planning the Activity

What activity would make it easier for students to use similes and metaphors to describe their personal response to an experience? First, we listed experiences students were likely to have had: visiting the dentist; incurring the anger of a parent, coach, or teacher; being lost or stranded; engaging in very strenuous activity or work; witnessing a bad accident or other terrible event. Then we remembered or imagined what those experiences were or would be like for us. When my father was angry, he never scolded or struck me, but he had a look of disdain for me that I would have crawled into a sewer to avoid. Possibly, asking students to remember or imagine a common experience would work.

Another possibility is to show pictures of catastrophes (the flood damage from a hurricane such as Katrina or the tsunami of 2004 in Indonesia) and ask students to develop figurative language to describe the pictures. (But we'd be careful about arousing upsetting emotions.)

Finding or Creating a Writing Sample

The following excerpt from *Black Boy* (Wright 1951) describes the author's experience at a new school:

> I was still shy and half paralyzed when in the presence of a crowd, and my first day at the new school made me the laughingstock of the classroom. I was sent to the blackboard to write my name and address; I knew my name and address, knew how to write it, knew how to spell it; but standing at the blackboard with the eyes of the many girls and boys looking at my back made me freeze inside and I was unable to write a single letter.
>
> "Write your name," the teacher called to me.
>
> I lifted the white chalk to the blackboard and, as I was about to write, my mind went blank, empty; I could not remember my name, not even the first letter. Somebody giggled and I stiffened.
>
> "Just forget us and write your name and address," the teacher coaxed.
>
> An impulse to write would flash through me, but my hand would refuse to move. The children began to twitter and I flushed hotly.
>
> "Don't you know your name?" the teacher asked.
>
> I looked at her and could not answer. The teacher rose and walked to my side, smiling at me to give me confidence. She placed her hand tenderly upon my shoulder.
>
> "What's your name?" she asked.
>
> "Richard," I whispered.
>
> "Richard what?"
>
> "Richard Wright."
>
> "Spell it."
>
> I spelled my name in a wild rush of letters, trying desperately to redeem my paralyzing shyness.
>
> "Spell it slowly so I can hear it," she directed me. I did. "Now, can you write?"
>
> "Yes, ma'am."
>
> "Then write it."
>
> Again I turned to the blackboard and lifted my hand to write, then I was blank and void within. I tried frantically to collect my senses, but I could remember nothing. A sense of the girls and boys behind me filled me to the exclusion of everything. I realized how utterly

I was failing and I grew weak and leaned my hot forehead against the cold blackboard. The room burst into a loud and prolonged laugh and my muscles froze.

"You may go to your seat," the teacher said.

I sat and cursed myself. Why did I always appear so dumb when I was called upon to perform something in a crowd? I knew how to write as well as any pupil in the classroom, and no doubt I could read better than any of them, and I could talk fluently and expressively when I was sure of myself. Then why did strange faces make me freeze? I sat with my ears and neck burning, hearing the pupils whisper about me, hating myself, hating them; I sat still as stone and a storm of emotion surged through me. (85–86)

For this activity, we might ask students, first, to find the figurative language Wright uses: *still as stone, a storm of emotion, freeze inside, muscles froze.* Then we might ask the class to recall times, when as young children, they were excruciatingly embarrassed. If I were teaching the lesson, I could describe an experience I had with forgetting the words when I sang in public. Better, I could type out the following and give them double- or triple-spaced copies to use, so the lesson could go on to teach revision.

Once, as an eight- or nine-year-old boy soprano, I was to sing a solo in church as the climax of the annual Children's Day service. I was to sing the words from memory. Usually memorizing words to music was not a problem for me. At home, the music seemed to carry me through. But with an audience, I was always dreadfully nervous and fearful of making mistakes. My mother was in the hospital at the time, so that a different pianist was accompanying me. That made me nervous. I began the first verse with a slight quaver in my voice. At the end of the first line, I looked at the balcony and saw my father sitting there. Suddenly, the words disappeared from my mind. I looked out to see hundreds of adults and children in the audience. I struggled in vain to find the words, every moment conscious of the eyes staring at me. I wanted to be anywhere but on this platform. The pianist continued alone through the first verse, and, when she reached the chorus, the words came back as suddenly as they had disappeared. I sang the second and third verses without a problem. When I finally finished, I turned from the congregation and walked to my seat at the rear of the platform behind the pulpit. Even partially out of sight, my face was red with embarrassment. I raised my hands to my head to hide my shame from the children around me. What would I say to my father? My body ached in anticipation of what he might say, how he might look at me.

I would also project this narrative on an overhead and ask the class to help me find figurative language to describe my intense embarrassment and shame. How might parts of the experience be described figuratively?

- When I saw the large audience, my stomach churned.
- My skin crawled with tiny creatures born of fear.
- My legs turned to rubber as I stood to take my place in front.
- The words disappeared into a sealed vacuum that I could not penetrate.
- My face burned with embarrassment.
- I was on fire with embarrassment.
- Molten lava seemed to be coursing through my veins.
- I wanted to disappear, to be vaporized.
- I felt as though I had been crushed by a ton of steel, squashed into the dirt.
- The weight of my shame was like a ton of steel on my shoulders.

Producing the figurative language ourselves provides hints about how to approach students for their inventions and suggestions—going through the experience step-by-step:

- How can I describe my fear and nervousness figuratively at the beginning?
- How might I talk about the loss of the words figuratively? Where might the words go figuratively?
- How might I describe my embarrassment and shame after forgetting?
- How could I describe my wish to be somewhere else figuratively?
- At the end, how might I describe the ache in my body figuratively?
- Can you think of any other points where I might use figurative language to be more effective?

As they made suggestions, I could insert them at the appropriate spots using carets.

Finally, I would ask students to write about their own experiences of great embarrassment or fear or some other strong emotion. At the conclusion of the class, I would call on students to share some of their ideas. Together we could explore ideas for figurative language to better describe the experiences.

Testing the Activity in Imagination

As I have written this lesson plan, I have tested it imaginatively. At this point, I am fairly certain it will work, although I know there will be rough places and detours and momentary failures.

Testing the Activity in the Classroom

The next step is to use the activity with real students in the classroom. The criterion for success will not be their ability to recall what figurative language is or to recall the figures used in some passage they have read, but their ability to *use figurative language in their own writing* to describe feelings, thoughts, and sensations.

Evaluating Success or Failure

In analyzing the successes and failures, we needed to evaluate each successive step of the lesson and the carryover. Does the model from Richard Wright have the impact we hope for? Does the teacher's model to be revised with the help of students have a useful impact? Are students actually able to invent figures to use in the piece? Or does it fall apart because it is too far removed from their own experience or for some other reason? Were students able to write about their own experience of great embarrassment or some other strong emotion and include successful figurative language? Even if they are able to do that, another test remains: Does writing about feelings and emotions carry over into assignments that do not call explicitly for that? Even if the lesson is relatively successful, we will need to ask how it might be more effective. How might we change it to reach more students more effectively?

Such planning and reflection is hard work and sometimes painful. But in my half century of experience, it has been the planning, anticipation of student response, and evaluation of those responses that have given me joy in teaching. When a newly planned activity or lesson fails, we might be very disappointed. But I believe that we learn at least as much from failure as we do from success. Failure forces us to question our basic assump-

tions, our teaching ideas and activities, the ways we relate to students in classrooms—
everything. If we think hard and sometimes long, we learn from those processes. But when
we see students learn from our teaching and use strategies that they did not formerly use
in their writing and reading, or (in the case of my MAT students) in their teaching, there
is no pleasure that can compare.

8

WRITING ABOUT PEOPLE AND ACTION

Student narratives rarely address the reader's need to know about how people appear, how they act, what their habits are, and so forth. The materials and activities in this chapter (which have been used, with variations, with students in seventh grade through college) help students notice details of appearance and action and apply them to the characters they are writing about in order to reveal something about the characters' personalities.

Writing About People

When I teach characterization, I often begin by showing the students the illustration in Figure 8.1, an engraving by John Gillray titled *A Voluptuary Under the Horrors of Digestion*.

The abundance of observable details in this 1792 caricature depicting the debauchery of the then prince of Wales, who would become George IV, enables students to practice connecting physical characteristics and outward behavior to *character* and provides a basis for them to develop the art of characterization in their own writing. (If you choose a different illustration, be sure to select one that has a comparable wealth of details about which much can be said and inferred. The people in most advertisements, for example, are not useful, since advertising is not concerned with people's character.)

The prince is very fat, with a huge stomach and thighs, his buttons bursting off his vest and trousers. The chamber pot to his left is spilling over onto unpaid bills from the butcher, baker, and poulterer; a bill from a doctor is on the floor below the pot. On the tiered tray farther to his left are various medicines; one on the top shelf is marked "For the Piles" and one on the second shelf has a tag inscribed "Drips for stinking breath." On one side of the tray stands a box of Leake's Pills, on the other a bottle marked "Velnos Vegetable Syrup," both famous quack cures for venereal disease. (One could tell younger students that these were purported to prevent an upset stomach.)

There is plenty of evidence that thoughts of food and drink pervade the prince's consciousness: the corkscrew instead of a watch on the fob in the pocket of his vest; the coat of arms consisting of a knife and fork, crossed on a plate, under the motto "Ich dien" (German for "I serve") on the band around the three feathers (the emblem of the prince of Wales); the wine-glass-and-wine-bottle candelabra; the bottles of port on the table; the wine bottles thrown away under the table; the bones and carcass of a bird on the table; and the man himself, picking his teeth with a fork. On the floor lie dice, a dice box, and

Figure 8.1 *A Voluptuary Under the Horrors of Digestion*

a book with the title *Debts of Honor Unpaid*. Another book with the title *Faro Market Account Self Archer Hobart & Co.* implies that he is a partner of two women who operated a notorious gambling house in the eighteenth century. Truly, this is a voluptuary, one who lives for every pleasure and as a result has become the epitome of gluttony, lethargy, and vice, not to mention apparent irresponsibility and wasteful spending.

Discussing A Voluptuary *with Seventh Graders*

My MAT students lobbied successfully for using the *Voluptuary* illustration when we taught this lesson to a class of inner-city seventh graders. I agreed against my better judgment. I thought it was too far removed from the children's culture, that too many of the details couldn't possibly speak to them.

Roger distributed copies of the engraving. I sat in class expectantly, prepared to save the day with backup pictures when *A Voluptuary* failed to launch the lesson. The class immediately began giggling, and three boys began making comments.

Ronald said, "This guy a fat slob."

Another boy said, "He ain't fat, he got a bowling ball in there."

"No," said Jefferson, "he pregnant. He gonna have a baby."

I was grateful that they were reading the picture and was eager to hear what else they would say, but Roger cut them short and began the planned discussion. "I hear a lot of you saying he's a slob. What makes you say that?" The kids pointed out his huge "gut," his thighs "like great big hams," his "popping buttons, 'cause he eat too much." They laughed about the monstrous bite taken out of the carcass on the table, the bones falling off the table, and the wine bottles under the table. They decided he must be a drunk. They spotted the dice on the floor and the dice cup. They read *Debts of Honor* on the book next to the dice but couldn't make out the word *Unpaid*. Roger told them what it was. They had no idea what debts of honor were. Roger explained that the phrase was a fancy expression used in eighteenth-century England for gambling debts.

"What else do you see?"

Ronakea said, "They a plate, knife, and fork on the wall. What they doin' on the wall?" Roger opened the question to the class. No one had an idea. Then Ronakea said, "He all about eatin.' Even put it on the wall."

Roger said, "You've hit it on the nose. He's all about eating so much that the plate and fork and knife are his coat of arms. Anyone know what a coat of arms is?" Someone said it was "like what a king or a duke has that show who he is." Roger explained that a coat of arms carries symbols and emblems indicating the history of a family or its associations with other important people. He asked, "So what do you think that this coat of arms shows about this guy?"

Ronald said, "It show he like food. The plate, knife, and fork must be his family."

Roger said, "Take a look at the three feathers above the coat of arms. They are coming out of a crown. And there's a little ribbon coming down from the crown. Can anyone read the words on the ribbon?" Students took some guesses, but their copies were not clear enough to make out the words. Roger told them that the words were a motto for future kings, *Ich* (on the left ribbon) *dien* (on the right). He wrote the phrase on the board and told the students it was German for "I serve." He told them that the feathers were the symbol of the Prince of Wales, the title of the man next in line to be king of England. He asked, "What do you think such a motto means for someone who is going to be king?"

Verita said, "I guess it suppose to mean 'a king serves the people'—but he not servin' anything but food." The class cracked up.

Roger said, "Well put, Verita. Everybody understand that?"

Jefferson had his hand up. "How come the words be German? You said he was English, right?"

Roger turned to the class. "Anyone know?" No one did. He explained that noble families in Europe often married their children to the children of noble families in other countries, sometimes as a way of gaining control of the other country. At this period, the kings of England were of German descent. "But I don't know all the details of that. Let's go back to the picture. Does anyone see anything else?"

Verita asked, "What's on the little shelf on the side of the picture? I see writing on them but I can't read any of it."

Since no one could make out the words, Roger explained what was written on the containers. Someone asked what Velnos Vegetable Syrup was.

Roger explained that in the eighteenth century Velnos Vegetable Syrup was a well-known quack medicine for sexually transmitted diseases. "It was really only a fake concoction that did not work, though," he said. "What does that tell you about this person?"

Hank said, "He a fool."

"Why do you say that?"

"For takin' fake medicine."

"Well, people didn't know it was fake. We do. But what does the fact that he needed it tell you?"

Hank volunteered, "He sleepin' around."

Roger said, "OK, what else do you see?"

Shaquita asked, "What that little tub beside him? On the stand?"

Roger explained that it was a chamber pot, which people in the eighteenth century, when there was no indoor plumbing, used for a toilet in the house. There was a general moan of disgust from the class.

Ronald said, "It runnin' over." There was a louder moan of disgust from the class.

Roger explained that perhaps the prince may have used it to throw up in so he could continue eating. Another moan. He then called the class' attention to the papers under the chamber pot. The students could read some of the words: *butcher bill, baker bill, doctor bill,* the *unpaid* at the bottom of two. Roger asked, "Why do you think they are under the chamber pot?"

Hank said, "He usin' 'em for toilet paper?"

Roger said, "Well, it's true they didn't have our kind of toilet paper in the eighteenth century. That is a fairly recent invention." The class moaned again; some laughed.

Hank reiterated, "So, he usin' his unpaid bills for toilet paper?"

"It appears so," Roger said. The class moaned again. "Can anyone see anything else we need to attend to?" Verita asked about the man in the painting on the wall. Roger explained that the man was L. Cornaro, a sixteenth-century Italian who wrote a book about living a life of self-denial and very strict dieting in order to achieve old age.

"Can anyone read the word on the glass he's holding?" Students did not recognize the word, but they could spell it. Roger wrote *AQUA* on the board. "Does that word sound familiar to anyone?"

"Do it mean water in Spanish?" Celine asked.

"That's close. It's the Latin word for water," Roger said. "What do you think the picture is doing on his wall? Here's the prince drinking wine and here's the old man drinking water. What's going on here? Any ideas?"

"To be on a strict diet, you suppose to drink water, not wine," Darlene said.

"Do you think the prince is leading a life of strict dieting?"

Students shook their heads no. Ronakea said, "He not strict about anything. He be doing whatever he want."

"So why do you guys think he has this picture of Cornaro up on his wall?" asked Roger.

"Maybe he has it on the wall to pretend he strict about eatin'," Ernest said.

"Any other ideas?"

"Maybe he has it up there to kind of hide what he doin' from his daddy. Like he don't want his daddy to know what a big pig he is. So he put this diet guy up on the wall to fox him," said Reynard in his first contribution to the class.

"Reynard says he's trying to fool his father. What do the rest of you think about that interesting idea?" Roger asked. After some discussion, the class decided the prince was trying to fool everyone with the picture, not just his father. Roger said, "If a person pretends to do or believe one thing and actually does the opposite, that person is called a *hypocrite*." He wrote the word on the board.

"He a phony," Hank said.

"Exactly," Roger said. "But *hypocrite* refers to the kind of phony who gives lip service to one set of values or ideas and acts according to another. Can one of you explain why the prince is a hypocrite?"

Ronakea and Verita had their hands up. Roger waited for more hands and then called on Reynard.

"He a hypocrite because the picture a man who believe in strict diet and the prince, he want people to think he that too. But he don't do nothin' but eat."

"Who can add to that?" Roger asked. No one did. "Who else can explain why this man may be a hypocrite?" (My MAT students and I had talked about using new words several times when they are first introduced.)

Exuberant as ever, Ronakea did not wait to be called on. "Ain't no maybe. He say one thing and he do another. Tha's what you said a hypocrite is."

"Would anyone add to that or say it in a different way?" Roger asked. He called on Verita.

"He is a disgusting hypocrite because he don't just eat, he eats so much that he got to throw up in the chamber pot. Then he eats some more, and he does it right there under the picture of the man who think strict diet important. Right underneath the picture of the man who represents strict diet."

"OK," Roger said, "it's time to take some notes. *Hypocrite* is a word you can use in your writing. So make an entry in your spelling pages for this word." He pointed to *hypocrite* on the board. "Then copy this definition and write an explanation of why the prince is a hypocrite. That will serve as an example for the definition. In your example, be sure to include enough to help you remember what a hypocrite is." He turned to the board to write the definition and then moved about the class, checking what the students were writing, stopping now and then to whisper suggestions.

After a few minutes, Roger said, "There are some aspects of the engraving we have not talked about—his face, the way he's looking out of the picture, his manner of sitting in the chair. How would you describe his face?"

There were several responses, including "round face," "double chin," and "don't care about nothin'."

Hank said, "Look like he on drugs."

"Why do you say that?"

Darlene volunteered, "His eyes glazed."

Hank said, "He ain't lookin' at nothin'."

Darlene said, "He don't care about nothin'."

Someone else said, "He just starin'. He in happy land."

Roger asked, "What do you think he thinks about other people?"
The students had a lot to say: "He don' care about anybody but him."
"He in happy land. He don't care about nobody."
"He lookin' down his nose at somebody."
"Naw, he lookin' down his nose at everybody."

Group Work on A Voluptuary

Roger then asked the students to work in groups on the following questions, which were written on the board, and prepare to report to the class on their ideas:

1.   What do all of the details we have talked about suggest about the Prince of Wales and his habits?
2.   How would you describe his character?
3.   What would it be like to visit this man, perhaps to ask for a job? Imagine you would find him the way he looks in this picture. What would be his attitude? What would he be doing? How would he treat you?

Roger visited the groups, answering questions. Some students didn't understand the second question. I listened to Roger explain that a person's character has to do with how the person behaves in relation to the world she lives in and to other people—with habits, attitudes, and the way a person thinks about everything. I wondered whether we should have put the second question last. After ten minutes the groups said they needed more time. Roger gave them five more minutes and then called for their reports. Jefferson's group volunteered first. Darlene was the spokesperson:

> Well, we think he not a good person. He eat too much; he drink too much; he got sexually transmitted disease; and he gamble too much 'cause he in debt. He got bad habits for health. He keep that filthy pot right next to his dinner table. We think he look down his nose at other people 'cause he think he all that. But he ain't no good. He a disgusting slob and hypocrite 'cause he pretends to be strict on a diet and he stuffs food in his mouth till it can't hold any more and he has to throw up. We would not want to go to see him for nothin'. We would not take a job from him. And tha's our report.

The other groups' reports, which were presented the next day, were comparable. I noted the possibilities for teaching new vocabulary this picture provided: *gluttony, profligate, sloth, arrogance, debauchery,* and a host of other words. The concrete referent of the picture stimulated and encouraged learning new words in a useful way, because they could be used to talk about the picture.

Individual Work: Writing About A Voluptuary

After the group reports on *A Voluptuary,* Sarah made the following assignment:

> Imagine that you have gone to visit the prince of Wales for lunch. Write a personal letter to one of your friends about his appearance and his room and how he behaved. Include your thoughts and sensations. Be as specific as you can so that your friend will be able to picture what you saw. Include lines of dialogue that indicate what you said to the prince and his replies.

Sarah told students how to begin and conclude a friendly letter—the date, the salutation, and the complimentary close—and encouraged students to include details that had been mentioned in the class discussion about the picture. They had the remaining twenty minutes of class to begin writing, and the letter was due the next day.

When we evaluated the letters they had written, we were particularly concerned to see how the students had described the appearance of the prince. We had assumed they would include plenty of details about the room, the items in it, and his clothing, and they had. But we were relieved also to find many effective details about the prince's face and behavior. Here are some of the descriptive phrases the students used:

RONALD: His cheeks were like tennis balls.
DARWYN: He is squinting his eyes with a smirk on his face.
RONAKEA: He raised his eyebrow and curled his lip.
JAMES: He has a double chin and no neck. He had bags under his eyes.
RUPERT: His eyes are halfway shut with bags under them, and his hair looks like a mop.
LETISHA: His lips are shaped like the letter M.
VERITA: He smirked at me and he belched and burped during our whole conversation.

We decided these students were ready to work on their own narratives. However, in most workshops we have to present additional lessons on writing about people. One of them centers on revising the letter to a friend to include more details about *A Voluptuary*. The students study the picture again and review any notes they may have taken in class.

Sara Spachman, one of my former MAT students and now a teacher at Chicago's Curie High School, recently used a comparable assignment with her ninth graders:

Imagine you're a writer who has accepted an assignment to meet and eat dinner with the Prince of Wales at his mansion. Imagine all the details of meeting this man and having dinner with him. When you return home, you decide to sit down and write about the prince. In your writing, describe the moment of your meeting, how the prince looks and acts, the meal you have together, the room you eat it in, and how your time with the prince concludes. Be sure to convey to your readers how you want to portray the prince. Is he as bad as Gillray depicts him or not?

She required all students to write two handwritten pages (one and a half pages typed and double spaced). She included a checklist of the features to be included: "description of the prince, including his face, body, clothing"; "figurative language"; "at least four lines of dialogue in correct story form"; and so on. Most students wrote more than the required amount. Here's about two-thirds of one piece:

Finally, I arrive at the dining room, I am seated by the attendant. There is an enormous crystal chandelier hanging over the long dinner table. At the head of the table is a wide, cushioned chair, smaller chairs surround the sides.

"The prince will arrive shortly," says the attendant.

The table is set with shining silverware, fine china, and golden wine goblets. A large door at the other end of the dinning room opens swiftly.

"Good evening, it is my honor to present the Prince of Wales," announces the attendant.

The prince enters the room, head held high, he is rather short, however he is a very large man. His weight prevents him from having any kind of speed or grace as he waddles over to greet me. He extends his stubby, jewel covered hand in my direction. I kindly shake his hand only to have mine covered in sweat.

"I am glad you decided to accept my invitation, I find your writing and ideas very intriguing," he says in an ambiguous somewhat unfriendly tone. He plops himself down in the chair.

The prince claps his hands and servers briskly float into the room, their trays piled with a variety of food. There are hams, chicken, roasts, assorted deli meats, bread, biscuits and different sauces, butter, cream and gravy. To drink, only wine.

"All this food, who else is joining us?" I ask naively.

"Is that your idea of a joke? I am the Prince of Wales, nothing is ever enough for me!" he boasts, as his body jiggles.

The prince rips a leg off one of the turkeys, smothers it in gravy, and it disappears into his mouth. The gravy streams down his chin onto his elegant clothes. Next, potatoes and gravy, then biscuits and butter, ham, beef, he takes a swig of wine, half of it spills on his trousers, he continuously shovels food into his mouth. Throughout the meal he stuffs his face, like a pig eating his slops. He barely stops to breathe let alone speak. As he unbuttons his trousers, his gut explodes over his waist. I sit astonished, watching the repulsive sight, I quickly lose my appetite. He belches loudly, the stench slaps me in the face, he makes no attempt to excuse himself.

"Why aren't you eating?" he growls as crumbs fly from his mouth.

"With all due respect sir, your table manners are appalling, you are rude, selfish, full of yourself and I do not wish to continue this dinner," I say.

"How dare you speak to the Prince of Wales in such a manner! Guards, take her away!" orders the prince.

Royal guards rush in and grab me by the arm.

Final Assignment: Writing About People

As the final stage in the writing-about-people sequence, the seventh graders either wrote about a person in one of their idea-sheet stories or added character descriptions to their developing narrative (see Chapters 3, 5, 6, and 7). (We didn't ask students to develop a full character profile as some teachers recommend; see Sperling and Freedman 1987. Our goal was for them to incorporate descriptive details about characters into their ongoing narratives.)

This is what Twila added about her dentist (the additions are underlined):

Another ten minutes go by. Finally, he comes in to my chair. He is a little, thin white man with a mustash. He wears wire rim glasses that look like they coming off his nose. He comes up close with his little pick and his little mirror. He leans over close to me, and I can smell the cigarettes smoke on his breath.

He says, "How are we today, Twila?"

I say, "I ain't good, I been here waiting 20 minutes. And it ain't no fun."

He says, "Well open your mouth and let me see the tooth that's bothering you." I see a nasty gleam in his eye. He is hoping I have a cavity so that he can make more money.

I tell him, "You been having a smoke, I can smell it." Then he jams his little mirror in my mouth and I do not get to say any more. He is smiling when he push that mirror into my mouth agains my gum so it hurts.

Here are Hank's additions about the first cop:

The first car slams into one of the posts for the el. Blam! Big crash. Little pieces of metal and glass tinkle into the street. You can hear a hub cap rolling down 63rd. The police car squeals loud to a stop about 40 feet behind the crashed car. A cop jumps out with his gun out. He is a fat cop with a belly hanging over his belt. He got a bright pink face. I think he must have high blood pressure. He creeps near to the crashed car. He looks at us. He has a little gray beard on his chin. I see it twitching up and down like he is chewing something. He is keeping his head down. He spits tobacco juice on the street. "You kids, get outta here. This guy got a gun. He ain't afraid to use it."

I tell the cop, "He looks dead from here."

The cop looks at me and asks, "What is he doing? Can you see anything?" He is chewing harder now. He must be nervous.

Describing Action

When it came to describing people in action, our students were fairly vague, confining themselves to generic terms and avoiding particulars. Frequently they provided highly abbreviated statements: *We had a fight.* Sometimes they provided slightly more detail: *She slapped me. I don't know why. So I hit her back. Then the principal came down the hall and broke up the fight.* But hardly anyone provided elaborated details like these: *She walked up to me with her mouth turned down and her chin out in anger. Suddenly, her hand shot up and slapped me across the face hard. The sting brought tears to my eyes, but I punched her as hard as I could in the chest to knock the wind out of her. She gasped for breath and I went in close and started hitting her in the same place with my fists, first the right and then the left. I landed four punches with each before the principal was suddenly between us. She grabbed my right arm and Trina's left arm and pulled us apart.*

To help our inner-city seventh graders include more and better descriptions of action, we used techniques similar to those in preceding chapters:

1. We read a sample from a student or professional writing.
2. We developed descriptions of actions in photographs (sometimes film clips) as a class.
3. Students developed descriptions of actions in photographs (sometimes film clips) in groups.
4. Students developed descriptions individually.
5. Students added descriptions of actions to their developing narrative.

Discussing Models of Action Writing as a Class

We have used a variety of models of action writing. I often use a passage from Jens Bjerre's book *Kalahari*, an account of life among the Bushmen of the Kalahari desert of southwest Africa. Here the author describes the actions of two hunters in pursuit of a gemsbok with bows and poison arrows:

With intense concentration they observe every clue which reveals the animal's movements—a bent straw, a hoof print in the sand, a broken branch, seeds shaken from the grass on to the ground, and many other signs which are invisible to me. Now they are moving more slowly. They stop, kneel down, and each take out an arrow. Then they proceed again at a slower pace, but they leave behind their quivers so the sound of rattling arrows may not give them away. . . . Suddenly I observe a movement only fifty metres in front of us. It is a buck gemsbok, and behind him there are two more, their heads in the grass as they feed. . . . Slowly and silently the two brown figures glide through the grass, drawing near to their prey until they are only about ten feet from the buck. Whenever the buck looks in their direction they stiffen. Its ears turn forward and it appears to be staring directly at them. Suddenly it looks the other way and gives its pursuers just the opportunity they have been waiting for. They swiftly fit the arrows into the bows. Tsonoma bends his bow, and is just about to stand up for the shot when Narni signals him not to move. The buck is looking towards them again. . . . For a long time the buck stands staring and sniffing nervously towards the hunters who remain motionless and prostrate in the grass. At last it decides that no danger is hovering near, turns away its head and takes a few steps. . . . Tsonoma and Narni rise and bend their bows. . . . At that instant the buck turns its head again and I glimpse the petrified horror in its eyes. As it stiffens for a split second, the two poisoned arrows fly through the air and bore into the flanks of the gemsbok. (1960, 121–23)

I like this passage because it is in the present tense (which is what we have been working in) and because it not only describes a very detailed action but also tells us a good deal about the hunters.

Our students liked it because it was unusual and let them see a bit of what life was like in Africa fifty years ago. For discussion, we posed this question:

The writer might have said, "Tsonoma and Narni track a gemsbok and shoot it with poisoned arrows." If he had left it at that, what would we have missed?

Our students responded with comments like these:

- We wouldn't know how they track animals.
- We wouldn't see how good they are at tracking and coming close to the animal.
- We wouldn't see how they work together.
- It wouldn't be as interesting.
- We wouldn't know about the gemsbok.
- We wouldn't know how important little details are to tracking.

They concluded that the detail is valuable to the reader.

I also used a piece of my own writing to demonstrate action. The following story is about my experience of walking too far along a narrow path on the face of a shale cliff in northern Ohio and finding that the path in front of me had ended and the path behind me had broken away. To keep from falling a hundred feet to the bottom of a gorge, I needed to climb up high enough to reach a sapling several feet above my head and to my right.

I move to the right cautiously, dig the inside of my right heel into the shale, dig my fingers in, and lift my left foot. As soon as I bring it down, the shale beneath my feet rolls away, and I begin to slide. I dig my fingernails into the crumbling stone and feel it cut in under the nails. I am certain I am going over the edge. After about three feet, my slide stops, and I freeze to the wall once again. My full pack feels as though it will pull me over backwards.

I think what a dumb idea it had been to take this path. I see myself sliding to the edge of the overhang and falling right to the bottom, flipping over a couple of times before I smash into the stone below. Slate is a soft rock, but not that soft. I clutch the cliff as tightly as I can.

Then I remember the hatchet on my belt. Maybe I can use it to hack steps into the shale. With difficulty I reach it and chop into the shale at the level of my knee and as far to the right as I can reach. Several blows gouge out a step. I feel guilty about the damage I am doing to the hatchet. Slowly I move my right foot over and up to the step. Then I bring my left foot up and hug the wall. Despite the cold spring air, I am sweating profusely. I think I feel the shale shifting under my feet. I quickly slip out the hatchet from its case, being careful not to drop it. Several blows cut out another step on my right. I carefully move up into that step clutching the cliff and this time, getting a mouthful of shale. I still cannot reach the larger sapling.

After reading this passage aloud, I asked whether anyone could pantomime the action, using the classroom wall as the cliff, as we read it again. Ronakea, of course, volunteered. She came to the front of the room, faced the wall, her feet apart, her hands raised above her shoulders, digging into the "shale," her fingers like claws. As I reread the passage, she pantomimed it flawlessly. She received a little round of applause and returned to her seat. The class agreed that without the detail, Ronakea would not have been able to pantomime the piece.

Jefferson wanted to pantomime hunting the gemsbok. I asked the students what they thought. They wanted to do it. Several boys volunteered to be the hunters. I picked Jefferson and Ronald. They went through the pantomime nicely, although the class found their signals to each other hilarious.

We then turned to copies of a painting by Peter Brueghel called *Children's Games* (Gluck 1936), which depicts more than eighty activities in all. I had copied it in four sections, so not all of the groups would be looking at the same games. I pointed out the game of leapfrog, and we wrote a description of the game as it was shown in the picture. We gave the children playing it names and wrote several sentences on the overhead describing what they were doing. I told them that they might not recognize some of the activities but they would recognize many. Each group's task was to describe the activities so accurately that students from groups working with a different section of the painting would be able to pantomime the activity even though they had not seen the visual representation of it.

Even these few activities help students write more specifically about the people in their own narratives. We have used pictures of people in action and sometimes character studies. The photographs must have enough detail to talk about. *A Voluptuary* turned out to be one of the best pictures we ever worked with because of its interest to students and their reactions to it. My fears were completely unfounded. Over the years we have found it to be one of those no-fail lessons, the kind you like to use when administrators visit your classroom.

9

WRITING ABOUT SCENES AND SETTINGS

Over the years my MAT students and I have used many different approaches to encourage students to write more about the scenes and settings of their stories. (We think of *settings* as natural landscapes and inanimate objects such as buildings and machinery. *Scenes* are settings that include people doing things, descriptions of *action*.) Our lessons on observing sensory impressions contribute to this, as do the lessons on setting scenes for dialogues and the work on people and action. However, we believed we needed something more. Examples of scenes and settings from other writers did not do the trick to our satisfaction. We needed activities that engaged students in observing and writing about something concrete.

Very early on we used locations from the students' everyday lives (both pictures and the real thing): the playground, the school cafeteria, the gym, a nearby supermarket, a shopping mall. The real scenes were difficult to negotiate: it was impossible to teach in the midst of the commotion of the cafeteria; a field trip to a supermarket or mall used up all of our class time. So we switched to assigning real settings as homework after we worked with pictures in the classroom.

Finding interesting pictures of scenes could be difficult. Students responded well to scenes crowded with detail—for example, Hogarth's *Beer Street* and *Gin Lane* and Brueghel's *Wedding Dance*, *The Peasant Wedding*, *The Census in Bethlehem*, *The Massacre of the Innocents*, *The Triumph of Death*, *The Fight Between Carnival and Lent*, and *Landscape with the Fall of Icarus*. But some of these are better with older students.

Settings Depicted in Photographs

Because I am an eager tourist, I have dozens of photographs of locations that are unusual for one reason or another: the glens, country houses, urban settings, and castles of Scotland; villages, marketplaces, churches, streets, and Aztec, Mayan, and Toltec structures in Mexico and Guatemala; streets, Buddhist temples, marketplaces, peasant huts, and urban homes in Thailand and Myanmar; streets, canals, rivers, houses, castles, and cathedrals in the Netherlands, France, Spain, and Germany; streets and homes (in both decaying and prosperous neighborhoods) and industrial sites in Chicago. All of these can be useful.

The problem with a single photograph of any site is that it presents a single fixed perspective that may hide many important features. As I write this, for example, I am looking at a picture of Tantallon, my favorite (but not widely known) Scottish castle. The picture shows the impressive front wall punctuated by three towers, one at each end and one in the center. In the afternoon sun the massive wall between the towers is pink, the towers an olive drab (the color of World War II army vehicles). The towers and connecting wall are built of many relatively small rocks laboriously stacked on top of each other and fixed with mortar. The tallest tower rises to six stories (relative to the person standing in front of the castle, it's probably sixty or seventy feet high). That's all I can tell from this one photograph.

In a class on describing settings, therefore, I would also use a photo showing that the walls are about twelve feet wide and have passageways and stairways leading to the rampart and one taken from the top of the wall showing that Tantallon is situated on a piece of land jutting into the North Sea, which crashes against the base of the cliff far below. The high cliff provides protection on three sides, so only a single towered wall was necessary at the front.

Many of my tourist photographs constitute pictures of settings (e.g., photos of castles in Scotland rarely include people doing anything interesting). Many others are scenes of people doing something: busy marketplaces in Mexico and Guatemala, a weaver working a loom in Oaxaca, Easter processions in Antigua, street musicians in Chicago, and so on. But paintings show more action than do my photos.

Describing Scenes Depicted in Paintings

Paintings, of course, do not provide multiple perspectives, but the vision of a painter like Brueghel makes up for that. In *The Massacre of the Innocents*, for example, the viewer looks down on what appears to be the central square or plaza of a small village, which is lined on two sides with sharp-peaked houses covered in snow. The ground is also white with snow, and the people in the square are in turmoil. In the lower left, a woman clutching an infant to her breast runs from a horseman with a spear. She looks back at him over her shoulder, her face contorted in terror. Farther back in the square stands a large group of horsemen, their spears jutting upward. They are watching six men who are thrusting their swords and spears into infants on the ground. A man kneeling on the ground before two red-jacketed horsemen raises his hands in supplication that his child be spared as a sword-carrying man behind him pulls a child from a mother. Holding her hands up to her mouth, a woman on the right begs for mercy, a small child clinging to her jacket. A man is reaching for the child, and another man carries a child toward the place of slaughter in the center of the square. On the far right, four men armed with hatchets and swords are breaking into houses. Two have climbed atop a tall barrel and broken the shutters to an upper window; two are kicking open a door.

Combining Sentences to Improve Students' Descriptions

In one class, students described the far-right section of the painting like this:

- On the far right, four men are breaking into houses.
- Two have climbed on a barrel.
- They opened the shutters.
- They are climbing through the window.
- The men are armed with hatchets and swords.

Once students had offered these sentences, we continued our work with syntax by showing them how to combine them using parallel verbs, adverbial clauses, verbal-phrase modifiers, and/or absolute modifiers. (We do not teach all of these together. Rather we concentrate on one pattern until students are able to use it correctly. Our goal in teaching grammatical principles is not naming and identification but *use*.) The following are listed in order of apparent difficulty.

- *Parallel verbs*: They have climbed on top of a barrel, have opened the shutters, and are entering the window.
- *Adverbial clauses*: After climbing on top of a barrel, two men have broken open the shutters and are climbing through a window.
- *Verbal-phrase modifiers*: Two men, having climbed on a barrel and broken open the shutters, are climbing in the window.
- *Absolute modifiers*: Two men have climbed on a barrel, have broken the shutters, and are climbing in the window, their hatchets and swords ready.

We then repeated this process with other clusters of sentences describing the actions of other people in the painting. For example:

- A woman on the right begs two men for mercy.
- She is holding her hands up to her mouth.
- A small child is clinging to her jacket.
- One man reaches for the child.
- The second man is carrying another child toward the place of slaughter.

These sentences can be combined in the following ways:

- *Parallel verbs*: A woman on the right holds her hands to her mouth and begs for mercy.
- *Adverbial clauses*: While a woman begs for mercy, one man is reaching for the child clinging to her jacket as a second man carries another child toward the place of slaughter.
- *Verbal-phrase modifier*: Holding her hands to her mouth, a woman on the right begs for mercy.
- *Absolute modifier*: A woman on the right begs two men for mercy, a small child clinging to her jacket.
- *Absolute modifier*: A woman on the right, hands held up to her mouth, begs for mercy.

Describing Scenes in Model Stories

After working with pictures until students were writing with great specificity, we pointed out examples of scenes in published stories. In the following passage, Richard Wright presents a montage of sensory impressions from his childhood—a collection of very concrete, vivid details that convey what his life was like at that time:

The days and hours began to speak now with a clearer tongue. Each experience had a sharp meaning of its own.

There was the breathlessly anxious fun of chasing and catching flitting fireflies on drowsy summer nights.

There was the drenching hospitality in the pervading smell of sweet magnolias.

There was the aura of limitless freedom distilled from the rolling sweep of tall green grass swaying and glinting in the wind and sun.

There was the feeling of impersonal plenty when I saw a boll of cotton whose cup had spilt over and straggled its white fleece toward the earth.

There was the pitying chuckle that bubbled in my throat when I watched a fat duck waddle across the back yard.

There was the suspense I felt when I heard the taut, sharp song of a yellow-black bee hovering nervously but patiently above a white rose.

There was the drugged, sleepy feeling that came from sipping glasses of milk, drinking them slowly so that they would last a long time, and drinking enough for the first time in my life.

There was the bitter amusement of going into town with Granny and watching the baffled stares of white folks who saw an old woman leading two undeniably Negro boys in and out of stores on Capitol Street.

There was the slow, fresh, saliva-stimulating smell of cooking cotton seeds.

There was the excitement of fishing in muddy country creeks with my grandpa on cloudy days.

There was the fear and awe I felt when Grandpa took me to a sawmill to watch the giant whirring steel blades whine and scream as they bit into wet green logs.

There was the puckery taste that almost made me cry when I ate my first half-ripe persimmon.

There was the greedy joy in the tangy taste of wild hickory nuts.

There was the dry hot summer morning when I scratched my bare arms on briers while picking blackberries and came home with my fingers and lips stained black with sweet berry juice.

There was the relish of eating my first fried fish sandwich, nibbling at it slowly and hoping that I would never eat it up.

There was the all-night ache in my stomach after I had climbed a neighbor's tree and eaten stolen, unripe peaches.

There was the morning when I thought I would fall dead from fear after I had stepped with my bare feet upon a bright little green garden snake.

And there were the long, slow, drowsy days and nights of drizzling rain. (1951, 53–55)

After reading the passage, students considered the following questions about it in small groups:

1. To what senses does Wright appeal in this passage? List as many examples of each as you can find.
2. What comparisons does he use? Make a list of as many as you find.
3. Overall, what do you think Richard thought about this time in his life?
4. What feeling did you have after reading the passage?

After sharing their reports on the questions, students individually chose a special event that they recalled with great pleasure and wrote a series of images similar to Wright's (the assignment is shown in Figure 9.1 on the following page). When they had finished, they shared their pieces in small groups. The groups provided feedback by answering the questions in Figure 9.2. Then the students applied what they'd learned about describing settings to their developing narratives.

Other Setting and Scene Activities

Naming Colors

This lesson was developed by Lori Huebner and Sara Spachman, who teach at Curie Metropolitan High School, in Chicago, when they realized that their students did not have a very extensive vocabulary for writing about colors. Using swatches collected from paint stores, they analyzed how colors are named and found that the basic colors (red, blue, yellow, green, orange, carmine, cyan, magenta, etc.) are usually modified in some way: canary yellow, sea green, barn red, burnt orange. The following brief passage from *Jaws*, by Peter Benchley, in which a man is submerged, protected by a large metal cage, uses some of these kinds of color descriptions:

> He glanced downward, started to look away, then snapped his eyes down again. Rising at him from the darkling blue—slowly, smoothly—was the shark. It rose with no apparent effort, an angel of death gliding toward an appointment foreordained. Hooper stared, enthralled, impelled to flee but unable to move. As the fish drew nearer, he marveled at its colors: the flat brown-grays seen on the surface had vanished. The top of the immense body was a hard ferrous gray, bluish where dappled with streaks of sun. Beneath the lateral line, all was creamy, ghostly white.

To introduce this lesson, Lori and Sara wrote the word *orange* on the board and passed out swatches of orange paint colors. They asked the students to think of synonyms for *orange*, objects or animals that are always thought of as orange, and specific adjectives signifying a particular shade of orange (*burnt* orange, *neon* orange). They then gave students the homework assignment shown in Figure 9.3 on page 118.

The next day, the class played the color relay game. The object of the color relay game, played by teams of three or four (each team was identified by a symbol they could stamp next to their suggestions), was to come up with the most original color names. At each color station was a set of paint swatches for that color and a game sheet. Moving from station to station in timed intervals, each team recorded (and stamped) their suggestions for names on the game sheet (no duplicates of names already there were allowed). The game rules are shown in Figure 9.4 on page 120.

After the game, volunteers compiled the words for each basic color on long scrolls of white paper decorated with designs and drawings, which were hung in the classroom for student reference. Sara Spachman maintains these lists on her website,

Pick a topic. Choose some period in your life that you remember fondly or some experience that you enjoyed very much. Here are some possibilities:

1. a day at an amusement park

2. a camping trip

3. a shopping excursion

4. a hike

5. a party

6. a school or professional athletic event

7. a fishing trip

8. a special holiday dinner or picnic

9. a parade

10. a visit to a museum or library

Prewrite. List all the things you remember about this experience. Include sights, sounds, smells, other sense impressions, and your reactions.

Write. Use this list of ideas to develop your montage of details. Try to capture the specifics of each idea so that your reader will share your pleasant memories. Use specific details and comparisons.

Figure 9.1 *Montage of Details*

1. How do you think the writer wants you, the reader, to feel?

2. What details are most effective?

3. What parts of the montage are unclear? How might they be clarified?

4. What questions should the writer answer by including more detail? Try to list three or four.

Figure 9.2 *Providing Feedback to Your Classmates*

Choose two colors (other than orange, which we used as an example in class) and list nine or ten synonyms for that color:

- actual words that mean the same color (for example, *tangerine* for *orange*)
- things that are universally known to be that color (for example, an orange *basketball* or an orange *sunrise*)
- specific adjectives that describe a certain shade of the color (for example, *burnt* orange)

Do not include

- generic words like *light*, *dark*, *medium*, and *pale*
- color adjectives like *red* orange and *yellow* orange

Try to be as creative as possible. The more interesting your synonyms, the better. You may use a thesaurus. Your homework will help your team when you play the color relay game tomorrow.

Figure 9.3   *Color Homework Assignment*

s.spachman.tripod.com/Narrative/StylizedNarrative/greatcolorlist.htm. The lists for red and green are shown below.

Red

apple red	like a pepper
blood red	like raw meat
brick red	like a robin's chest
burgundy	like a Santa suit
cardinal red	like spaghetti sauce
cherry	like a stop light
crimson	like a stop sign
fire	like a sunburn
fire-truck red	like a sunset
fruit punch	like a clown's nose
garnet	like a tongue
hot sauce	like a Valentine
ketchup	lipstick red
like a Coke can	lobster
like a devil	maroon
like Dorothy's slippers	pepperoni red
like embarrassment	raspberry
like a flame	rose
like a heart	ruby
like Hell	rust
like Kool-Aid	scarlet
like a lady-bug	strawberry
like Mars	tomato
watermelon	

Green

algae
apple green
army green/camouflage
avocado
broccoli green
cabbage
chartreuse
chalkboard green
cilantro
clover
cucumber
emerald
evergreen
Exorcist green
fern green
forest green
frog green
grape
grass
guava
hunter green
jade
jalapeno
kelly green (Irish green)
kelp
kiwi
lake-water green
leaf green
leprechaun green
lettuce
like a dragon
like a garden
like a grasshopper
like a lizard

like a pickle
like a parrot
like unripe bananas
like a willow tree
like Godzilla
like money
like oregano
like Oscar the Grouch
like the Statue of Liberty
like a watermelon rind
lime
mint
moldy green
monster green
moss
olive
parakeet green
pea green
pear
pine
sea green
sea weed green
spinach
spring green
string-bean green
swamp green
teal
traffic-light green
turquoise
turtle green
verdant
vomit green

The Abandoned Farmhouse Lesson: The Power of Setting

This lesson was developed by Seth MacLowry, a teacher at Maine Township West High School, in Des Plaines, Illinois, to help his students incorporate sensory details and figurative language in narrative and learn how the setting of a story can play an important role in developing a story. It goes beyond lessons presented earlier in that it relies on students' imaginations to conjure up the concrete imagery, just as they must do in writing about their own experiences. Here Seth describes it in his own words:

> I tell my students to close their eyes, put their heads down on their desks, and imagine in their heads the following scene as I describe it. (I always turn the lights off as well. Also, I never read the visualization verbatim but improvise.)

1. You may start writing when I say go and you must stop writing when I say stop.

2. You must write at least ONE idea at each station. Your team will lose five points for each station you miss.

3. You may not REPEAT what another team has already written. If you do, a point will be deducted from your team's overall score for each duplication.

4. Your synonyms must be genuine synonyms (like *tangerine* for *orange*) OR a specific adjective-noun combination (*light yellow* is NOT specific; *vomit yellow* IS specific).

5. Your synonyms must make sense (*vomit black* doesn't make a whole lot of sense to most people).

6. Your similes and metaphors must be universal enough to make sense beyond this classroom. (You shouldn't write "purple like Monica's shirt," because Monica's shirt isn't always purple and not everyone knows who Monica is. "Purple like Barney" is much more universal.)

7. You may use your homework to help your team during the game.

Figure 9.4 *Color Relay Game Rules*

Imagine that you are in the countryside, maybe a lake house that you've visited in Wisconsin or Michigan or a farm in Iowa or rural Illinois. You are on vacation with two or three of your best friends or maybe your brothers and sisters. It is an absolutely perfect fall morning, the temperature is in the seventies, no humidity, the sky is clear, and you decide to go for a bike ride. Really picture the exact bike that you are riding. As you leave the house where you are staying, you hear the crunching of gravel under your tires, and you head out onto a one-lane country road that you've never explored before.

The rich smell of dark earth mingled with manure fills your nostrils. As you look around, you can see, on both sides of you, cornfields lined with chest-high corn ready for harvest. Sometimes you pass a field that has much smaller, darker green plants that look like they might be soybeans. Once in a while you pass a rundown barn by the side of the road, the kind of barn that is leaning heavily to one side and sagging inward. On the roof is an old advertisement for 7-Up that has faded in the sun. You see solitary red silos off in the distance, and every once in a while, you can see the dust of a pickup truck in the distance. You can see the dust before you hear the truck, but as the dust trail comes closer, you can hear the rumbling, and you pull to the side of the road as the pickup rattles by. Then it is silent again. A hawk circles high above you, floating on the wind.

After you've been biking for a couple of hours, you decide to take a rest, and you hop off your bikes. There is no one else in sight. This is the kind of place where you can just put down your bikes, and you don't have to worry about them getting stolen or damaged. You look off into the distance across a field and see that there seems to be an abandoned farmhouse. You decide to explore. You cross through a cornfield until you get to what must have once been a gravel driveway but is now filled with knee-high grass and weeds that scratch against your exposed legs as you walk closer to the house. You get to the front of the house and stop. To the left of the house is an old oak tree. The house looks like no one has lived there for fifty years. Really picture the house in your head, every detail of it. Now open your eyes, but keep the image of the house clearly in your minds.

I tell students to open their eyes and I ask two of my better students to come to the board to write down details so that I can focus on monitoring the discussion. I also explain that this is a "yes, and" game, which means if someone says that the shutters are blue, you don't say, "No, they are red!" but rather "Yes, the shutters are blue, and each slat on the shutters has a layer of dust on it."

I start calling on students, asking for one specific detail about the house. My job is to encourage them, compliment them on the really specific details ("the forest-green paint on the shutters is peeling up like wood shavings, exposing the rotting gray wood beneath"), and push them to be specific when they use general terms. If a student says that the door looks "old," I ask for specific details that show that it is aging. If he says there are steps leading up to the porch, I ask how many steps. If she says the oak tree is big, I elicit a specific height ("thirty feet tall" or "its branches reach above the second story of the house"). This activity gets kids so excited that it is very easy to make sure that every student contributes details; in fact, the two students writing on the board usually struggle to keep up.

Once I've spent about ten minutes collecting details on the outside of the house, I tell the students to put their heads down on their desks again and continue the visualization:

You decide to explore the inside of the house, so you walk up the three steps [I use whatever details they've just suggested], and they creak and sag under your feet. As you pull the screen door open, it tumbles off the one hinge holding it up and rattles to the ground. You jump back, but then push the heavy door open. You enter the front foyer, and you see to your left a flight of stairs leading up to what you assume would be the bedrooms. There is a long hall that leads down to a kitchen area. But what strikes you most is when you turn to your right. There is a living room that is fully furnished, and it seems as though the family who lived there must have just picked up in a moment of haste and left everything behind. All the furniture looks like it must be at least fifty years old. Imagine every last detail in the room, every item that they left behind. Now open your eyes.

I repeat the same process I went through with the outside of the house, focusing on all of the little items that might be around: photographs, newspapers, desks, and so on. I make sure to try to direct students to sensory details (smells, textures) and also to similes ("the dust caught in the ray of light that slants through the hole in the roof danced like ballerinas in the light").

I try to leave at least ten minutes at the end of class for students to write down as many of the details as they would like. Then I hand out the homework assignment [see Figure 9.5]. I let students know that they can use any or all of the specific details that we generated in class. They have creative license to start the story whenever they want, make up whatever plot that they want, and so forth. The only requirement is that *every sentence* must have at least one specific detail.

This lesson was inspired by the poem "Abandoned Farmhouse," by Ted Kooser (1980). (Kooser received the 2005 Pulitzer Prize for poetry for his 2004 book *Delights and Shadows*. He is currently serving his second term as poet laureate at the Library of Congress.) I show the poem to my students after the writing assignment, and we look at how Kooser literally uses setting details to tell the story of the family that used to live there. I often begin the short discussion by saying with a smile, "You'd never believe it, but I was reading some poetry yesterday, and I came across this poem called 'Abandoned Farmhouse.'"

Abandoned Farmhouse

He was a big man, says the size of his shoes
on a pile of broken dishes by the house;
a tall man too, says the length of the bed
in an upstairs room; and a good, God-fearing man,
says the Bible with a broken back
on the floor below the window, dusty with sun;
but not a man for farming, say the fields
cluttered with boulders and the leaky barn.

Write a narrative of at least two pages, double spaced and typed, that describes the abandoned farmhouse. (Many students write four or five pages—or more—and you will receive *extra credit* if you get fired up and write an entire story.) You have a lot of freedom in this assignment. You can use some or all of the details that we listed together on the board. You can make up all new details if you prefer. You can include yourself as a character in the narrative, or you can just describe the house and let the house be the main character of the story. You can create characters if you prefer.

However, *every sentence* in the narrative must contain *at least* one specific detail or contain at least one simile or metaphor!

Remember, the details of the story and the objects that you describe will tell the story of this house and why it was abandoned! Let the setting tell the story!

Figure 9.5   *Abandoned Farmhouse Assignment*

A woman lived with him, says the bedroom wall
papered with lilacs and the kitchen shelves
covered with oilcloth, and they had a child
says the sandbox made from a tractor tire.
Money was scarce, say the jars of plum preserves
and canned tomatoes sealed in the cellar-hole,
and the winters cold, say the rags in the window frames.
It was lonely here, says the narrow gravel road.
Something went wrong, says the empty house
in the weed-choked yard. Stones in the fields
say he was not a farmer; the still-sealed jars
in the cellar say she left in a nervous haste.
And the child? Its toys are strewn in the yard
like branches after a storm: a rubber cow,
a rusty tractor with a broken plow,
a doll in overalls. Something went wrong, they say.

Oftentimes I will also read one or two paragraphs of a story written by a former student. I remind students that they can begin their story on their bike, or in front of the house, or just leave themselves out altogether and let the house tell its own story. I want students to know that they have complete creative control. I reemphasize that the *only thing* I will grade is whether they have at least one specific detail in every sentence. They don't have to finish the story as long as they submit the two pages required.

While students get one day in class to work on the computer, I usually have the papers due a few days after that so that students have a chance to develop their stories thoroughly. Before I have my students turn the assignment in, I have them reread their story in class and underline and/or number what they consider to be their top ten or fifteen details. It works as a fun little self-evaluation. Sometimes I have each student share aloud one of his favorite details to the class.

I don't use a scoring rubric for this assignment: if my kids write for the required length and have strong details throughout, they get an A. For whatever reason, the archetype of the abandoned farmhouse seems to span race and class in a way that I don't understand. This has always been one of my no-fail lessons. (I've tried the same guided visualization with a haunted house, and it doesn't work nearly as well. For one thing, the haunted house has been so overused in movies that students' work ends up being very clichéd instead of original.)

The following are the first five paragraphs of a paper written by a ninth grader in response to the Seth MacLowry's abandoned farmhouse prompt. It appeared in the high school literary magazine.

Discovering Jonis
by Erin Harrington

I woke up in my truck, in a ditch, next to a corn field. It must have been night, because it was very difficult to see. I tried to recall what happened, how I got to where I found myself. Suddenly my eyelids became heavy again, and immediately I was asleep.

"Why must I be a teenager in love?" I sang to myself, along with the fuzzy radio of my rusted, "almost-as-old-as-I-am" Toyota Pickup. I was on my way to a barn party at my cousin Jack's farm, at a quarter past five. I was cruising well over the speed limit, but not nearly as fast as most of my other high school friends drive. However, I couldn't tell exactly how much slower I was going because the speedometer on "Loraine" had been broken for years.

The sun was beginning to set on an absolutely majestic warm September evening. As I gazed thoughtfully into the crimson sunset, I began to wonder what my religious father would say if he knew that I was on my way to a party that would almost definitely result in a barn full of drunken teenagers. Guilt began to swim in the pit of my stomach. I noticed a hawk circling over the cornfield to my left. It reminded me of my father with its noble authority and admirable strength. I looked up to my father, which is probably why I was feeling such guilt.

I whizzed past a car for the first time in ten miles, which woke me from my trance. All of the sudden I screamed as a man walked out of the sea of corn stalks in front of my car. In slow motion, my truck swerved sharply to the left and landed in the ditch. The man walked casually toward the wreckage that was once Loraine, looked inside, saw that I was alive and conscious, and walked back into the depths of the yellow-brown corn.

I woke up from my dream startled because it was like reliving what had happened just hours before. I got out of what used to be my truck, and wandered onto the road. I noticed an area where the corn parted, and it beckoned me to investigate. As I drew closer I saw a gravel path, about six inches wide, that led into the field. I followed the path, hoping to come across some help. The stars above me seemed to shimmer and gleam brighter than I had ever seen them. They created a friendly contrast to the corn stalks that looked like short sickly people begging and bowing in the wind. They looked deathly and they made rustling noises that continued with the breeze. My eyes were unexpectedly drawn to a black silhouette in the darkness. It was an old abandoned farmhouse.

10

TEACHING STUDENTS HOW TO REVISE

Teachers of writing know only too well that students do not like to revise. Many do not like to write in the first place, but to insist that they revise is to add insult to injury. Janet Emig has concluded that "students do not voluntarily revise school-sponsored writing" (1971, 93). However, such a conclusion does not explain anything, and other research contradicts it. In a carefully designed study, Bridwell (1980) focused on the nature, extent, and quality of revisions made by one hundred randomly selected high school seniors and found that, given the opportunity, students make fairly extensive revisions. For this experiment students were asked to write about something they knew well in a way that another twelfth grader reading it would "be able to recognize the thing or place if he or she ever got the chance to see it for real" (202). They were encouraged to write down facts they wished to remember on specially provided sheets they could bring to class with them. They did the writing over a series of three class periods. On the first day they recorded any ideas they had for the essay. On the second day they wrote a draft in blue ink, crossing out the material they changed as they wrote. On the third day they considered their first draft, made revisions on it if they wished, and wrote a final draft, this time using black ink.

Overall, the students in the study made 6,129 revisions, or on average, about 61 per student, almost half of which were made on the first draft. Most of the revisions (56 percent) were at the surface and lexical levels. Surface-level revisions included changes in mechanics such as spelling, punctuation, and capitalization. Word-level changes included the addition, deletion, or substitution of single words. Another 18 percent of the revisions had to do with changed phrases. The remaining 26 percent were at the sentence level or the multisentence level: additions, deletions, and reorderings. However, no revisions were made at the text level—changing the overall organization or the major ideas of the text, substantially reordering or rethinking the ideas in a text, or rejecting a topic and writing about another.

An important question relative to revision concerns the effects of the revision: Does it result in a better piece of writing? Hansen (1978) concludes that revising is a waste of time. Bracewell, Scardamalia, and Bereiter (1978) even find evidence that revisions by eighth graders make their compositions worse. However, Bridwell (1980) also examines differences in the quality of the first and second drafts and finds highly significant differences in favor of the revised drafts, indicating that at least older students can revise effectively.

The Process of Revision

Nold (1981) argues that revision involves evaluating a text against the writer's plan as it relates to the writer's intended audience, persona, meaning, and semantic layout. She claims, "The complexity of the review sub-process is bounded by the depth of the planning sub-process that has preceded it: writers cannot match the text against their intentions if they have not elaborated upon them" (73). She also points out the corollary that texts that involve minimal planning, such as freewriting exercises, "can be reviewed only against criteria that are constant across all [written] communication tasks" (73)—spelling and legibility, for example.

Revision, of course, involves more than evaluation. The successful reviser must note deficiencies *and* "think of a good way to change them" (74). Hayes and Flower (1980, 18) present a similar model with one major difference. They discriminate between editing and reviewing. Editing is defined as a subprocess that "is triggered automatically and may occur in brief episodes interrupting other processes." Reviewing, on the other hand, involves a decision "to devote a period of time to systematic examination and improvement of the text" that has already been produced. Both, however, rely on matching text to intentions *and* producing a change when needed.

Scardamalia and Bereiter (1983) argue that the failure to revise might lie with problems in the production system. Their model posits an "executive routine" for switching from generating text to assessing it. However, because writing is so complex, making that switch from generating to critiquing may be very difficult for children. The model also posits the following sequence of tasks:

- comparing or evaluating the actual text against the intended text
- diagnosing the problem underlying the perceived mismatch between the actual and the intended text
- deciding whether or not to change the plan
- choosing a tactic to solve the problem
- generating a change in the text

Failing to revise might stem from failing at any of these tasks.

These analyses assume that the writer's intentions for a text are formed prior to writing. I suspect that is not completely accurate. Rather, I suspect that intentions may change as the piece of writing develops and that changes in intentions may not be recognized, because they are hidden in the mental processes of the writer, which are not evident to researchers. I suspect that students who acquire criteria for judging writing may be able to apply them in revisions more efficiently than those who have no or underdeveloped criteria. In the instruction presented in the previous chapters, criteria for judging texts are explicit. They are conveyed by the focus on the strategies that students are learning to use. I would argue that if teaching does not make the criteria explicit, no amount of revision will be helpful. If we want students to include dialogue in narratives, we need to teach them how to include dialogue. One of the criteria is that dialogue should be included. Knowing that and knowing how to produce it, students can include it in revision. If they know neither of these things, no amount of revision is very likely to produce dialogue. In other words, *instruction should be both the impetus for revision and the guide to it.*

Kinds of Revision

Students in all of our classes were typically concerned with revision as a process of making their papers neat. I was always tickled to see three or four bottles of correction fluid circulating among groups of students. When we collected their pretests, we discovered that the correction fluid had been used to remove misspellings and words and punctuation marks about which they'd had second thoughts. However, these were what researchers call cosmetic revisions. Our students did not make substantive revisions involving the addition, removal, or rearrangement of large chunks of text.

Students need to learn that revising (*revision*) is a process of *reseeing* what has been written. If writers can *see* what they have written in a different way, they will be able to improve it. If they cannot resee what they have written, they will have no need to change it. For many writers, the best aid to reseeing and revising is having others respond to what they have written.

Feedback from others often lets a writer know how material can be added, cut, or rearranged to clarify meaning or to make the writing more effective. When my MAT students and I concentrated on teaching revising, we usually provided a composition written by one of us and asked students to help us revise it by asking us questions and making suggestions. Here is one of the pieces I wrote for this purpose:

A Close Call

My Scout troop was part of an organization that owned a camp about forty miles east of Cleveland, Ohio. The camp was a mile or so from a ruined maple sugar shack. The large, rusty pans for boiling the sap are still there. But the roof and doors are gone. About a mile and a half from "our" camp is the Fifty-Foot Falls. It probably is the highest waterfall in Northern Ohio.

One Saturday in March many years ago, twelve of us Boy Scouts left our base camp, about forty miles east of Cleveland, Ohio, to hike to the Fifty-Foot Falls. The skies were dark with clouds, and it was cold, not freezing, but only in the mid-thirties. We carried sleeping bags, ponchos, food, cooking gear, first-aid kits, and other equipment because we planned to camp overnight on the banks of the Grand River. We hiked for at least two hours across farmland and finally began to follow a small stream. The stream bed dropped more and more steeply so that, before long, we were in a shallow gorge. When the top of the bank was about twenty feet above our heads, we stopped to listen for the sounds of water falling.

The leaders and other Scouts started up a steep path to the right. I continued along the lower path along the face of the nearly vertical cliff for a hundred yards or so. It narrowed to about twelve inches wide at a point where the gorge turned gently to the right. At that point I was about thirty feet below the top and could hear the unmistakable sound of water falling. The path leveled out, and I as I rounded the bend I could hear the loud clatter of water falling against stone. I knew I was close, and I wanted to get closer. I edged carefully along the path for another fifty feet. At this point the path was about six inches wide and becoming even more narrow. It was so narrow I soon had to give up walking forward. I put my chest tight against the wall of crumbly shale, feet spread out, left foot facing forward along the path and right foot facing backwards. I could inch my left foot forward and bring the right foot up to meet it. Since my backpack was heavy, I hugged the cliff and could smell the pungent oily shale. The crashing sound of the falling water was quite loud now.

Then, turning my head carefully to the left, I could see the whole waterfall. The snow had been melting for a few days, and the stream was swollen with the water. It tumbled over boulders and a fallen tree for about thirty feet into a giant shale dish. From there it streaked to the bottom, for another fifty feet, splashed high, formed a stream, and continued at the bottom of the gorge. What a sight! I felt like an explorer discovering something for the first time.

Suddenly, I heard the voice of our Scout leader. "Hillocks, where are you?"

"Down here, sir. You should see the falls from here. It's great."

"Are you on that narrow path?"

"Yes, sir. But I'm OK."

"You only think you're OK. I told you that's a dangerous path. It tapers completely out a few yards from you. Come back the way you went in. You can't go farther forward."

I looked forward. He was right. The path narrowed to nothing about ten feet away. "I see," I said. "I'll move back along the path."

"Well, make it snappy. No one knows how long that shale will hold anyone up. You are on what amounts to a little ledge. So move carefully. Try not to dislodge the shale. Or you'll go to the bottom."

I took a deep breath and moved my right foot back the way I had come. I pulled my left foot along after it. Then I took a long step with my right foot, put my weight on it and began to pull the left foot along. Suddenly I felt my right foot going through the shale. I looked down to the right and watched a three-foot section of the path sliding down. It slid for ten feet and then fell to the bottom. Then I realized that I was perched on some sort of overhang. If I slipped ten feet, I would fall to the bottom, just like the shale. I froze to the wall of the gorge. When I looked to the left, I saw that the section I had stood on no more than a minute before had also broken off and fallen away. I had about a three-foot ledge holding me up. I tried to dig my fingertips into the little crevices of the shale for a handhold. I could feel the shale cutting into my fingers under the nails, but there was no hold to be had. I reached far above my head to a tiny oak sapling. I could just grasp it with my left hand, but when I tried to pull myself up, it came out of the shale. I let it drop. My brain seemed numb with fright. I had no idea what to do. I could feel myself shaking. I wondered what would happen if I could not get off the cliff. I actually thought about staying put through the night. I did not know what else to do, but I also feared that the shale would give way under my continued weight.

Finally, when my brain began working again, I looked about for some solution. I could see a maple sapling, four or five feet to my right and twelve feet above my head. It was about six feet tall. I hollered as loudly as I could to the guys on top, "You guys have any ropes?" Every Scout was supposed to have a rope about twelve feet in length. It was a troop rule. I could hear them talking above. At the same time, I could hear lumps of shale breaking off and sliding before dropping off into the air.

Someone yelled, "We've got three ropes." Great, I thought, eleven guys up there and only three ropes. Really prepared. Somebody above yelled, "Go to the sapling. We'll tie one end to a tree and throw the other end down there." If I could reach that, I could reach the rope. The problem was, I couldn't see any way I could reach the sapling.

I moved to the right cautiously, dug the inside of my right heel into the shale, dug my fingers in, and lifted my left foot. As soon as I brought it down, the shale beneath my feet rolled away, and I began to slide. I dug my fingernails into the crumbling stone and felt it cut in under the nails. I was certain I was going over the edge. After about three feet, my slide stopped, and I froze to the wall once again. I wondered if I should drop my backpack.

I thought what a dumb idea it had been to take this path. I saw myself sliding to the edge of the overhang and falling right to the bottom, flipping over a couple of times before I smashed into the stone below. Slate is a soft rock, but not that soft. I clutched the cliff as tightly as I could.

Then I remembered the hatchet on my belt. Maybe I could use it to hack steps into the shale. With difficulty I reached it and chopped into the shale at the level of my knee and as far to the right as I could reach. Several blows gouged out a step. I felt guilty about the damage I was doing to the hatchet. Slowly I moved my right foot over and up to the step. Then I brought my left foot up and hugged the wall. Despite the cold spring air, I was sweating profusely. I thought I felt the shale shifting under my feet. I quickly slipped out the hatchet from its case, being careful not to drop it. Several blows cut out another step on my right. I carefully moved up into that step clutching the cliff and this time, getting a mouthful of shale. I still could not reach the larger sapling.

I kept thinking the shale was crumbling, as I began to cut another step. I became impatient and brought the hatchet down too hard at an oblique angle. It bounced off hard and the vibration of the blow went through my forearm. I nearly dropped the hatchet. I clutched the shale with my free hand.

I could feel the shale under my left foot crumbling, and I hurried to bring the hatchet back into action. I managed a new step in five or six blows and put the hatchet back in its sheath at my waist. As I moved my right foot toward the new step, the shale beneath my left foot broke away, and I was left clutching the cliff again. I felt stranded on my right foot, my left dangling below. I closed my eyes and pulled with all my strength. My left foot scraped against the cliff wall trying to make it to the step. Finally, my left foot was on the new step. I stood up on the step. I reached as high as I could but still could not reach the sapling. I was a few feet short. Suddenly my legs went rubbery, and I hugged the cliff. I looked down and then up. I slipped my hatchet out of its sheath and slammed it into the shale, one, two, three, four, five blows to cut another step. Then I reached as high as I could above the step and struck into the shale to cut a handhold. I did not want a repetition of my last step that left me dangling. I put my right hand on the handhold, hugged the cliff, and lifted my right foot to edge it onto the step sideways. I did not want only a toehold. As I shifted my weight to my right foot, the shale under my left broke away. But the new step held and I could just reach the sapling with both hands.

I wondered if it would hold me and my full backpack as I tried to pull up on it. I saw it was going to be impossible. I pulled out the hatchet again and cut three toeholds into the face of the cliff above me. Then I pulled hard and put my right toes into the first hold. Then the left. Then the right again. Suddenly my left leg was over the sapling and I pulled myself up to straddle it. I leaned back in relief and felt the sapling bend backward over the overhang. I quickly leaned forward.

"Grab the rope! Grab the rope!" the boys above me yelled. They heaved the rope down toward the sapling. At this point, the slope of the gorge was only about forty-five degrees. I could crawl to the rope. As I did, the shale beneath my knees slid away and went over the edge. The boys above shouted, "Get the rope. Get the rope." I finally reached the rope and tied a bowline around my waist. I took the rope gratefully in both hands and pulled and walked myself to the top. When I reached the top, I sat down exhausted. "I'm sure glad you guys had ropes," I said. When I looked down, I could see the whole waterfall just as well from there. But I thought I would never forget seeing it from my narrow perch on the face of the cliff.

Adding

Writers add material during revision for two main reasons: (1) to clarify and (2) to increase interest or impact on the reader. After reading my story, students generally had a number of questions. Most had never seen shale or a shale cliff eroded away by streams. They did not understand that shale is a very soft sedimentary rock made of layers of fine compressed sand laid down thousands of years ago. The layers are usually very thin, break easily from a cliff or stream bed, and crumble in the fingers. Readers who did not know what shale was did not know a cliff face could crumble so easily. In response to their questions, I made up the following addition and asked students to help me decide where it should be placed:

> The walls of the gorge on either side of us were made of thin layers of shale, a soft, blue-gray and sometimes reddish-brown sedimentary rock that crumbles easily in your fingers. The layers were no more than a quarter to a half inch thick, most much thinner. Here and there grass, saplings, and other little plants grew out of the shale.

This addition provides a picture of what the shale was like and prepares the reader for its important role in what is to come.

My student readers also questioned other points. One girl asked, "Why did you take the path down when the others went up? Didn't the leaders tell you it was dangerous?" To deal with these questions, I wrote:

> "OK, you guys," one of the leaders said, "we'll head up to the top here. That low trail is washed out up ahead. It gives you a good view of the falls, but it's too dangerous without ropes." I looked ahead at the lower trail. I went straight along until it curved around a bend in the face of the cliff. I wanted to see what lay beyond the bend. So I followed the lower path for another hundred yards or so.

I let students help me find a place to insert this added material.

Cutting

Young writers frequently include material that is irrelevant to the story. Donald Graves (1983) talks about the "bed-to-bed" stories of middle school students. A character gets out of bed in the morning, goes through his daily routine, finally encounters the main event of the story, and continues on with his day, finally going to bed at night. The first paragraph of my story is an example of irrelevant material. I may have been fascinated by the sugar camp, but my fascination does not make it relevant.

In early drafts, our students often included such unrelated details at the beginning of their stories. Some writers had difficulty getting started on what they really wanted to say. They might first write several sentences that were not very closely related to their main idea. A good way to test the relatedness of a sentence is to ask these questions: *What does this sentence tell the reader that is important to the main point of the writing? Would its removal interfere with the reader's understanding or appreciation of something important in the writing?* If the answers are *nothing* and *no*, then the sentence should probably go.

Let's test two other sentences in the story:

1. It probably is the biggest waterfall in Northern Ohio.
2. As I rounded the bend, I could hear the loud clatter of water falling against stone.

How high the falls are is important. But that the falls may be the largest in Northern Ohio is not important to the main point. Even if the sentence is removed, readers learn later how high the falls are. Therefore, since the answers are *nothing* and *no*, this line can surely go. What about the next sentence? My reaction to the falls is also important, but if I take it out, readers will still understand the main point of the writing. Nevertheless, it indicates that I am coming closer to the falls: I can hear it but not see it. This sentence does contribute to a better understanding or appreciation of the story. It should stay.

Rearranging

Often writers move large parts of their writing around. After writing a first draft, they find themselves dissatisfied with the sequence of the material. They may move several paragraphs or even several pages because they believe this new arrangement will be more effective. In writing about their own experiences, writers tend to provide a great deal of background information at the beginning. Often this background information is not really part of the story. In fact, it stands like a barrier between the reader and the story. It may be necessary to understanding some part of the story, but it may not have to appear before the story begins. In the following example, the background information comes first. As you read, think about how the writer might rearrange the material to make it more interesting right from the beginning.

The Contest

I started racing bicycles a long time ago when I was in third grade. I can't really remember, but I'll bet I was racing on tricycles long before that. As long as I can remember, I've wanted to go faster than anyone else on a bike. Those days were great. We'd line up on the street. I could hardly wait for someone to shout. "On your mark, get set, go." I would shoot off the mark and go like crazy.

But one day last June was different. I straddled my bike, waiting. Was it too high? Yeah, the seat was too high. My stomach churned. I should probably adjust the seat. But the race would start soon. Suddenly, I realized that my hands hurt me. I looked down at them. I had squeezed my fingernails into both palms so hard that a line of little half-moon marks showed. What a difference a real race makes, I thought.

The following version of the previous introduction rearranges the parts.

The Contest

I straddled my bike, waiting, my stomach churning. Suddenly, I realized that my hands hurt. I looked down at them. I had squeezed my fingernails into my palms so hard that a line of little half-moon marks showed. What a difference a real race makes, I thought.

I had started racing my bicycle in the third grade, and probably I had raced tricycles long before that. But this was a real race with officials, a starting gun, judges, spectators, and timers.

The second introduction begins with the tension experienced by the writer and brings the reader close in to the action. Most readers are more immediately pulled in by the second. They feel the dramatic tension right away and want to know what will happen. In the first, however, no tension develops for the first several sentences.

Let's look at my story "Close Call" again. Would the story be improved by removing the first two paragraphs? If so, would any parts of those paragraphs have to be reinserted later in the story? Where and how would those parts be repositioned?

After working through these important ideas about revising using examples similar to those given here, we provided students with the guide to revising in Figure 10.1.

Revising a Story's Beginning

During eighteen years of teaching classes at inner-city schools, we had worked hard at helping our students use more interesting openings for their stories. We showed students models of good openings, we led discussions, we taught criteria, and we asked students to apply the criteria. Our efforts, by and large, were unsuccessful in the sense that most students did not write strong openings on the posttest. A few did, but only a few.

In 1995, we worked with ninth graders at Chicago's Curie High School. We rethought our work on beginnings and realized that we had been concentrating on declarative knowledge but had not taught the procedures for bringing strong introductions into being. We invented new lessons that had much greater effect.

Lesson 1

The first of the lessons concentrating on procedures for inventing beginnings came after more general work on revision. It was qualitatively different from activities we had used in the past, because students had to use strategies of selection. For the lesson, Sarah Ruth Levine, now a teacher at Curie High School, produced a story with four alternate

---

Adding. Test the adequacy of what you have included by asking these questions:

> Will additional details help readers understand more fully?
> Will additional details help the writing achieve an impact on the reader?

If the answer to either is *yes*, add the necessary details.

Cutting. Test the relatedness of sentences and ideas by asking these questions:

> What does this sentence (passage) tell the reader that is important to the main point of the writing?
> Will its removal interfere with the reader's understanding or appreciation of something important in the writing?

If the answers are *nothing* and *no*, the sentence should probably go.

Rearranging. Test your arrangement by asking the following questions:

> Does the arrangement of sentences and ideas interest the reader and generally evoke the response the writer wishes?
> Does the arrangement highlight important ideas?

If the answers are *no*, then rearrange the material.

Figure 10.1   *Guide to Revising*

beginnings. The students' task was to rank these beginnings from weakest to strongest and try to explain their reasons. Sarah explained that they would first read the narrative without the beginning. She said, "Before we can begin to look at the beginnings, we need to know what the main event of the narrative is." She asked why we needed to know that. Students were not sure, but some thought that the beginning should be related to the main event. She asked students to make up a title for the story. This focused their attention on the theme of the story and helped them identify the major event. They summarized the main event and wrote their summary at the top of their copy of the story, along with a title.

Next Sarah distributed the beginnings she'd written and asked students, in small groups, to decide which beginning was best, second best, and so on. She asked them to write down as many reasons as they could for ranking the beginnings as they did. She explained that later on in class, groups would compare their choices and determine what kinds of things make a good beginning.

Ms. Levine's Narrative—No Beginning

One day we skated for about a half hour. Then we stopped for a break and hot chocolate. When we stepped back onto the ice, my aunt said what she always said: "Don't skate too fast! You'll knock yourself right out!" That was it. I decided to play a trick on her.

I don't know why. Maybe it was the laughter that I heard from the two girls in green sweaters who did figure-eights near the middle of the rink. Maybe it was the way my friend Eva rolled her eyes. Whatever it was, I found myself skating faster and faster around the ice rink. I could hear my skates scraping the ice beneath me. I could feel the wind on my face, fluttering in my ears like a flag. I felt the cold and then heat surge to my fingertips, and from across the rink I heard my aunt call my name. Then I put one skate in front of me and fell onto the ice. I slid halfway across the rink, scraping frost from the ice onto my clothes as I slid. Then I screamed "Aaah!" and pretended that I had knocked myself right out.

I opened my eyes just in time to see my aunt skidding out onto the ice in her street shoes. Her mouth was open and her hands were stretched out toward me. I sat up and said, "Just kidding!" But my aunt didn't laugh. She stood on the ice, pointing her finger and yelling at me. I remember her saying that it was a rotten joke to play. "Come on, Aunt Em, I was just kidding," I said.

My aunt's lower lip began to quiver and her eyes filled with glassy tears. I sat on the ice, feeling the cold and wet seep through my sweatpants. Around us skaters stopped and stared. I was sorry about the whole thing, sorry for scaring my aunt and making her cry. My aunt didn't even talk to me for the rest of the day.

Possible Beginnings

Beginning A: When I was nine, I used to go ice skating every Wednesday at an ice rink near my house. My aunt would drive my friend Eva and me to the ice rink and pay the two dollars to rent our skates. At the rink, we would change into sweatpants and sweatshirts, and then we could skate for an hour. On some days, my friend's mother would take us.

Beginning B: If there's one thing I used to love it was skating fast around the ice rink. I loved speeding up until my face and fingers grew cold and I could hear the wind make a fluttering, voom-voom sound in my ears. I have been ice skating since I was seven years old. By the time I was eleven, I was pretty good, even though I knew that I would never be good enough to be a professional. Still, I enjoy skating, and I used to go every week.

Beginning C: In general, I'm not the kind of person who plays tricks on people or tries to scare them on purpose. But there was something about the way my aunt kept nagging me when we went to the ice rink that made me feel a little bit evil. I felt like I had to teach her a lesson. That's why I did what I did.

Beginning D: I loved ice skating, but I hated going to the rink with my aunt. She always sat in the bleachers with a cup of watery hot chocolate, and every time my friend Eva and I skated by, she cupped her hands to her mouth and yelled, "Don't skate so fast! You'll knock yourself right out!"

In the class discussion following the reading and group work, groups disagreed about the best opening. Some had decided on C, but most had chosen D. None had chosen either A or B as the best. We were pleased with that result. Those who had chosen D, with C in second place, said C had too many sentences that were not related to the main point of the story. Students who had chosen C liked the sentence about Ms. Levine's feeling "a little bit evil." They argued that that was important to the story because it showed why she did what she did. All students agreed that A and B were not related much to the theme or the main event. But most thought that A was stronger than B, because B did little to develop the main event or even the characters.

Lesson 2

Our next activity was invented by Greg Lundberg, who is now a teacher at Maine Township East High School in Illinois. Greg wrote a narrative that required many revisions. After reading the composition, he projected it on the overhead and asked for suggestions. Here is the original:

> The first thing I did that morning was pour myself a bowl of Cap'n Crunch. I munched away for a while, watching cartoons until it was time to go to basketball practice.
>
> Afterwards, I was hungry, so I headed over to the local shopping mall. I went inside. I grabbed a candy bar and put it in my pocket. I looked right and left. I saw no one, so I made a bolt for the door. As soon as I stepped outside, I felt a hand on my shoulder. It was the security guard. He asked me to empty my pockets, but I said no. His voice was scary. He was angry and looked at me in a mean way.
>
> It really bothers me a lot when people look at me that way. I remember this other time when my teacher caught me spitting a spitball. She looked at me the same way.
>
> The security guard grabbed my arm and led me to a small room. He made me sit down in a chair. Then he left the room. I heard his footsteps disappearing down the hall, echoing like distant thunderclaps. He called my parents from the other room. I listened to the conversation through the wall. I could hear my father yelling at the other end of the phone.
>
> Then the guard came back. He told me that my parents would be by to pick me up in an hour and to stay where I was. I was scared and embarrassed. I didn't know what to do. The guard gave me one last look and left the room, closing the door hard behind him.

The students were enthusiastic and had many ideas about how to revise the piece. They insisted on cutting the opening three sentences; they wanted a more exciting opening. Greg crossed out the objectionable lines and asked them about other possibilities, making notes on the margins of the overhead. Students wanted to hear more about the guard, about the room where Greg was held, about his father's reaction, and what happened. Someone made a special request for dialogue. They also wanted to cut the lines about the teacher who had caught Greg with a spitball.

The next day, Greg brought back his revised piece of writing and thanked the students for their help. Here is the revision:

> It only took an instant to slip that big fat Snickers bar into my coat pocket. My mouth was already watering as I looked up and down the aisles of the brightly lit Osco in which I stood. Seeing no one, I made a move for the door. I measured my steps carefully, all the while wanting to break into a mad dash just to get out of there. No sooner had I stepped outside, though, than I felt a gargantuan hand clamp down on my shoulder, holding me back. It felt like the icy hand of the grim reaper.
>
> "All right, sonny boy," the security guard said in a low-pitched growl. "I know what's in your pocket. Hand it over and then let's take ourselves a little walk." His beady eyes seemed to penetrate my jacket like laser beams, focusing directly on the Snickers bar I had so carefully nestled there. The cheap tin star on his blue uniform was right in front of my eyes. I could not refuse. As I reached into my pocket for the hidden loot, my face flushed red.
>
> The guard led me to a small room with nothing else in it but a gray metal chair. He indicated, with a long, knobby finger, for me to sit down. The walls of the room were painted a dull white, but they were covered with scuff marks and cracking paint. There were brown water stains on the ceiling. A single fluorescent lamp dangled above me, throwing a cold white light on everything. It buzzed insistently like an electronic bumble bee.
>
> After sitting me down, the guard shot me another stare with his cold laser-beam eyes. "I'll be back," he boomed. "But first, I'm going to call your parents." He turned around and walked out. His footsteps echoed like thunderclaps as he walked down the hall to another room.
>
> "I'm dead meat," I thought, shuddering. In the distance, I heard the faint beep-beep-beep of the touch-tone pad as the guard dialed my home number. I strained my ears to listen to the conversation. I couldn't make out what my father was saying at the other end of the phone, though I heard the guard recounting my crime in vivid detail, adding words like "shocking" and "disappointed."
>
> The guard reappeared with a second chair in his right hand. He pulled the door shut, hard, sending a shockwave through the room that vibrated all the way up into my chair. "Your parents will be here in an hour," he said, his voice rumbling, as he proceeded to take a seat opposite me. "Stay put. And don't make a sound. I'm going to sit right here with you, too, just to make sure you follow the rules."
>
> The minutes ticked by like sludge through a flour sifter. I didn't look at that guard once in the next hour, though he stared at me almost without blinking. Just at the moment that I was sure I couldn't take it any more, the door opened. It was my father. And though I saw him mouthing the words, "Son, you're grounded," I knew that anything was better than another minute with the security guard with the laser-beam eyes.

Students Revise Their Own Beginnings

The next step in this series of lessons was to ask the ninth graders to select one of the three narratives they had written so far and revise it. In their small groups, they read their compositions aloud and made suggestions to one another in the same way they had made suggestions to Greg.

There were two tests for the resulting revisions:

1. Did the revision improve the selected piece?
2. Would the work on revision transfer into writing better beginnings on the posttests?

We evaluated the revisions carefully and decided that they had improved. Later, we were pleased to discover that the improvement had transferred to the students' subsequent work. Even though the posttest was a first draft, eighteen of twenty-seven students had the improved openings that we had tried to teach, the best result we had ever had. And the gains from pretest to posttest were significant.

The following compositions exemplify changes in students' ability to write strong introductions, even in test situations, after instruction of the kind described. The first pair is from ninth grader Louisa.

Louisa's Pretest

The event that touched me most was our family reunion. Ever since I was ten I never knew my family very well. As I was turning twelve I had an idea. I would have a reunion to unite my family together. The idea of a family reunion was mine because, when people called my house I never knew who they were. After all the arrangements were set for the reunion, we sent out invitations. All total I sent out three hundred and nineteen invitations. When the reunion was here I met so many people, I never even knew. The reunion was a success, and now when people call my house I know who they are.

Louisa's Posttest

"No," I screamed as I ran to the large window on the fourth floor. My cousin Pauly who was short and skinny, no taller than me, fell out the window. We were playing a game of tag and we used the window as base. As I seen my cousin let his little body up on the ledge, my heart grew cold. I knew he would lose his balance, but I was frozen and couldn't move. There was a smile on him that covered his whole face, but slowly turned to a grin as he looked down. I wanted to say something but my mouth was dry, like I ate a can of powder. My body grew numb as I seen the terror in his eyes. His face went from a smile to a frown like he knew he was going to fall. His shoes lurked of little pieces of gravel which made him unstable. He reached for the sides of the walls, but he lost his grip. Sure enough he fell. Racing to the window I saw his body falling down four flights of windows. Screaming, running down the stairs shouting "No," I ran to my mom. Fully out of breath I told her, "Pauly fell out the window." We dared to look out the window where Pauly lied. He wasn't there. He landed on the stop sign. His jacket went over the pole breaking his fall. Unfortunately he had about five surgeries, but it's better than dying. Now Pauly and I are closer than ever as he came close to this near death accident. The doctor calls it a "freak" accident. "Bad luck," I call it.

In the posttest, Louisa uses an in medias res opening so that the reader is pulled immediately into the action. The pretest piece takes several sentences to get into the story, which is quite simple and unelaborated. We saw this posttest as a vast improvement.

The second pair is from an eighth grader. You have already seen the posttest from Andreanna, in Chapter 2. Here is Andreanna's pretest:

This is the day that I had my gymnastics competition. It was at Independence Park on Saturday. When we went to the park we had to go change into our body-suits and practice before the competition starts. It was 4:00 P.M. the gymnastics meet started, so we sat down and waited for them to put us in groups. After they put us in groups we waited for them to call us up to do our rutein. When she called me I was scared I might mess up but I didn't and all of my team members were clapping for me. When it was time for them to give out the 1st, 2nd, 3rd metals and the 4th, 5th, and 6th ribbons my name was called for 2nd place metal. When I heard my name I jumped so happy and all of my teammates were happy too. After that my gymnastics teacher took all of us out to eat.

On this paper, Andreanna earned a score of 6—a 1 for episodic elaboration, a 2 for specificity, a 1 for style, and a 2 for mechanics. It tells about very general events and includes no dialogue or figurative language. She takes several sentences to get to the main event and does very little with it.

Her posttest does not provide an in medias res opening, but it gets into the tension of the runner within a sentence, and a few sentences later, into the action. Here again are the opening lines:

In the middle of July, 1994, I was stretching out for a big track race. I was very nervous and I had butterflies in my stomach. There was a lot more teams getting ready to race. Me and my teammates were ready to race. It was almost time to start. We had shirts that said "Independence Park." That was where we were at. The coaches split all of us into groups with other kids. My friends wished me good luck, and I wished them good luck too. It was my group that was going first. We all lined up at the starting line. It was hot and sunny and I was sweating to death. It was very dusty through the track field. All you could hear was people talking, and see kids stretching.

Well, we were all ready, and next thing you know, "On your mark, get set, go!" He blew the whistle. I was sweating so much and running so fast.

Andreanna's score on the posttest was 13—a 4 for elaboration, a 4 for specificity, a 3 for style, and a 2 for mechanics—a gain from the pretest of seven points.

One of the largest gains among our inner-city students came from a seventh grader named Verita. Her pretest, scored a 6, follows:

My birthday is coming up. I hope I get almost all the things I asked for, and maybe the rest of the things I didn't get for my birthday I can get for Christmas. I know I'm getting an electronic game. My brother is giving it to me. I don't know a single seventh grade girl who has a wild fire, but since my brother doesn't have his ten dollars anymore . . . I'm assuming he bought it with his own money, and I'd hurt his feelings if I didn't take it. So I'll take it, and thank him for it. I really try not to pick on my brother, or any seven year old, for that matter, but sometimes they get in your way. I guess my favorite holiday is my birthday, so I hope I get what I want.

This writing lacks detail and focus. There is no dialogue, no figurative language, and no episode at all. But the mechanics are good.

Now check out Verita's posttest:

My First Day

I was half scared and half excited. All night I had practiced my times table chart. I got up and walked to the bathroom and took a nice hot shower. I thought about how I would like my new teachers, or how they would like me. I got out of the shower and started to dry myself. The thing I wanted most was to be in the same class as Tracy. She wasn't one of my best friends, we had gotten in plenty of fights, but still when you're going to a new school, anyone you can pal around with would be great.

Our doorbell rang. It was 8:25 just as I popped the last bit of toast into my mouth. I ran to the front hall and opened the door. There was Tracy. She said, "C'mon, or we'll be late!" Marian, Tracy's mom, had brought her car around. I hopped in and we drove off.

As we got nearer and nearer to school, my heart started pounding like a volcano about to erupt. We got out of the car, and someone told us that if we were new we should go to the auditorium. So we finally found it, and there were already about one hundred people there. The lady on the stage was dressed in black and white. Her hair reminded me of the Gloria Vanderbilt lady. She had spectacles on and was talking about rules and regulations. We sat down near the edge. She went on with her lecture for about forty-five minutes. It was really boring, but I listened. Finally, at the end, she called out names and room numbers. I was in 314 and Tracy was in 315. I felt my heart jump, and I could tell Tracy wasn't the happiest person on earth either. This guy came down to our row and told us to follow him to the room.

By the time I got up to the third floor, my feet felt like a ton each, and the rest of my body was well exhausted. We walked into a room marked 314, and the man left. I was all alone with everyone staring at me. Finally, my teacher broke the silence and said, "Find a seat. I'm your home room teacher, Mrs. Lanier. I will tell you what you need for this room."

I sat down in back of a girl. She turned around and said, "Hi. Welcome to the school. I'm Clara."

Verita's opening begins immediately with the tension she felt in anticipation of a new school. There is no exposition up front. All of the exposition is integrated into the ongoing action. This piece scored 4 for elaboration, 5 for specificity, 5 for style, and 3 for mechanics, for a total of 17. Verita had a gain of eleven points. We used this piece for many years as a model for other classes.

Gains like these are the result of the kinds of instruction described in this and the preceding chapters. They depend on thoughtful analysis of the tasks involved; careful design, evaluation, and revision of activities that help students learn the strategies for producing the effects that make a good personal narrative; and positive reinforcement at each juncture of the teaching. These gains were accomplished in less than a month. Imagine the progress that might be achieved in a year of such teaching.

11

Evaluating the Impact of Teaching

One important set of strategies I tried to teach my MAT students has to do with evaluating instruction. These strategies have to come into play every teaching day as well as over a longer span of days, months, and even years of teaching. If teachers care whether their teaching is successful, they must critically examine the goals, means, and effects of their teaching and be prepared to revise the goals and means of the teaching process even as it is in progress. This is reflective teaching.

Analyzing and Critiquing Goals

Before instruction begins, we must assess whether our goals are appropriate and useful. After instruction has begun, we must determine at each stage whether our teaching is working. Are students responding as we had hoped? Are they gaining the knowledge we intended? If not, we have to revise or move on to something more productive. We need to evaluate the effects of each day's instruction. Did the activities for the day produce any evidence of progress? Since instruction should build over a period of days, at the end of a unit of teaching we should be able to see changes in student writing. If not, we must go back and rethink our plans.

Initial Analysis

In our initial critical analysis of our goals, we need to ask whether a particular goal is appropriate and worthwhile for our students:

1. Are our students likely to be able to attain the goal?
2. If the goal is attained, are the students likely to be able to put the knowledge gained to any use? (Is the knowledge a stepping-stone to further knowledge?)

When teachers teach the short story in middle and high school, they may, often using plot diagrams, show students how to identify the *exposition*, *rising action*, *conflict*, *climax*, *falling action*, and/or *denouement*. Are these goals attainable? Probably. Once the students have mastered this knowledge, does it lead anywhere? I would argue that it goes nowhere. It is an end in itself and therefore of relatively little value. For example, the traditional thing to say about conflict is that there are three kinds: man against man, man against nature, and man against himself. Teachers ask students to identify the kind of conflict in a story. But once we know the story's conflict is man against nature, where does that knowledge lead? What do we do with it? The nature of the conflict in Jack London's story "To Build a Fire" (1986) is obviously man against nature, but that fact does not provide any insight into the meaning of the story except at the very lowest level. A much more important question is *What brings the conflict in the story about?* This question might prompt thoughtful readers to consider the arrogance of the man (London does not name him) and the power of nature and perhaps lead them to the writer's underlying message. But the simple question about the kind of conflict goes nowhere.

Reflecting on the Effects of Teaching in Action

Unfortunately, we do not always have research to rely on when we test our goals for attainability and for likelihood of effect. But as long as we have clear goals, we can test our teaching at every step of the way.

When the objectives are not clear, however, there is no way to judge whether or not students are approaching them as teaching proceeds. One of the schools in which I recently observed language arts classes had mandated daily journal writing. The teachers had a formula. They put a topic on the board. Students understood that for five minutes or so they were to write whatever they wanted about the topic. Then the teacher called on some of them to read aloud what they had written and offered a few comments. I could not tell what the object of the writing was or what focus the comments had. Pieces that students read were short, simplistic, and banal. All responses received praise. The teachers had no clear goals for the journal writing. They were satisfied with anything the students produced. Indeed, they reinforced whatever the students wrote. In essence, the teachers were telling their students every day that writing simplistic, mindless stuff is fine.

The shell game described in Chapter 4 is based on clear goals: producing language—especially figurative language—to describe the shells in detail. At each stage of the instruction, a teacher can determine whether to move forward or try again. Clear goals make reflection in action possible.

My MAT students had to learn how to judge student progress as they moved through lessons. When we had planned a daily lesson carefully, most followed the plan. However, sometimes they were so worried about covering everything that they ignored obvious clues to students' need for more or clearer teaching, plowing ahead and missing opportunities for rectifying problems early. Some of the chief mechanical problems included

- talking over their students instead of waiting for quiet
- forgetting to give instructions before moving students into groups
- failing to involve 50 percent or more of the students in classroom discussions
- failing to ascertain whether students were ready to move on to the next part of a lesson

When problems like those occur, a lesson will not have achieved its planned effect.

However, the constant presence of friendly observers with whom they could review the class within minutes of its conclusion made a great difference in helping them improve. Teaching partners who share clear goals and who are not afraid to acknowledge problems and venture suggestions go a long way in helping us develop more effective reflection in action.

Judging Student Progress After Teaching

In the MAT program, we worked together for four hours each morning. Before teaching a forty-five- or fifty-minute class, we spent about forty minutes reviewing what we would do and making last-minute adjustments. After teaching the class, we spent about two hours examining what had happened: what the MAT students had done as teachers and what our young charges had done and learned as a result of the teaching. Assessing the daily learning allowed us to plan for the next day, to decide if we should continue with more of the same kind of activity, work with students in small groups or as a class, invent new activities with the same goals, or move on to our next goal. (To make these assessments, we needed some concrete work from students to review or some evidence about their learning from their oral work as a class or in small groups.) Usually this examination after teaching allowed us to move ahead with our learning activities. Occasionally, however, we were stymied.

In our first attempts to help students write better introductions to their stories or to find better places of entry to their stories, we thought we were making progress as we moved through the activities and materials we had designed. One such activity involved a set of student-written models we thought would illustrate the difference between an elongated introduction and a snappy one, between one that failed to get to the story and one that got right into it. Students seemed able to make the distinctions. When we asked them to write opening paragraphs for their stories, they responded reasonably well with a little help and coaching. Another activity involved examples of various openings and a scale and criteria for judging them. When we coached students in writing their openings and provided feedback along with suggestions, they did reasonably well. However, their posttest writing revealed that our students had not learned what we had hoped.

We spent only four and a half weeks in a school each year.[1] The result was that even when we predicted that our activities would not have the effect we hoped for, we could not do much about it. I believe that if something is important, we should keep trying to teach it until our students learn it. But the structure of the program made that impossible, and we had to be satisfied with whatever we had accomplished in any given year. The following year, a new group of MAT students could try new ideas.

Not until we developed the lessons for use with ninth graders described in Chapter 10 did we see a significant change in the openings of stories. After those lessons our ninth graders seemed able to apply what they had learned to their own writing without much coaching. Posttest writing revealed that a number of students had learned strategies for providing an arresting opening, strategies they were able to use on their own.

Suggestions for Teachers Working Alone

Unfortunately, the structure of most schools does not allow the kind of workshop collaborations that were central to the MAT program at the University of Chicago. But if you are

---

[1.] We did not want to ask to spend an inordinate length of time in a school, and the MAT students needed time to complete their work in their regular classes. (The workshop did not count as a class until the final years of the program. Until then, it was a requirement for which students received no class credit.)

a teacher and you have read this far, you are probably wise enough to be reflective on your own. Following are some guidelines.

Break Down Each Activity into Segments

First, think of each activity as an experiment framed by the amount of time you have predicted the activity will take. You have something you hope the activity will accomplish, some result you hope to observe. The first step is to decide what will count for evidence that the result has been achieved. Let's assume that you decide to try the shell game described in Chapter 4. It can be broken into five little experiments:

- teacher-led talk about a large shell
- group writing about one of two shells
- group feedback on that writing
- individual writing about a shell
- individual feedback on that writing

Determine Evidence to Collect and Decisions to Make for Each Segment

Teacher-Led Talk About a Large Shell

The evidence indicating that students understand the goals of using specific language and figures of speech to describe the shell is their oral response. You should expect twenty or twenty-five responses about color, shape, and patterns and eight or more figures of speech. The responses should be distributed over the whole class. Do not move to the next activity until you have responses from at least half of your class.

Group Writing About One of Two Shells

The evidence for the group activity will be the writing produced. You will be monitoring the writing in progress as you coach the groups. Do not move to the feedback stage until each group has several sentences about a shell. After the feedback, collect the group writing for closer examination. Evidence of progress will be detail and figurative language. In the example in Chapter 4, we had both, but because the sentences were very simple, we added an activity on sentence combining and asked students to revise. If the groups' compositions are very weak, you might want to add a teacher-led activity in which you write about the large shell on the overhead followed by a group activity in which students write together about a different set of shells.

Group Feedback on Writing About One of Two Shells

Appropriate evidence is simple underlining of specific detail and strong figurative language from at least half of the groups.

Individual Writing About a Shell

The evidence is dense, specific language about color and shape and figurative language used in describing the shell. If the detail and figures are not very strong for most students, it might be wise to make comments on the writing and provide time for revisions in class while you coach individuals who have had trouble.

Individual Feedback on Writing About a Shell

Evidence of success is that most students have underlined good detail and figurative language. If they have not, you should assume that they do not recognize what you have been trying to teach.

Act on What You've Learned

Once you see the results of these little experiments, figure out what to do next. If you do not see the results you expected, it will be important to reteach or find another activity to help reach the goals you set. You need to consider carefully what you did and how students reacted. The following questions might help you think through why an activity or series of activities did not work well:

1. Were the goals clear to you? Were the goals appropriate for your students at their level of development as writers?
2. Were the goals clear to the students?
3. Were the tasks to be learned clearly defined and laid out?
4. Were the gateway activities structured so that students could do the tasks with help at the beginning?
5. Did the activities move students to increased independence, from teacher support to peer support to independent work?
6. Were most students on task during most activities? If not, why not?
7. Were the materials used in the activities accessible to the students?
8. Were the materials and activities interesting to the students?

Questions such as these should help you think about how to improve your activities for another day. They should also help you generate additional activities and/or materials to make up for whatever failed.

I have observed thousands of classrooms. It is easy to spot a classroom in which no learning is going on. The goals are unclear, both to the teacher and to the students. The tasks are not laid out in a thoughtful manner. There is no gateway activity; instead, there is a gap between abstractions mouthed by a teacher or set forth in a book and what the students are to do.

Overall Evaluations

Every year of the MAT composition workshops, which took place all but my first year as director, I insisted on a pretest and posttest evaluation. I believed it was our responsibility, in return for the favor granted us by the schools we worked with, to ensure that we had taught something. In addition, the tests gave me the opportunity to teach my MAT students how to evaluate writing systematically, how to establish rater reliability, and how to test the results of their teaching.

Nearly every year our tests showed that our students had made statistically significant gains. There were only two exceptions. One year, unknown to us, our seventh graders had decided to have a party for the MAT students who had taught them. These youngsters were too excited about the party to write much of anything, and they wrote quickly so that they could get to the cake and cookies. The result: *no gains*, or at least no significant gains. Another year we made the mistake of giving the posttest on Halloween, with many kids sitting and writing in costume. Many chose to write about various Halloween adventures, which included many clichés and little detail.

Our assessments were fairly formal and used comparable pre- and posttest writing prompts and comparable testing conditions. (A description of one of these formal assessments appears in Appendix A.) Examples of pre- and posttest writing appear at the end of the previous chapter. While these provide some insight into the gains achieved, a more formal assessment is necessary to reveal gains (or losses) for the class as a whole. A formal assessment requires administering a pretest and a posttest with comparable prompts and conditions, because they allow making specific claims about the results of your teaching of a class, claims that are defensible. In my experience, these evaluations are useful in dealing with school administrators who want to see evidence of learning. And they provide a ready defense of your practice. In that sense, the study in Appendix A is an integral part of this book.

The results of our assessment were very impressive. There were significant gains for all groups of students who received the kind of instruction described in this book. I am proud of these results, not least because my MAT students achieved them in 1994 and 1995 while the University of Chicago MAT program in English was still thriving. I believe they are important, or should be, for anyone who cares about the teaching of writing to inner-city children (or any kids for that matter). They demonstrate that significant gains are achievable among students who have "suffered the slings and arrows of outrageous fortune" and for whom little in the way of achievement is the standard expectation.

APPENDIX A

AN ASSESSMENT OF TEACHING NARRATIVE IN INNER-CITY SCHOOLS

The following study was undertaken a few years ago as part of the MAT program in English at the University of Chicago. The teaching involved has been described in this book.

Design of the Study

The study consisted of five trial groups and three control groups. The trial groups included a sixth-grade, a seventh-grade, and an eighth-grade class from a school I will call LeGrand, the population of which at the time of the study was approximately 45.7 percent Latino, 34.7 percent African American, 14.3 percent white, and 5.4 percent Asian American. Approximately 92 percent of the students were eligible for free or reduced-cost lunches. The other two classes in the study were ninth-grade classes from Curie High, a school whose population was approximately 18.2 percent white, 32.8 percent African American, 46.4 percent Latino, and 2.6 percent Asian. Eighty-nine percent of students in the school were eligible for free or reduced-price lunches.

The control groups were unfortunately somewhat different. The school I will call Arco had, like LeGrand, a high level of students from low-income families, 98 percent. However, the population, unlike LeGrand's, was more than 98 percent Hispanic. Two eighth-grade classes were from this school. The third class of eighth graders in the control was from a blue-collar suburban school, the population of which was only 23 percent low income and more than 95 percent white.

The control classes at Arco were working on writing autobiographies and wrote nearly every day. They were taught the writing process, including brainstorming and mapping, which they made use of over the four weeks of their participation. The autobiographies were to be narrative in form, focusing on important incidents in the lives of the authors. The third control group, from the blue-collar school, Hoover, worked on narrative also. However, the teacher used material from two standard writing textbooks and focused on the development of paragraphs through what the books called elaboration. She also required that students write three longer narratives of several paragraphs during the twenty-two days of the study.

All groups were administered pre- and posttests using the following prompt.

> Write a story about an event and its consequences that was important to you in some way. Be as specific as you can in describing the event and its consequences. Try to write so that a reader of your story will see what you saw and feel what you felt.

All classes received the same writing prompt for both the pretest and the posttest. The MAT program had used this prompt for many years to evaluate the progress made in writing narrative. One criticism of writing prompts is that some require students to write about something they do not know about (Langer 1984; Polio and Glew 1996). This open-ended prompt gives students complete control over the specific topic and is intended to ensure that they can select an experience for writing about which they know a good deal. It has served its purposes well.

In the evaluation of the writing, I included two class sets of pre- and posttest compositions from an earlier study, several of which had been given the highest scores on the scale. Even though these would not be included in the analysis of the study data, the presence of compositions likely to receive ratings of 14 to 18 would help ensure that raters would use the full range of the scale.

Limitations of the Study

The study had several limitations. Among the chief of these is the fact that there were only three control groups and that they did not match the trial groups in ethnicity and one did not match in socioeconomic status. In addition, students could not be assigned to treatments randomly. Nor did the teachers have equivalent skills. The three control teachers were all skilled teachers with advanced work in teaching writing and several years of experience, while the teachers of the trial groups were all neophytes. All of the control teachers were following the writing curricula imposed by their schools. Finally, the researcher was involved in the teaching of two trial groups by virtue of being the MAT supervisor for one trial group in each year.

If this were a funded study, I would say that there would be no excuse for conducting the study with these problems. However, since it was not funded, the researcher had to make do, to find teachers who were friends and willing to cooperate in the control groups. Since the initial goal was to evaluate the effectiveness of the MAT teaching with minority students, there was no choice but to use neophyte teachers. Additionally, the researcher felt he could not abdicate the supervision of his students just because he was conducting a study. At any rate, the results of the study will have to be examined with these shortcomings in mind.

Rating Scale

For this study, we used the analytic rating scale that appears in Chapter 2 with the addition of a scale for mechanics, which follows. The scale for mechanics was, I thought, simple. Using it involves estimating the number of errors per line, including spelling, punctuation, and usage.

> *Score 1*: an estimated average of one error or more per handwritten line
>
> *Score 2*: an estimated average of between less than one error per handwritten line and one every three lines
>
> *Score 3*: an estimated average of fewer than one error in three handwritten lines

In practice, this simple scale turned out to be difficult to use for several reasons. Some raters detect more errors than others. The scale leaves undefined what counts as errors in usage. A third problem is that some students write an average of five words per line while others write many more per line. A better scale might involve an actual count of errors in relation to the number of words in each paper. However, this would involve a great deal of time. I decided to use the simpler scale shown here even though it might not be as reliable as one would wish.

Scoring

I recruited five MAT students for scoring. All had used the scale for rating papers as part of a course. One graduate student coded the papers, removing the names of the students and any dates after assigning the codes. Following the coding, the papers were randomly mixed as thoroughly as possible. I trained four raters until they were coding with high reliability ($r = .86$, $p < .0001$). The raters sustained their high correlations throughout the rating sessions. During rating, correlations ranged from .866 to .943 with $p < .0001$.

Correlations on subscales were lower. The average of six correlations on episodic elaboration was .79, with a range of .79 to .89 with $p < .01$; for specificity, average correlation was .87 with a range of .80 to .95 with $p < .01$; for style, average correlation was .84 with a range of .80 to .88 with $p < .01$; for mechanics, average correlation was .69 with a range of .61 to .80 with $p < .01$.

Results for Trial and Control Groups

Nearly all groups in our study made some gain, as indicated in Table 1. All of the trial classes made gains of more than a point, but none of the control classes did. The mean gain for the trial classes was 2.1, but for the control classes the mean gain was only .036. Analysis of covariance, using individual students as the unit of analysis, revealed that the differences between the experimental and control groups were highly significant ($F = 23$, $p < .0001$). Results for this ancova appear in Table 2A. More conservatively, using class as the unit of analysis, an analysis of covariance also yields statistically significant results with $F = 11.9$ and $p = 0.018$.

My second question was whether gains appeared in all subscales. Table 3 shows the mean differences for each subscale in each class. Even a cursory glance at Table 3 indicates that the mean differences for elaboration, specificity, and style were much greater for the trial groups than for the control groups. The mean for elaboration for all trial groups was .606, while for the control groups it was only .073; for specificity, the mean for trial groups was .916 as opposed to .133 for control groups; for style, .594 as opposed to .07. The difference for mechanics was clearly not so great, −.05 for trial groups and .063 for control groups.

Results for Race and Ethnicity

Given the history of African American and Hispanic students falling below white students on nearly all tests by nearly a standard deviation, I thought it important to determine the role played by race or ethnicity in any gains we might see. Therefore, the racial group, as indicated by each student, was recorded and coded into our database. Our total trial group

TABLE 1   MEANS AND STANDARD DEVIATIONS FOR ALL CLASSES

Trial Classes		Pretest Total	Post Total	Difference
LeGrand 6	Mean	4.64	6.88	2.24
	Standard Deviation	.86	2.42	2.11
	Number	25	25	25
LeGrand 7	Mean	4.73	5.91	1.18
	Standard Deviation	.94	1.48	1.26
	Number	22	22	22
LeGrand 8	Mean	5.75	8.05	2.3
	Standard Deviation	1.83	3.22	2.52
	Number	20	20	20
Urban High 9A	Mean	6.5	9.5	3.0
	Standard Deviation	.95	2.31	2.15
	Number	20	20	20
Urban High 9B	Mean	6.0	7.6	1.6
	Standard Deviation	1.73	1.88	2.41
	Number	15	15	15
Control Classes				
Arco 8A	Mean	5.88	6.08	.20
	Standard Deviation	1.8	1.38	1.74
	Number	26	26	26
Arco 8B	Mean	6.32	7.00	.68
	Standard Deviation	1.68	1.79	2.18
	Number	28	28	28
Hoover 8	Mean	6.88	6.18	−.70
	Standard Deviation	2.32	1.81	2.68
	Number	17	17	17

included 102 students, of which 36.3 percent were African American, 46.1 percent were Hispanic, and 17.6 percent were white or Asian. In addition, school data revealed that more than 80 percent of those students were from a population designated as low income. Unfortunately, we could not code that into our database for individual students. My question was this: Does the kind of instruction described earlier affect racial or ethnic groups differentially? To answer this question, I examined differences among students of different racial groups in our five trial classes. Because there were relatively few white and Asian students, the two were grouped together. Table 4 indicates the mean pretest, posttest, and difference scores for three groups: African American, Latino, and white/Asian students.

Clearly, there was not much difference in the gains achieved by the various groups. All gained an average of 2 points or a bit more. Analysis of covariance indicated that the differences among them were not significant, $F = .172$, $p = .842$.

At the same time, however, the differences from pre- to posttest writing were quite large. To estimate the size of the gain, I computed an effect size for each racial group. The

TABLE 2A   ANALYSIS OF COVARIANCE FOR TRIAL AND CONTROL GROUPS WITH INDIVIDUAL AS UNIT OF ANALYSIS

Source	Type III Sum of Squares	df	Mean Square	F	Significance
Corrected Model	216.351	2	108.175	25.707	.000
Intercept	150.226	1	150.226	35.701	.000
Pretest Total	169.774	1	169.774	40.306	.000
Experimental/ Control Differences	96.804	1	96.804	23.005	.000
Error	715.349	170	4.208		
Total	9,620.000	173			

effect size was the trial group's gain minus the gain for the control group divided by the pooled standard deviation for all groups on the posttest (see Cooper and Hedges 1994). The effect size for African American students was .76, for Latino .65, and for white/ Asian .66. According to Cohen (1977), differences of .2 standard deviations are small, those of .5 are medium, and those of .8 and over, large. Clearly all of these were good-sized gains. When compared with the effect sizes for other composition studies, they are even more impressive. In a review of composition studies (Hillocks 1986) that computed effect sizes for seventy-three treatments in sixty studies, effect sizes ranged from –.45 to .82. The mean effect size for all treatments was .28. Of the seventy-three treatments, only five had effect sizes over .6 and only three had effect sizes over .7. The results for each racial group here rank with the strongest effect sizes in that analysis.

TABLE 2B   ANALYSIS OF COVARIANCE FOR TRIAL/CONTROL GROUPS WITH CLASS AS UNIT OF ANALYSIS

Source	Type III Sum of Squares	df	Mean Square	F	Significance
Corrected Model	7.519	2	3.759	6.873	.037
Intercept	.019	1	.019	.034	.861
Pretest Total	4.961	1	4.961	9.069	.030
Experimental/ Control Differences	6.511	1	6.511	11.903	.018
Error	2.735	5	.547		
Total	419.234	8			
Corrected Total	10.254	7			

TABLE 3   MEAN DIFFERENCES ON EACH SUBSCALE BY CLASS

Trial Classes	Elaboration	Specificity	Style	Mechanics
LeGrand 6	.44	1.04	.76	.00
LeGrand 7	.64	.64	.23	−.32
LeGrand 8	.90	.85	.75	−.20
Urban High 9A	.45	1.45	.90	.20
Urban High 9B	.60	.60	.33	.07
Control Classes				
Arco 8A	.35	.35	−.04	−.23
Arco 8B	.11	.11	.18	.36
Hoover 8	−.24	−.06	−.35	.06

Results for Gender

Previous research indicates that boys do not respond to teaching of writing as well as do girls or, for some other reason, lag behind significantly (Hedges and Nowell 1995). Given these differences, it seemed important to ask if the gains in the present study were significantly different for boys and girls. Table 5 indicates the pretest, posttest, and difference means for boys and girls in the trial groups. The difference between males and females was .66, which, divided by the standard deviation of trial group pooled posttests (2.08),

TABLE 4   DIFFERENCE IN GAINS FOR GROUPS BY RACE

Racial Group		Pretest Total	Posttest Total	Difference
African American	Mean	5.84	8.08	2.24
	Number	37	37	37
	Standard Deviation	1.818	3.077	2.362
Latino	Mean	5.11	7.09	1.98
	Number	47	47	47
	Standard Deviation	1.127	2.125	2.125
White/Asian	Mean	5.5	7.5	2.00
	Number	18	18	18
	Standard Deviation	1.249	2.114	2.144
Total	Mean	5.44	7.52	2.08
	Number	102	102	102
	Standard Deviation	1.460	2.605	2.156

TABLE 5   MEANS FOR GIRLS AND BOYS

Gender		Pretest Total	Posttest Total	Difference
Female	Mean	5.61	7.97	2.36
	Number	59	59	59
	Standard Deviation	1.543	2.525	2.107
Male	Mean	5.21	6.91	1.70
	Number	43	43	43
	Standard Deviation	1.319	2.617	2.188
Total	Mean	5.44	7.52	2.08
	Number	102	102	102
	Standard Deviation	1.460	2.605	2.156

produced an effect size between them of .32, which is relatively small and stands in contrast to the large effect sizes that Hedges and Nowell (1995) found. Analysis of covariance indicated that the difference was not significant, $F = 2.365$, $p = .126$.

Discussion

Given the well-known and very large gaps between African American and white, Latino and white, and economically disadvantaged and the economically advantaged students in reading and writing achievement (Hillocks 2006), I can think of few, if any, more important problems facing American education. In an article entitled "Dispositions Toward Language," Ball and Lardner (19) examine the hypotheses that, first, speakers of African American English are at a disadvantage in school because their language is a barrier to learning and, concomitantly, that increased teacher knowledge of African American English (AAE) will result in greater success for those speakers in language arts. Ball and Lardner argue cogently that the simple process of becoming more knowledgeable about AAE is not likely to make much difference. They argue that what makes a difference in the performance of African American students is the efficacy of teachers, defined as a "teacher's beliefs about the power she or he has to produce a positive effect on students" (422). They further argue that "having high expectations and good intentions is not enough; these intentions and expectations need to be evident to students in observable or, we might say, audible behaviors in the classroom" (424).

Ball and Lardner (2005), in *African American Literacies Unleashed*, pursue the same themes in greater detail and explore a variety of what the authors call "models of participatory literacy" in community-based organizations, such as a "dance program for inner-city girls" (61). These models take many forms, but all of them "provide writing and composition teachers four avenues for broadening and enriching the participation patterns in their classrooms. The teachers in the community-based programs (1) "create opportunities to play multiple roles," (2) "integrate performance into . . . literacy activities," (3) "make optimum use of students' oral and vernacular resources," and (4) "encourage students to make maximum advantage of their community knowledge by positioning students as informers/interpreters" (75).

I believe that these qualities and characteristics in classrooms help to enhance learning for all students, not just poor African American students. While increasing participation is necessary to gains in writing achievement, it is probably not sufficient. Although Ball and Lardner do not explicate what form their "four avenues for broadening and enriching the participation patterns" might take in composition classrooms, the activities described in preceding chapters provide all four avenues of participation. That is, they provide for students' playing multiple roles, integrate performance, make use of students' oral and vernacular resources, and require that students make use of their community knowledge. But more importantly, the activities are so designed that the engagement and participation of the students is focused on learning and rehearsing strategies for developing and shaping the content of writing. Over the years, when our activities have failed to engage students in that way, our students have failed to learn much.

I believe that, with appropriate pedagogical content knowledge, teachers can use such activities effectively in their own classrooms. However, such gains are not likely to occur under standard teaching practices or changes in curricula brought about in the current passion for reform. Over the past several years, I have witnessed a large city's board of education make almost yearly demands for curricular reform. The demands are passed on to teachers, who make lists of topics to be covered, lists concerning the elements of narrative, or the use of thesis statements and introductory paragraphs or the structure of paragraphs, or the elements of literature, and many other abstract concepts. And these are all conceptualized as pieces of information that have to be learned to be successful in English. They always amount to declarative knowledge that can be tested in relatively simple tests of recall. But I have never seen anyone conceptualize the strategies that students need to learn to become better writers or better readers of literature. I have never heard anyone say, "We need to think about what students have to be able to *do* to be proficient writers of narrative or persuasion or exposition or argument." Nor have I heard anyone say, "We have to think of activities that will help students learn those strategies so that they can *use* them." And I never, never hear anyone say, "How can we assess our own teaching in order to determine how successful we are in teaching the important strategies?" It is so much easier to bemoan the poor preparation of students than to examine the necessary dimensions of teaching for improvement.

Knowledge for writing is task specific, and different writing tasks require knowledge not only of different forms of writing but of task-specific procedures or strategies for dealing with both content and form necessary to produce good writing. Smagorinsky and Smith (1992) argue that such knowledge is important at the middle school level through college. I would argue that this study indicates that the specific knowledge of procedures for writing effective narrative can be taught to minority students from low-income families, even by neophyte teachers. All that is required is the knowledge and patience on the part of teachers to take students through activities designed to lead them to the strategies, and to provide the environment that enables students to put those strategies to use with aid from peers and the teacher and then independently. It seems to me that reform efforts would be well advised to aim at bringing teachers to this knowledge and helping them use it rather than reinforcing ideas of curriculum that are stagnant and stagnating.

A NOTE ABOUT GRAMMAR

Many administrators and teachers believe that knowledge of grammar is the basis of writing and must be taught as a prelude to writing. This appears to be true particularly in schools in which students do not speak Standard English. For example, Dawn Burnette, an English teacher writing in the *Atlanta Journal Constitution*, says, "To help students communicate more effectively, teachers and students must share a common lingo, and that lingo is grammar. Students who know the lingo understand why we use *who* for subjects and predicate nominatives and *whom* for objects, indirect objects and objects of prepositions" (2006, B4). That means that if we know grammar, we know the nominative and objective cases. The notion of cases in language comes to us through Latin, a highly inflected language with nouns varying in inflection with the nominative, accusative, dative, genitive, and ablative cases for both singular and plural and three separate groups of nouns: masculine, feminine, and neuter.

The Latinate grammars for English that began to be published in the eighteenth century followed in the footsteps of their Latin predecessors and demanded that students identify the cases of English nouns that, with the exception of plural and genitive, had not been inflected since the days of Old English (see *Sweet's Anglo-Saxon Primer* [Davis 1955]). Modern English nouns have no inflections for nominative, dative, or accusative, or ablative, for that matter. Today we have only plural and possessive inflections for nouns. It makes sense to speak of nominative and accusative (objective) for only a small set of pronouns including *I, me, we, us, he, him, she, her, they, them, who, whom,* and their derivatives.

But the Latinate traditional school grammar (TSG) books are prescriptive and tell us the proper positions for the uses of this small group of words. However, anyone paying attention to modern speech, even of educated people, will recognize that the rules are generally ignored, if known at all. It is common to hear "between him and I," "It's me," "That's her," "That's him," and "It's us." All of these are incorrect according to the TSG books. However, many people think of the correct forms as uppity and phony. Further, some distinctions seem to be disappearing altogether. I seldom hear anyone using *whom*. Would you say, "Whom are you bringing to the party?" Even the singular versus plural distinction for third-person pronouns seems to be changing. Statements such as "Everyone should bring their books tomorrow" are common, even among English teachers.

Linguists, the professionals who study language, distinguish between grammar and usage. A grammar is a description of how people use the language. A descriptive grammar would include all of the forms as people use them. School grammars are prescriptive and tell people what to use and how. The "correct" forms tend to be used by the upper, educated

classes and are considered to be Standard English. The forms used by the lower, unedu-
cated classes and minority groups are dismissed as incorrect or nonstandard. In effect, such
dismissals suggest that the upper classes have a right to impose their dialect upon others.

The proponents of teaching traditional school grammar, grammar as it appears in most
contemporary texts on grammar and composition, argue that without grammar instruction,
people cannot understand sentence structure and therefore cannot write clear sentences or
punctuate them correctly. Recently, I conducted a study of thirty English classes (sixth,
seventh, and eighth grades) in one urban metropolis and two smaller cities (Hillocks, in
progress). One school with a 32 percent African American population had mandated the
regular teaching of grammar and had adopted textbooks that focused on TSG. In a pattern
of instruction no doubt influenced by the textbook being used, the teacher would read or
ask students to read a passage from the text defining or explaining some aspect of grammar:
subjects, verbs, participles, and so on. Next, students would be given a set of sentences in
which they were to underline subjects, verbs, participles, or whatever the target of instruction
was that day. When they had finished, the teacher would solicit the correct answers in a class
recitation, and the students would correct their own papers and pass them in.

Each of the observed lessons had an implied goal: to identify the grammatical en-
tity in question. Could the students attain that goal? And if so, where did this knowledge
lead? Did learning to identify participles in textbook sentences lead to the use (or better
use) of participles in writing or speaking? Teachers usually believe that it will, but my study
showed that the teaching of grammar was negatively related to the improvement of writing.
The more grammar in classrooms, the lower the scores on writing.

In my first year of teaching, I taught grammar because it was required. I quickly
recognized that it had little appeal for my seventh graders and that even those who appeared to learn it (they passed my tests) were unable to apply it to their writing. Part of
the difficulty lay in the ambiguity of the definitions that were proposed in textbooks. For
example, a noun is defined as the name of a person, place, or thing, or, some books add,
an idea. But verbs are identified as showing action or a state of being. A student trying
hard to learn these definitions would likely call *explosion* a verb showing action and *exist-
ence* a verb showing a state of being. There are many other problems with the analysis of
language in TSG (see Fries 1952 and Hillocks and Smith 2003).

Was the goal attainable? Probably not. One of my favorite studies is beautiful in its
simplicity. Macaulay (1947) wanted to find whether or not students were able to identify
parts of speech. He presented sets of sentences to Scottish students at various educational
levels and asked them to identify the nouns, verbs, adjectives, and adverbs. He administered the test to 131 students who had completed primary schooling that included thirty
minutes of grammar instruction daily for four years. He set the passing score at 50 percent; only one student passed on all four parts of speech. (Thirty-seven percent passed
on nouns, 21 percent on verbs, and only 5 and 4 percent passed on adjectives and adverbs, respectively.) He administered the same test to students completing the elite senior
secondary school, which in Scotland at the time admitted only the top 20 percent of junior secondary school graduates. These students had studied grammar for nine years. Of
these top students, only 42 percent were able to identify 50 percent of the items correctly.
In other words, a majority of even the most capable students failed to learn what teachers
think of as fundamental concepts of TSG.

Where does grammatical knowledge of this kind lead? If I can identify 100 percent
of nouns, verbs, adjectives, and adverbs in running prose, what does that enable me to

do? It is arguable that such knowledge leads to better production of sentences or better editing of sentences. But does it? I fail to see how it could. Identification is merely the application of definitions to examples. It is no more than declarative knowledge. It does not provide the procedures for creating good writing or editing it.

As long ago as 1963, Braddock, Lloyd-Jones, and Schoer asserted, "The teaching of formal grammar has a negligible or, because it usually displaces some instruction and practice in actual composition, even a harmful effect on the improvement of writing" (37–38). This statement was based on a comprehensive review of studies of teaching writing from as long ago as the 1890s. My own review of research on the teaching of writing and a meta-analysis of composition studies completed between 1963 and 1983 (Hillocks 1986) strongly reinforced this conclusion. In fact, the meta-analysis determined that of the several foci of instruction examined (grammar, study of model compositions, sentence combining, study of criteria for judging writing, freewriting, and inquiry), every treatment was more effective than grammar in improving writing. Indeed, grammar had virtually no impact on the improvement of writing at all.

But what about correctness? Although the study of grammar might not be expected to result in better writing, surely one would expect it to result in higher levels of correctness. The most impressive study of the effects of teaching grammar on writing is by Elley et al. (1976), in which the researchers examined the achievement of a group of New Zealand high school students moving through the third, fourth, and fifth forms and again one year after the completion of instruction. This was a lengthy study and used a large sample (248 students at the outset and 166 after three years). The study was also carefully controlled, with students divided into eight classes matched on the basis of test scores, sex, ethnicity, contributing school, and subject option. Three classes studied the Oregon curriculum, which includes generative grammar. Three studied the same curriculum but replaced the study of generative grammar with extra literature and creative writing. The final two classes studied traditional school grammar. No one method was taught by the same teacher for more than one year. The researchers used a variety of measures after each year of the study—tests of reading, listening, English usage, spelling, English literature, and sentence combining; criterion-referenced scales on essays the students had written; and attitude surveys. The most significant difference was that students who studied generative grammar had considerably more negative attitudes toward English than the other students. However, there were no significant differences in the quality or correctness of students' actual writing. That is, students in the group that had not studied grammar wrote as well and as correctly as the students in the two grammar groups. The research on the effects of teaching grammar on the quality of writing and on correctness, then, forces us to reject both traditional and generative grammar as means to improving the quality of writing or correctness.

What can be done? I have a few strong recommendations, one don't and three dos.

Don't teach grammar through a traditional school grammar book.

Do examine your students' writing to discover their needs.

Do teach syntactic structures through the kind of pattern practice that appears in Chapters 4 and 6, in the context of real writing.

Do teach items of usage separately and as soon as possible incorporate them into real writing.

REFERENCES

Applebee, A. N. 1981. *Writing in the Secondary School: English in the Content Areas.* NCTE Research Report No. 21. Urbana, IL: NCTE.

———. 1984. *Contexts for Learning to Write.* Norwood, NJ: Ablex.

Aristotle. 1947. *Nichomachean Ethics.* Trans. W. Ross. In *Introduction to Aristotle,* ed. R. McKeon, 308–543. New York: Random House.

Bahktin, M. 1981. *The Dialogic Imagination: Four Essays.* Ed. Michael Holquist. Trans. Caryl Emerson. Austin: University of Texas Press.

Ball, A. and T. Lardner. 1999. "Dispositions Toward Language: Teacher Constructs of Knowledge and the Ann Arbor Black English Case." In *On Writing Research: The Braddock Essays 1975–1998,* edited by L. Ede, 413–76. New York: Bedford/St. Martin's

———. 2005. *African American Literacies Unleashed: Vernacular English and the Composition Classroom.* Carbondale, IL: Southern Illinois University Press.

Benchley, P. 1974 . *Jaws.* New York: Fawcett.

Bjerre, J. 1960. *Kalahari.* New York: Hill and Wang.

Bracewell, R. J., M. Scardamalia, and C. Bereiter. 1978. *The Development of Audience Awareness in Writing.* Paper presented at the 58th annual meeting of American Educational Research Association. ED 154 433.

Braddock, R., R. Lloyd-Jones, and L. Schoer. 1963. *Research in Written Composition.* Champaign, IL: NCTE.

Bridwell, L. S. 1980. "Revising Processes in Twelfth Grade Students' Transactional Writing." *Research in the Teaching of English* (October): 197–222.

Burnette, D. 2006. "Who Needs Grammar?" *Atlanta Journal Constitution* April 9, B1, B4.

California Department of Education. 1994. *Scoring Autobiographical Incidents.* Sacramento, CA: Author.

Cisneros, S. 1991. *The House on Mango Street.* New York: Vintage.

Cohen, J. 1977. *Statistical Power Analysis for the Behavioral Sciences.* New York: Academic.

Cooper, H., and L. V. Hedges, eds. 1994. *The Handbook of Research Synthesis.* Washington, DC: Brookings Institution.

Csikszentmihalyi, M., and R. Larson. 1984. *Being Adolescent: Conflict and Growth in the Teenage Years.* New York: Basic Books.

Davis, N., ed. 1955. *Sweet's Anglo-Saxon Primer.* 9th ed. Oxford, UK: Clarendon.

Delpit, L. 1995. *Other People's Children: Cultural Conflict in the Classroom.* New York: New Press.

Dickens, C. 1970. *David Copperfield.* Vol. 1. N.p.: Heron Books Centennial Edition.

Dudley-Marling, C., D. Abt-Perkins, K. Sato, and R. Selfe. 2006. "Teacher Quality: The Perspectives of NCTE Members." *English Education* 38 (3): 167–91.

Elley, W., I. Barnham, H. Lamb, and M. Wylie. 1976. "The Role of Grammar in a Secondary School English Curriculum." *Research on the Teaching of English* (Spring): 5–21.

Emig, J. 1971. *The Composing Process of Twelfth Graders.* Urbana, IL: NCTE.

Fowler, H. W. 1965. *A Dictionary of Modern English Usage.* New York: Oxford University Press.

Freedman, S. W. 1987. *Response to Student Writing.* NCTE Research Report No. 23. Urbana, IL: NCTE.

Fries, C. C. 1952. *The Structure of English.* New York: Harcourt, Brace, and World.

Gluck, G. 1936. *Peter Brueghel the Elder.* New York: George Braziller.

Graves, D. 1983. *Writing: Teachers and Children at Work.* Portsmouth, NH: Heinemann.

Hansen, B. 1978. "Rewriting Is a Waste of Time." *College English* 39: 956–60.

Hayes, J. R., and L. Flower. 1980. "Identifying the Organization of Writing Processes." In *Cognitive Processes in Writing: An Interdisciplinary Approach,* ed. L. Greg and I. Steinberg, 3–30. Hillsdale, NJ: Lawrence Erlbaum.

Heath, S. B. 1983. *Ways with Words: Language, Life, and Work in Communities and Classrooms.* New York: Cambridge University Press.

Hedges, L. V., and A. Nowell. 1995. "Sex Differences in Mental Test Scores, Variability, and Numbers of High-Scoring Individuals." *Science* 269: 41–45.

———. 1998. "Black-White Test Score Convergence Since 1965." In *The Black-White Test Score Gap,* ed. C. Jencks and M. Phillips, 149–81. Washington, DC: Brookings Institution Press.

Herrnstein, R., and C. Murray. 1994. *The Bell Curve: Class Structure and Intelligence in American Life.* New York: Free.

Hillocks, G. 1975. *Observing and Writing.* Urbana, IL: ERIC and NCTE.

———. 1979. "The Effects of Observational Activities on Student Writing." *Research in the Teaching of English* 13: 23–35.

———. 1982. "The Interaction of Instruction, Teacher Comment, and Revision in Teaching the Composing Process." *Research in the Teaching of English* 16: 261–78.

———. 1986. *Research on Written Composition: New Directions for Teaching.* Urbana, IL: National Conference on Research in English/ERIC Clearinghouse on Reading and Communications Skills.

———. 1999. *Ways of Thinking, Ways of Teaching.* New York: Teachers College Press.

———. 2002. *The Testing Trap: How State Assessments of Writing Control Learning.* New York: Teachers College Press.

———. 2006. "Middle and High School Composition." In *Research on Composition,* ed. P. Smagorinsky, 48–77. New York: Teachers College Press.

———. In progress. "The Impact of Classroom Activities on the Learning of Writing: A Qualitative/Quantitative Study."

Hillocks, G., and M. W. Smith. 2003. "Grammar and Literacy Learning." In *Handbook of Research in Teaching the Language Arts,* 2d ed., ed. James Flood et al., 721–37. Mahwah, NJ: Lawrence Erlbaum.

Hunt, K. 1965. *Grammatical Structures Written at Three Grade Levels.* Champaign, IL: NCTE.

Jencks, C., and M. Phillips. 1998. *The Black-White Test Score Gap.* Washington, DC: Brookings Institution Press.

Kooser, T. 1980. "Abandoned Farmhouse." In *Sure Signs: New and Selected Poems,* 63. Pittsburgh: University of Pittsburgh Press.

Labov, W. 1972. *Language in the Inner City: Studies in the Black English Vernacular.* Philadelphia: University of Pennsylvania Press.

Ladson-Billings, G. 1994. *The Dreamkeepers: Successful Teachers of African American Children.* San Francisco: Jossey-Bass.

Langer, J. 1984. "The Effects of Available Information on Responses to School Writing Tasks." *Research in the Teaching of English* 18 (1): 27–44.

———. 2001. "Beating the Odds: Teaching Middle and High School Students to Read and Write Well." *American Educational Research Journal* (38) 4: 837–80.

London, J. 1986. *To Build a Fire and Other Stories*. New York: Bantam.

Macaulay, W. J. 1947. "The Difficulty of Grammar." *British Journal of Educational Psychology* 17: 153–62.

McAdams, D. P. 1989. *Intimacy: The Need to Be Close*. New York: Doubleday.

Morrison, T. 1987. *Beloved*. New York: Penguin Putnam.

National Assessment of Educational Progress. 2002. *The Nation's Report Card: Writing 2002*. Washington, DC: National Center for Education Statistics.

Nold, E. W. 1981. "Revising." In *Writing: The Nature, Development, and Teaching of Written Communication*, ed. E. H. Frederiksen, M. F. Whiteman, and J. F. Dominic, 67–79. Hillsdale, NJ: Lawrence Erlbaum.

Nystrand, M., with A. Gamoran, R. Kachur, and C. Prendergast. 1997. *Opening Dialogue: Understanding the Dynamics of Language and Learning in the English Classroom*. New York: Teachers College Press.

Poe, E. A. 1984. "The Tell-Tale Heart." In *Edgar Allan Poe, Poetry and Tales*, 555–9. New York: Literary Classics of the United States.

Polio, C., and M. Glew. 1996. "ESL Writing Assessment Prompts: How Students Choose." *Journal of Second Language Writing* 5 (1): 35–49.

Rickford, J. 1999. *African American Vernacular English: Features, Evolution, Educational Implications*. Oxford, UK: Blackwell.

Scardamalia, M., and C. Bereiter. 1983. "The Development of Evaluative, Diagnostic, and Remedial Capabilities in Children's Writing." In *The Psychology of Written Language: A Developmental Approach*, ed. M. Martlew, 67–95. London: Wiley.

Shulman, L. S. 1986. "Those Who Understand: Knowledge Growth in Teaching." *Educational Researcher* (March): 4–14.

Smagorinsky, P., and M. W. Smith. 1992. "The Nature of Knowledge in Composition and Literary Understanding: The Question of Specificity." *Review of Educational Research* 62: 279–305.

———. 2002. "Whose Who?" *Research in the Teaching of English* 36: 305–308.

Sperling, M., and S. W. Freedman. 1987. "A Good Girl Writes Like a Good Girl: Written Responses to Student Writing." *Written Communication* 9: 343–69.

Stein, N., and T. Trabasso. 1982. "What's in a Story: An Approach to Comprehension and Instruction." In *Advances in Instructional Psychology*, ed. R. Glaser, 213–67. Hillsdale, NJ: Lawrence Erlbaum.

Stotsky, S. 1995. "The Uses and Limitations of Personal or Personalized Writing in Writing Theory, Research, and Instruction." *Reading Research Quarterly* 30: 758–76.

Twain, M. 1880. Letter to D. W. Bowser. March 20. twainquotes.com/Writing.html.

———. 1962. *The Tragedy of Pudd'nhead Wilson*. New York: Harcourt, Brace, and World.

University of Chicago Press. 2003. *The Chicago Manual of Style*. 15th ed. Chicago: Author.

Vygotsky, L. S. 1978. *Mind in Society: The Development of Higher Psychological Processes*. Ed. M. Cole et al. Cambridge: Harvard University Press.

Western Reserve University, Euclid Central Junior High School Project English Demonstration Center. 1964. *Concepts of Man: A Curriculum for Average Students*. ED 017 492. Euclid, OH: Author.

Wilhelm, J. 2003. *Reading Is Seeing*. New York: Scholastic.

Wright, R. 1951. *Black Boy*. New York: New American Library.

INDEX